WE ARE ALL HEALERS

Sally Hammond

HARPER & ROW, PUBLISHERS
NEW YORK, EVANSTON, SAN FRANCISCO, LONDON

ISBN: 0-06-063694-7

LIBRARY OF CONGRESS CATALOG CARD NUMBER: 73-6331

Dedication

To my sister, Marcelle, who was healed by the best of medical treatment in combination with the power of spiritual healing sent to her through individuals and groups, to which she added her own self-healing and in so doing lived the message of this book.

CONTENTS

Part Three   Probing the Healing Mystery

Introduction by Edgar D. Mitchell

WE ARE all psychic healers, says Sally Hammond. It is a view I share. While I can neither confirm nor deny the experience and accounts which she records here (except for my own), I can say that personal experience with the field of psychical research leads me to see more than a nugget of truth in this book.

But psychic abilities, even healing abilities, do not necessarily equate to spiritual enlightenment, as Miss Hammond has indicated. This lesson has been sounded over and over in the history of psychical research. The reason is simple : psychic energy, like all physical energy, is devoid of an inherent value system. It can be used as the consciousness of the person directing it desires. This is not to imply that one can use their abilities with impunity, however. Egotism, ignorance, self-aggrandisement are no basis on which to activate psychic forces. Otherwise, like a child playing with fire or a nation playing with nuclear energy, psychic abilities which have greater potential than either are likely to be used in ways that hurt people rather than help them.

Thus the psi process must be grounded in the highest moral and ethical principles. And parapsychology, which studies the psi process, must be seen in the perspective of transpersonal psychology, the study of humanity's ultimate potential.

Psychic healing is the area where parapsychology and transpersonal psychology come closest together. It is an area of great significance because in this application psychic energy is being used in the service of mankind—an ethic repeatedly given us by all spiritual masters.

In addition to the concept of service, psychic healing is important because it offers one of the strongest challenges for the paradigm underlying current science. We do not have clear answers from scientists—or from psychics themselves—which explain the psychic healing event. But the evidence of psychic healing is unavoidable. The spontaneous remission of large tumours in a terminal cancer patient, a shortened leg that grows four and a half inches to normal size in a few days, the restoration of sight in a woman whose optic nerves were shown by X-rays to be totally atrophied : these observations cannot be dismissed as psychogenic or emotional disorders, especially when the one healed professes total scepticism about it before the healing takes place. How such dramatic changes take place is a mystery to science, and it may be that entirely new laws and forms of energy must be recognised before the mystery is solved. In any case, science and orthodox medicine can no longer ignore the fact of psychic healing.

I must add a note of caution, however : it would be unwise to seek any sort of psychic healing in lieu of regular medical treatment —at least in this stage of our knowledge. For the moment, I think, psychic healing can best be seen as an adjunct to conventional medicine. In the past, unscrupulous and inauthentic practitioners of psychic healing have been a source of discredit to the tradition. That is why I began with a word of warning about the difference between psychic development and spiritual growth, and why I advocate a certification process for psychic healers. With those lessons in mind, though, I look hopefully for the day when healers work hand in hand with the medical profession.

Until then, we will need more of the pioneering efforts of the sort given us by The Academy of Parapsychology and Medicine in Los Altos, California, and by The Foundation for Parasensory Investigation in New York City. These organisations have made great efforts to educate the public in general and the medical profession in particular. Conferences on psychic healing sponsored by these organisations are good examples of what can be done. They have been responsible, scientific and duly cautious but by no means timid.

Conference audiences are quite limited, however. Books such as this one fill a strong, immediate need in the process of informing the public and those in the healing sciences. I believe *We Are All Healers* will quickly become an important document in the literature of psychic healing. Therefore I am pleased to introduce the work of Sally Hammond and to say that I look forward to other books by this capable reporter.

Author's Note

IT TOOK little time for New Age researchers and observers of the psychic scene to agree that, of all the psychic faculties, the ability to heal by the laying-on of hands and at a distance promises the greatest benefits to mankind, offering the glowing hope of widespread relief for sufferers from chronic illness beyond the help of orthodox medicine. And now, to reinforce that hope, comes growing evidence that the ability to heal psychically may be innate in all humans—although dormant in most of us—and that it can be developed to greater or lesser degree. The only requirements for that development, it appears, are a sense of caring or compassion, and a willingness to acquire the necessary training.

My extensive inquiries in the United States and in England regarding the universality of the healing gift turned up no serious opposition to the idea. Even the many healers I interviewed were, without exception, convinced of it. I had not expected them to so readily agree that they were not uniquely gifted. Their mood was more that of revolutionaries, under fire in some quarters, who welcomed more recruits to their ranks. Indeed, it was a healer who, by her spontaneous remark, gave me the title for my book. The premise was fully accepted by such people as Harry Edwards, England's charismatic healer of nearly forty years' experience, who has written many books covering every aspect of his work, and Dr Robert Laidlaw, the well-known New York psychiatrist, for several years chairman of Life Energies Research, Inc., a distinguished group of doctors, physicists and other professionals seeking scientific proof of psychic healing and other parapsychological phenomena.

Naturally, not everyone can become a great healer—a Harry
Edwards or a Kathryn Kuhlman—merely by virtue of their love
and concern for their fellow humans and by applying themselves to
training techniques. As Edwards expresses it with a twinkle, 'Some
people have the ability or the gift to be better than others, like a
good violinist. Some can fiddle while others can play.' He suggests
that 'since the origin of healing is divine' its wider practise in the
world will advance 'the spiritualisation of mankind'.

The questions then arise : where can would-be healers find the
proper training, and to what standards should they aspire? With
few training facilities in the United States, I went to England, where
thousands of spiritual healers practise in a free and tolerant atmosphere, to discover their sources of training. Interviewing a number
of well-known, lesser-known and unknown practitioners—all people
of remarkable simplicity and sincerity—I found that many had
attended the classes or development circles sponsored by the
Spiritualist Association of Great Britain at their imposing headquarters on Belgrave Square or at the little Spiritualist Church
round the corner. Several thousand, I was told, have taken the
correspondence courses in healing (including a cram course in
general anatomy) distributed by the National Federation of Spiritual
Healers, the professional society of Great Britain's healers. On
another level is the College of Psycho-Therapeutics directed by
Ronald Beesley at his lovely country estate in Kent, where groups of
students spend a fortnight at a time exploring a wide range of healing
studies, including the esoteric art of detecting disease in the auric
patterns, along with natural healing and self-healing.

Many Britons appear to prefer training themselves to heal. At all
these centres I visited, and at the College of Psychic Studies in South
Kensington, I found a rich assortment of books, tapes, pamphlets
and instructional records in meditation giving guidance on various
methods of attunement, the widely acknowledged basis of spiritual
healing.

When a few of England's older healers expressed concern to me
that the fast proliferation of their numbers might be lowering the
standards of healing in their country, I realised that as the practice
grows in the United States in the expanding spiritual consciousness
of the Aquarian Age much can be learned from the English experience. I hope the information I gathered will be helpful to those who
will be guiding the expansion of spiritual healing in America, so that

it will be encouraged sensibly and not unduly restricted, bringing the fullest benefits to the many in need.

My liveliest hope is that this book will help to remove psychic healing from the category of 'the Occult' and bring it within range of everyone's experience. While not a great many will have the desire or the freedom of choice to become full-time healers, the ability to relieve a friend's migraine, a mate's lumbago or a child's bruises is within the power of all who are willing to be used as channels for God's healing energy. And, in situations where a doctor is unavailable, anyone who can lovingly apply spiritual healing to a stricken friend or stranger may mean the difference between life and death.

Note: The workshop lecture by the Reverend Alex Holmes quoted herewith is from a series of lectures he gave at Emory College in Oxford, Georgia, and the selections are quoted with his permission. They will appear in fuller form in his book, *You Too Can Heal.*

Ronald Beesley sets forth his theory of Chakra healing in these terms:
  'Man is an inter-dimensional being poised between heaven and earth—the bridge between his astral body and earth counterpart are the centres of activity we know as Chakras. Every function and system depends on the energy of balance of these centres, and for this reason are highly important in the transference of the vital forces we know as life. Healing is the transference and releasing of these energies that enable the body life to get the house in order. Any breakdown in these co-ordinations means the function or system they serve will be dis-eased.
  'The healer's work is to restore this balance, so knowledge of these centres and their work is part of his training in spiritual therapeutics. He, himself, is a temporary bridge to enable the life force to renew and replenish the one in need.'

PART ONE

On the Psychic Trail

1. A Link Across the Atlantic

IT WAS 1948, and I'd travelled by boat and by train from New York to Luxembourg to take part in a congress of World Federalists, their idea of a stronger United Nations equipped to outlaw war having strongly attracted me after my husband was killed in service. And now, in that smallest of European capitals, I was being exposed to a new idea of equal power—psychic healing.

About a dozen of us had met for refreshment between conference sessions at a little café on the city square. Coffee and pastries had been served and the atmosphere had mellowed when a fellow delegate named George Rogers—genial, black hair, jaunty moustache—brought up the subject. A Labour Party MP, one of a British Parliamentary group attending the conference, he approached it from a religious viewpoint, starting off by asking if we'd mind going around the table letting each one name their church affiliation, if any; an odd little game to which nobody objected.

When it came Rogers' turn, he announced somewhat dramatically that he was a Spiritualist, and that one of their chief concerns was healing the sick by a method he termed 'spiritual healing'. Explaining that it was an ancient psychic therapy applied by the laying-on of hands or by prayer directed to the ill person at a distance, he proceeded to enthrall us with accounts of cures performed by spiritual healers which might have come straight out of the Book of Acts.

His wife, Mary, was a gifted healer, Rogers said, and she had successfully treated people with such chronic ailments as arthritis and multiple sclerosis, who had been given up by medical doctors. She had also put in place the slipped discs of several policemen in the neighbourhood and mended the cracked bones of dancers in the Royal Ballet.

Most impressive, however, was the MP's claim that Mary Rogers could disperse cancerous growths by the psychic method. He told us he had seen tumours, X-rayed before and after healing treatments, disappear completely, making surgery unnecessary.

Winding up his impromptu lecture, Rogers said he had himself participated in a 'development circle' with others wanting to develop the healing ability, and that they met regularly under his wife's guidance at their home in Sudbury.

We listened to Rogers with rapt attention, the subject being far beyond the experience of every one of us. And, considering his solid credentials as a parliamentarian representing North Kensington, London, I, for one, was inclined to take him seriously.

But the idea that a divine power unidentified by science could intervene through medically untrained healers and ease the suffering of human beings was too mysterious for my world-political mood of those early post-war years. And so, as we headed back to the conference to tangle once again with the legal aspects of arms control, I put psychic healing to the back of my mind.

Ten years later (I had recently found a job I liked as a newspaper reporter on the *New York Post*), a surgeon, examining a small lump I had discovered in my left breast, warned me that if a biopsy proved it to be malignant he would have to do extensive surgery.

In the chilling fear of that moment I remembered what George Rogers had said psychic healing could do in such cases. And, having no idea how to reach Mary Rogers to arrange for treatment, I sent a note by air mail to her husband at the House of Commons. Did he, I asked, remember telling a group of World Federalists about spiritual healing just ten years ago in a little café in Luxembourg? And hadn't he said his wife could remove tumours without surgery? If so, I said, and she would agree to take me as a patient, I would gladly catch the next plane for England.

By return mail, George Rogers wrote, cordially: 'You won't need to come to England. My wife will be happy to send you absent healing, which in many cases is just as effective.' But he wanted me to understand that the length of time required was variable. The growth might dissolve instantly, he said, or it might be reduced gradually over a period of time. He gave me their telephone number in Harrow-on-the-Hill, Middlesex, and suggested I call his wife at a certain hour when she would be home waiting to hear from me.

A few days later, picking up her phone in England, Mrs Rogers said in a pleasant voice that she could see me clairvoyantly, and, after giving an accurate description of my colouring, noted correctly that I was wearing a pink shirt! She then gave me her prescription for treatment : 'Just link up with me once a day at 10 p.m., our time, and we'll keep it up for a week.' (That would be 5 p.m. in New York.)

My doctor had scheduled the operation for only two weeks ahead, so I determined not to miss a single link-up and to follow her instructions precisely. It wasn't easy. I was to find 'a quiet place'—hardly the City Room of a metropolitan daily—and to 'reach out' mentally to her for twenty minutes.

Exploring the upper floors of the building at 75 West Street, I found a fire escape where I could be completely alone, and that week I managed to get all my interviews and phoning done by mid-afternoon so I could be back at my desk and free by five o'clock. After leaving a message at the switchboard that I'd return in twenty minutes, I buzzed a lift and went up to my spiritual rendezvous with Mary Rogers.

On that lofty parapet with traffic humming below me, it was surprisingly hard to link up with someone I'd never seen on the far side of the Atlantic. But I tried hard to imagine her from the brief description she'd given me—a thirtyish mother of two, with blue eyes and pale blonde hair that looks almost white (her forebears, she said, were Norwegian)—and I tried to recall her hearty telephone manner. It took an intensive effort to keep my mind from wandering back to the story I'd just been writing.

If I'd stopped coolly to analyse what I was doing I might have dropped the whole thing, but in my predicament, with mutilating surgery a grim possibility, almost any kind of positive activity seemed better than allowing myself to feel trapped and helpless. So, as the date of my operation drew closer I concentrated on the only reality that could uplift my spirits, that I was simply experimenting with an unknown force that had apparently helped others, and that someone who hardly knew me cared enough about my well-being to 'send' that force across the ocean in an attempt to spare me disfigurement.

Meanwhile, to give the treatment more time, I asked my surgeon if it would be all right if he withheld the knife for a week or two longer, and confessed to him my reasons. He did not laugh as I had expected him to, but rather sternly advised me not to waste any more than two weeks more with it because he could assure me that 'faith healing' was a delusion. It was useless to argue with him considering my sparse knowledge of the process, nor did I want to. He was a gentle, dedicated man, who had skillfully removed a similar lump from my forearm just a year earlier without damaging the nerves in my fingers. I don't remember clearly, but I might have informed him that the treatment I was getting in absentia from Mary Rogers must be different from 'faith healing' since my faith in God or in any religious or spiritual concept had never been brought into the picture as necessary to my recovery.

But I did not take lightly the surgeon's warning of the danger of further delay. That night I wrote Mrs Rogers asking for more information and, if it was possible, to speed things up a little. She replied with the following message :

July 29, 1958

'Dear Sally,

'I had your letter only yesterday. I am keeping up the contact. There is no need for you to link up other than at 10 p.m. our time. I do hope you are benefiting from it. Of course the doctor is sceptical, it is only natural. I do wish that we were able to meet so that I could give you contact healing. If only he could see some cures, he would, perhaps, think differently. However, doctors are necessary for prescribing and helping where all else fails, and my own view has always been that the patient should take the best from both healer and doctor.

'It would take an awful long time to write about healing. You ought to try to get Harry Edwards' books on the subject. He is the most famous healer in England and only the other day performed some wonderful cures at Albert Hall before an audience of 8,000. My husband was speaking for him from the platform.

'By actual laying-on of hands I have had some very good cures to bones, etc., and slipped discs are chicken-feed. No

manipulation, either. In the case of absent healing I sit quietly and link up with the patient, whom I then see clairvoyantly. Then I "will" rays to the affected part. It sounds "daft" but has had startling results. At any rate, let us go on praying and hoping. If by the 3rd the doctor says you must have the operation, do not have any fear. You will be fine! Keep writing to me and keep praying for help to be given to you and to me . . .
My love to you,
(Signed) Mary Rogers'

It helped that she could be so calm and relaxed, but I had to face the fact that the size of the lump had not changed perceptibly with two weeks of absent healing, and the new deadline was now only a few days away. Hoping still to stave off surgery, I gave Mary one more call. 'It is not now malignant. I can tell you that for sure,' she said confidently. 'But if your doctor wants it out, better to get rid of it.'

That same week I made my final attempt to obtain an instant, non-surgical healing. Happening to meet a young minister of the church where I was an occasional attender, and mentioning my long-shot experiment with Mary Rogers, I was told that there were a few priests of the Episcopal Church who were willing to administer the early Christian rite of the laying-on of hands, and he was one of them. Inviting me to meet him in the chapel of his church, the Church of the Ascension, at Fifth Avenue and Tenth Street, he asked me to kneel on a cushion and, after a prayer, performed the service for the Unction of the Sick from the *Book of Common Prayer.*

But the miracle I was seeking so anxiously—that my affliction would disappear in a twinkling—did not occur, and with no time remaining and with wilting faith, I signed in at New York Hospital and put myself in the hands of surgical science.

Mrs Rogers was right, I found, in her prediction that the growth was benign. But had it always been benign? I will never know the answer. I learned the good news when under local anaesthetic and putting all my faith in the surgeon. (In retrospect I think he might have told me it would be so painful and I would have preferred to be unconscious!) In any case, I did come through it well, as she had assured me I would, and the orderly, wheeling me out of the operating room, cheered me up by congratulating me for my bravery. Curiously enough, the operation left no mark, while a cousin of mine who had the same operation that summer was left with a deep scar.

To show my appreciation to Mrs Rogers for her time and efforts, I sent her a pink knitted stole, not knowing what fee, if any, a spiritual healer expected. In late August her buoyant reply suggested that in her view the outcome did not at all imply failure for spiritual healing. On the contrary, she seemed convinced that the spiritual treatment had influenced the good result. It would have been in bad taste, I thought at the time, to ask her if the lump had ever been malignant. But if there is truth in current theories that cancer may have psychosomatic origins, and that hopeful states of mind can spur regressions, she may have been ahead of her time in her conviction. Here is her letter :

August 28, 1958

'My dear Sally,

'What a beautiful stole, and as I am silver-blonde colouring, the colour is wonderful. I did not deserve such a reward. To know that you are better is quite enough . . . I had a very interesting case this week, a man who has a wasting of the nerves, resulting in a semi-paralysed leg and arm. Specialists told him there was no cure (after two years' treatment) and that he would just get worse and worse. He had to see him every six weeks. I gave him one healing and restored the use of both arm and leg. Going for his check-up last week, the specialist had thirty students lined up to see this hopeless case and demonstrate the various reactions of the limbs. He was very puzzled and finally said to them, "This patient *had* so-and-so." He told Mr Scott it must be one of his good days and that he need not come back for six months. . . .

'I am convinced that our "link" was not accidental. Let us keep up the letters. . . . I hope you are feeling good and remember to link up occasionally, at any time. Once again, so very many thanks for that lovely gift, and love from,

Mary R.'

Over the next year or two we exchanged several friendly letters. Then she had an illness and I remarried and our correspondence trickled out. In summing up the experience, my first test of the mysterious power of psychic healing having been inconclusive, and my understanding of theories behind the treatments being so minimal, I obviously needed a clearer demonstration of its effectiveness before I could accept it—if not in myself then in someone else. And I hoped for more assurance that it was truly 'spiritual'. A few months later, a sharp turn in the psychic trail led me in dramatic fashion to that assurance.

2.   Group Healing at the ARE

My next resort to psychic healing for a physical ailment—this time a bad case of bronchitis rather than a surgical problem—provided all the proof I needed that the healing power described so dramatically in the Scriptures was still available today. I was healed at a distance of twenty-six blocks and in just one treatment. It was the beginning of my search into a seemingly limitless new field of inquiry and came about like this:

Some time back in 1959, a friend gave me a biography* in paperback to ease the boredom of a long train ride, and the book kept my eyes pinned to the pages for most of the trip from Florida to New York. Simply written and not at all sceptical, it recounted the strange life and amazing mental/psychic powers of Edgar Cayce, a small-town Kentuckian and Sunday School teacher who was able accurately to diagnose and recommend effective treatment for a wide range of serious illnesses while in a sleeplike trance, using complex medical terms and phrases. When awake, the book claimed, he could not remember a single word he had said.

In the back of the book was a note saying that a Foundation based in Virginia Beach was indexing the 14,249 Cayce 'readings' recorded live by his secretary between 1910 and 1944, the year he died. And it gave the address of their New York headquarters. I stored the information away for the time being and, finally, in 1967, I was able to follow it up. One slow summer day when the assistant City Editor

* *There Is A River* by Thomas Sugrue

at *The Post* was looking for feature ideas, I proposed that we take a look at the local activities of the organisation carrying on Cayce's work, known as the Association for Research and Enlightenment. Given a go-ahead, I made an appointment with the director.

Arriving at the ARE's plain but hospitable quarters on two floors above a Chinese Restaurant at 34 West 35th Street, I was met by Dan Livingston, a soft-voiced, undramatic spokesman, a man in his forties who struck me as intelligent and independent-minded. Taking me into the lounge, lined by bookshelves, he suggested that only scientists who have actually experienced or observed psychic phenomena are likely to be open-minded about Edgar Cayce. A number of respected university professors had studied Cayce's work with interest, Livingston said, and he mentioned Dr Ian Stevenson, the University of Virginia School of Medicine psychiatrist, and Dr Gardner Murphy, the George Washington University psychologist who had been president of both the Society for Psychical Research in England and the American Society for Psychical Research.

A note on the bulletin board in the hallway caught my eye when I came in—announcing a 'Meditation for Healing' group meeting. Livingston explained that it was a major activity of the centre and that one group had been meeting faithfully every Wednesday night since the New York Centre opened in the 1950s. Could I attend? I asked. 'Certainly,' Livingston said, and he assured me that by joining with others it was possible for untrained people like myself to raise a healing vibration of a strength they couldn't muster acting individually.

'If you are ever sick, just call the office before six o'clock and ask to be put on the list,' Livingston said as I was leaving. And I did not forget his invitation. (Unfortunately I never got to write the feature story since the City Editor discovered that a Sunday page was already being devoted to a subject he considered too closely related.)

Later on that year, when I was feeling miserable with the worst case of virus bronchitis I'd had in years, I suddenly thought of the Wednesday night healing group. It was Monday, and I'd been in bed with a fever and deep cough for nearly two weeks, and I was not a bit better on Wednesday when I phoned in to be put on the list.

An office staffer answering instructed me to find a quiet place where I could 'keep time' with the healing group between 8.00 and

9 p.m., the period during which they would be in meditation and sending out healing. 'And be sure to send us a report of your condition before next Wednesday,' she said.

It wasn't much quieter than the *Post*'s City Room in our small apartment with my husband, a busy free-lance writer, attacking his typewriter non-stop. And the only way I could find a measure of privacy and silence was to lock myself in the bathroom and turn off the light. Using the bathmat as a kind of prayer-rug and imagining myself in a sanctuary, I tried to link up with the healing group just as I'd done nine years earlier with Mary Rogers. It was much easier this time to relax and quiet myself. I didn't yet know how to meditate, but I was able to feel warmth for the good-hearted people in that plain little room who were sending out healing to sickrooms and hospitals all over the city.

I kept an attitude of hopeful expectancy, although no particular attitude had been prescribed. About twenty minutes slipped by. With considerable effort I kept my wayward mind focused on the group, which I had to imagine since I'd never seen it operating. Then, all at once, I felt a gentle jolt like a weak shock of electricity in the area of my chest, and a glow of well-being filled me. After a few prayerful moments and, judging the time to be well past nine, I got up, feeling unmistakably stronger and better. That night I stopped coughing and my fever left me. In a day or two I was well enough to go back to work.

The next day I wrote an exuberant report and, along with others, it was read to the healing group the following Wednesday. I wish it had been saved (no effort is made to preserve such records) because it would have helped me recapture that momentous night when the unseen healing power I'd read about in the *Book of Acts* was relayed to me by a devoted band who had been encouraged by Edgar Cayce to develop their spiritual gift of healing.

I know there are those who will say I might have got well anyway, that the illness had reached a natural turning-point, but I can't agree. I had suffered attacks of bronchitis all through my life, and recovery had always been a long drawn-out process with the cough hanging on for weeks. This time all my symptoms disappeared within hours.

I hoped that somewhere in the mass of Cayce's readings I might find a description of what happens in psychic healing—a famous psychic's inside view of the phenomenon. I knew of no medical or scientific research being done in this area. On the other hand, a psychic diagnostician and healer should be able to supply some highly interesting theories, unavailable to most people, that might be tested out!

How is the power activated and transmitted? What factors help or hinder it? What part do spiritual attitudes play in both healer and patient? Are there any shortcuts to developing the healing ability? These were some of the questions I wanted answered, but my fast-paced life as reporter-wife-housekeeper and a tragic death in the family forced me to put the matter aside for the time being, and I didn't return to it until my entire lifestyle changed unexpectedly two years later.

I had picked up enough information from Dan Livingston to know that Cayce's approach to healing emphasised self-healing and indeed a thoroughgoing mind-body-spirit balance that required study and practise. A pamphlet entitled *Adventure in Soul Growth* gave the impression that the ARE's various group activities were like sensitivity groups, in which people are encouraged to be open and responsive to each other, but with a spiritual element added. 'Members try to help each other relate more fully to God and all mankind by extending love and service to others', the text read, 'The sharing of concerns in the group can reduce personal anxieties. Expressing thoughts in understandable words often clarifies them as nothing else will. This is particularly true in groups where a warm sense of belonging has developed'. And so, when my second marriage struck a crisis and a psychologist seemed bent on tearing it apart rather than helping to put it together, I arrived in a forlorn state at the ARE one Wednesday night in the fall of 1969 looking for several kinds of spiritual healing, and a 'warm sense of belonging' along with it.

I found right away that the healing of heart-breaking life situations was a primary concern of a good many others in the group. Among the regular attenders, for example, were a red-bearded young artist who had been in a car crash that hospitalised him for a year and intensified a case of fatherly rejection; a TWA executive constantly concerned about his retarded child and a far-reaching shake-up in his company; and a Negro mother of four abandoned by her husband, whose oldest son was a drug addict and frightened her younger children. But these were balanced by at least as many less weighed-down types—a tall Irish lad who did skyscraper construction work and came in his heavy boots; a young bushy-haired photographer given to hugging people; shaggy-haired and bearded youngsters in colourful clothes wearing crucifixes and lovebeads, and a svelte ballerina from the Harkness Ballet.

Arriving alone at the door of the meeting room on my first visit, I introduced myself to the healing group leader, Sid Weinstein, who made me feel welcome by saying he remembered the letter I wrote reporting my healing two years earlier! I then found a seat in the circle of chairs and admired the colourful variety of types and ages. I learned this was a fairly new group and that many were beginners like myself. We began with an hour of informal discussion (sample topics: 'How do you handle impatience?' 'How did you show love the past week?'), and as we went around the circle of about fifteen people, each making a thoughtful and occasionally an eloquent contribution, I was pleased to sense a spirit of openness to the ideas of others, no matter how simple or unenlightened.

When the time came for the healing meditation at 8 o'clock, the newcomers were reminded that we ourselves did not do the healing; we were serving as channels for the healing power which comes from God. Our goal was to become clearer channels, which meant overcoming such spiritual obstructions as greed, resentment, pride, egotism, in order to reach a higher state of consciousness or 'attunement'. There were 'Search for God' study groups recommended for this purpose or we could study on our own. There was a well-stocked library and bookshop upstairs where we could borrow or buy the best books and pamphlets on healing and on psychic or spiritual development in general.

In starting the meditation, the leader described the preparatory exercises as we did them, for the benefit of the new arrivals: first, the head and neck exercises—three nods forward, three backward, three to each side, three very slow rotations of the head clockwise and three counterclockwise. Second, the breathing exercises—three breaths through the right nostril, exhaling through the mouth, and three breaths through the left nostril, exhaling through the right nostril. Lastly, a chant suggested by the Cayce readings for raising the body's vibrations that sounded like Aaaarrrreeeeoooommmm. Then, to raise the spiritual consciousness, an 'affirmation', repeated three times. (Some samples: 'Be still and know I am God.' 'Not my will but Thine, O Lord, be done in me and through me.' 'As the Father knoweth me, so may I know the Father, through the Christ

Spirit, the door to the kingdom of the Father. Show thou me the way.' All recommended by the readings.)

The meditation itself lasted about twenty minutes, a peaceful, uninterrupted silence. But with no prior study and no one person to link up with, I felt as though I were adrift without a paddle. We'd been told that if our minds strayed we were to gently nudge them back to a spiritual level by repeating the affirmation, but we weren't to let it become a mechanical exercise nor concentrate so hard on the words that we lost the spirit behind them. For me, it was a battle all the way to keep my personal anxieties from crowding in.

When Sid broke the silence to read the names of the people who had asked for healing, we were to try mentally to direct the healing power to each one. And as we went down the list I repeated each name to myself and tried to visualise it on a mental screen. These were the people who were 'keeping time' with us, whose names were on our 'target list'. He then read names from another list known as 'the rounds'—people whom we were only to 'surround with light', since they had not asked for healing. Sid explained that, according to Cayce, healing should only be sent to people who expressed a desire for it. The 'light' would help raise that person's spiritual awareness so that they would want to get well and be open to healing power, otherwise they couldn't be helped.

The laying-on of hands followed, after most of the group had left. This was an intensification of the earlier effort, in which lights were dimmed, the door locked, and about five or eight formed a smaller circle, placing a chair in the middle for the person wanting contact healing for himself or to beam out to a particular person. Sid stayed to lead, and after a prayer and several minutes of deepening silence we sat, one by one, in the centre chair, after tapping the person we wanted to give us healing.

There was something clandestine about celebrating this ancient rite practised by Christ and his disciples and traditional in the church for centuries without any member of the clergy present and substituting our own service for that prescribed in the *Book of Common Prayer*. When we stood in a closed circle, arms linked, in silence, the love feelings that were generated made me think of the love-feasts of the Early Christians I'd read about. The experience was unforgettable and, if there is such a thing, soul-warming. I was back the next week and I became a regular member of Meditation for Healing Group No. 2. And I began digging determinedly into a stack of books and pamphlets about healing and the healing philosophy of Edgar Cayce.

In the pages of *Venture Inward*, by Hugh Lynn Cayce, the psychic's son—a much newer book about Cayce than the one I had read on the train—I was surprised to discover the text of a *New York Times* story of October 9, 1910 that revealed interest in respected, orthodox medical circles in the Cayce phenomenon. Here are some excerpts:

'The medical fraternity of the country is taking a lively interest in the strange power said to be possessed by Edgar Cayce of Hopkinsville, Ky, to diagnose difficult diseases while in a semi-conscious state, though he has not the slightest knowledge of medicine when not in this condition.

'During a visit to California last summer, Dr W. H. Ketchum, who was attending a meeting of the National Society of Homeopathic Physicians, had occasion to mention the young man's case and was invited to discuss it at a banquet attended by about thirty-five of the doctors of the Greek letter fraternity in Pasadena.

'Dr Ketchum made a speech of considerable length, giving an explanation of the strange psychic powers manifested by Cayce during the last four years, during which time he has been more or less under his observation. He stimulated such interest among those present . . . that one of the leading Boston medical men who heard his speech invited Dr Ketchum to prepare a paper as part of the programme of the September meeting of the American Society of Clinical Research. . . . Its presentation created a sensation and almost before Dr Ketchum knew that the paper had been given to the press he was deluged with letters and telegrams inquiring about the strange case.

'It is well enough to add that Dr Wesley H. Ketchum is a reputable physician of high standing and successful practice in the homeopathic school of medicine. He possesses a classical education, is by nature of a scientific turn, and is a graduate of one of the leading medical institutions of the country. He is vouched for by orthodox physicians in both Kentucky and Ohio, in both of which states he is well known. In Hopkinsville, where his home is, no physician of any school stands higher . . .

'Dr Ketchum wishes it distinctly understood that his presentation of the subject is purely ethical, and that he attempts no explanation of what must be classed as mysterious mental phenomena.

'Dr Ketchum is not the only physician who has had opportunity to observe the workings of Mr Cayce's subconscious mind. For nearly ten years his strange power has been known to local physicians of all the recognised schools.'

The *Times* story then quoted from Ketchum's paper which had caused such a clatter:

' "About four years ago I made the acquaintance of a young man 28 years old who had the reputation of being a 'freak'. They said he told wonderful truths while he was asleep. I, being interested, immediately began to investigate, and as I was 'from Missouri' I had to be shown.

' "And truly, when it comes to anything psychical, every layman is a disbeliever from the start, and most of our profession will not accept anything of a psychic nature, hypnotism, mesmerism, or what not, unless vouched for by some MD away up in the profession and one whose orthodox standing is unquestioned.

' "My subject simply lies down and folds his arms, and by autosuggestion goes to sleep. While in this sleep, which to all intents and purposes is a natural sleep, his objective mind is completely inactive and only his subjective is working . . .

' "I next give him the name of my subject and the exact location of same, and in a few minutes he begins to talk as clearly and distinctly as anyone. He usually goes into minute detail in diagnosing a case, and especially if it be a very serious case.

' "His language is usually of the best, and his psychological terms and descriptions of the nervous anatomy would do credit to any professor of nervous anatomy. . . . He handles the most complex 'jaw-breakers' with as much ease as any Boston physician, which to me is quite wonderful, in view of the fact that while in his normal state he is an illiterate man, especially along the line of medicine, surgery or pharmacy, of which he knows nothing.

' "After going into a diagnosis and giving name, address, etiology, symptoms, diagnosis and treatment of a case, he is awakened by the suggestion that he will see this person no more, and in a few minutes he will awake. Upon questioning him, he knows absolutely nothing that he said, or whose case he was talking about. I have used him in about 100 cases, and to date have never known of any errors in diagnosis except in two cases where he described a child in each case by the same name, and who resided in the same house as the one wanted. He simply described the wrong person . . .

' "The cases I have used him in have, in the main, been the rounds before coming to my attention, and in six important cases which had been diagnosed as strictly surgical he stated that no such condition existed, and outlined treatment which was followed with gratifying results in every case . . .

' "Now, in closing, you may ask why has a man with such powers not been before the public and received the endorsement of the profession, one and all, without fear or favour? I can truly answer by saying they are not ready to receive such as yet. Even Christ himself was rejected, for 'unless they see signs and wonders they will not believe.' " '

Toward the end of the *Times* interview with Dr Ketchum was this nugget—Cayce's own revelation of the source of his knowledge which Ketchum and his associates had elicited from him while in his sleep-state! Cayce refers to himself in the third person :

' "Edgar Cayce's mind is amenable to suggestion, the same as all other subconscious minds, but in addition thereto it has the power to interpret to the objective mind of others what it acquires from the subconscious mind of other individuals of the same kind. The subconscious mind forgets nothing. The conscious mind receives the impression from without and transfers all thought to the subconscious where it remains even though the conscious mind may be destroyed." Continuing, Cayce added that since the subconscious mind is in direct communication with all other subconscious minds, he is able to gather all the knowledge possessed by millions of other subconscious minds.'

Dr Ketchum's paper wound up with an appeal to his colleagues to 'give their advice and suggestions' as to the best method of 'putting my man in the way of helping suffering humanity' and he added that if they would send him the name and address of their most complex case he would gladly try to prove 'what I have endeavoured to describe'. Apparently there was no pell-mell rush to co-operate, and I read elsewhere that Dr Ketchum had to put up with a good deal of ridicule from a number of his medical colleagues.

What of Cayce's standing with the medical profession today? I found that the ARE runs its own clinic in Phoenix, Arizona, where patients are given treatments that combine Cayce concepts and remedies with modern medical knowledge that harmonise with it. Staffed by four MDs, its director, Dr William McGarey, has tested Cayce therapies in his private practice for ten years! There is also a medical research division of the Edgar Cayce Foundation, custodian of the original verbatim transcripts of the Cayce readings. It sponsors annual medical conferences that bring Cayce concepts before the medical profession, encourages research on Cayce therapies, and circulates the results to an interested coterie of about 250 medical doctors, psychologists, psychiatrists, osteopaths, chiropractors and nurses.

Perhaps my most important reading at this time was the two ARE pamphlets highly recommended for would-be healers: *That Ye May Heal* and *Gifts of Healing* and especially the important source-work known as the *281 Series,* a bound transcript of all the readings Edgar Cayce gave to the original Meditation for Healing Group over a thirteen-year period beginning in 1931. The first members of that group had never done any healing before Cayce undertook to guide and teach them, and so the readings are particularly helpful to beginning healers. The concepts are often expressed in the language of the old-time prophets, however, and the style of expression is notoriously complex.

At a point when I was trying to condense into clear, simple terms the densely worded descriptions Edgar Cayce gave of the spiritual healing process to his prototype Meditation for Healing Group, I followed a Cayce formula and made a strong prayer-suggestion before going to sleep, asking for clarification of the mechanics of healing as laid out in Cayce's *281 Series.* That night in a dream I saw clearly typed on white paper these two lines:

Open yourself up to God
Let the healing power flow through you to the ill person.

I couldn't believe I was being directed by my Higher Self to discard the entire *281 Series* and accept this explanation instead! Then it slowly dawned that this 16-word phrase was like the clear, precise theme of a fugue around which I could weave the complex counterpoint of Cayce's healing philosophy.

The dream-directive clearly suggested four areas that needed separate explanations: (1) How do you 'open yourself up to God?' (2) What factors help or hinder the flow? (3) How is the healing power conveyed to the ill person? (4) What attitude is best for the person receiving the healing?

Boiled down and with some words of my own added, here is the gist of Cayce's answers to the above questions:

(1) In meditation, with the aid of breathing exercises, attune the inner self to a consciousness of the oneness of individual life with Universal Consciousness. Through this attunement, the body's vibrations will begin to rise. The body then becomes like a magnet as spirit answers to spirit.

(2) In order to raise the body's vibrations high enough so that they flow out of self to the person for whom healing is intended there must be unity of purpose in the group. Each member should look into himself and overcome attitudes such as cynicism, selfishness, envy and resentment and develop virtues such as love and patience, the desire to be of service to others. In other words, one must heal himself in order to heal others, but conversely, one heals himself by healing others. It helps to feel oneself surrounded by divine love while healing.

(3) The vibrations raised in the body are emanations of the life force from within and are material expressions of a spiritual influence. These spiritualised emanations are sent out through the pituitary gland as thought waves, by suggestive force, or by visualising the healing activity on the ill person.

(4) The ill person should seek help and have a sincere desire to be healed. It is best if he has faith that he will be healed and if he co-operates wholeheartedly with the Healing Group by co-ordinating his meditation and prayers with theirs so that his consciousness will be raised at the same time.

This is my understanding of the healing process through a laborious study of the *281 Series*. I had been following much the same steps more or less consciously in our Meditation for Healing Group, but only after reading this source book did I understand why my body would gently tip from side to side or make a circular motion sometimes when I was giving the laying-on of hands! Cayce explains this, in reading *281*-12, as the result of the vibrations being raised in the body.

3. Incident in a Subway

A FEW WEEKS later, returning home on a spiritual wave from our healing group session, I stopped as usual at 14th Street to wait for a local underground to take me to Sheridan Square. I happened to look idly downward, and a plain white piece of folded paper lying on the platform caught my eye . . . It had been stepped-on and was not at all tempting, but for some reason I picked it up and unfolded it. I stared in disbelief. It was a letter from Mary Rogers to someone in New York who wanted healing! It was addressed to 'Dear Friend' and she was asking them to link up with her at a certain hour. After her signature was a Sussex rather than a Middlesex address, but I had little doubt it was the same person. I dusted off the letter and returned it by air mail with my note asking if she was the same Mary Rogers I had last corresponded with over eight years ago. I got a swift reply:

'My dear Sally,

What a fantastic happening! Obviously arranged, and a great story. I was interviewed by the London correspondent of your weekly paper, *The National Enquirer,* and now I seem to be healing America. I *may* be coming over later but I would need a good write-up in a good magazine that would explain the kind of healing work I do. I have lists of total cures by absent healing . . . I'd love to see you . . . George is now retired from the House . . . I am busier than ever and was "told" that I had a lot of work to do in the USA.

In haste,

(signed) Mary Rogers'

Of all the millions of people in New York City, for me to be the one to pick up Mary's letter was so remarkable that it didn't seem at all outlandish that I might have been 'guided'!

In our next few exchanges, I offered to write the magazine article about her work and she was delighted. We had several expensive talks on the overseas phone, corresponded heavily, and a New York friend travelling to England took down a face-to-face interview on tape. Mary also sent me a large envelope full of clippings suggesting that both she and her husband had been making an impact on the public.

A number of news stories reporting George Rogers' campaign for re-election in 1966 spoke of his demand that a government commission be appointed to verify the psychic cures of his wife and her colleagues. (Mary said he failed in his bid to introduce a private member bill to that end, however, a motion which must be won by ballot.)

I learned that in his twenty-five years in Commons, Rogers had worked tirelessly to upgrade the status of spiritual healers. In 1951, co-operating with Tom Brooks, the only other Spiritualist MP, he helped repeal an archaic Witchcraft Act and update other old laws that had for years persecuted both mediums and healers, succeeding where other MPs failed in 1930 despite Sir Arthur Conan Doyle's influential support.

Appearing on a platform at a huge 'Healing Teach-In' at Central Hall, Westminster, in 1966, Rogers challenged the British Medical Association to change its official policy of non-co-operation with spiritual healers. 'People are dying and suffering needless pain because the medical profession will not take the blinkers off their eyes. It is criminal irresponsibility', Rogers was quoted as saying, and he asked that healers be 'respected and treated as the valuable citizens they are, and healing removed from the doubtful fringe of charlatans who exploit it for their dubious ends'.

The publicity generated by her husband's successful re-election campaign in 1966 put Mary in the limelight. Under the headline, 'MP's Wife With A Healing Touch', the *Sunday Telegraph*, a staunch Tory newspaper, reported in straight journalistic style that 'by laying-on hands, she claims, she has cured paralysis, blindness and slipped discs which have failed to respond to hospital treatment,' and, without naming names, noted that 'several of her husband's fellow MPs are her patients'.

Mary explained that unfortunately none of the thirty or so MP friends of her husband who come to her for treatment or send their wives and children would want their names to be used in such a story. Nor could she name the government minister whose crippled daughter she cured. 'People in high places still consider spiritual healing offbeat,' she said regretfully. 'They rush to seek for help but are very coy about admitting that God can and has healed them.'

On the other hand, she said a Nassau government official, Dr Doris Johnson, was not afraid to stand up in Chapel and tell the congregation that spiritual healing had corrected her slipped disc. A clipping from the *Nassau Guardian* and *Bahamas Observer* of December 7, 1968, told the lively story of Mary's visit there when Dr Johnson, unable to walk more than a few steps at a time because of a painful back condition, was healed within seconds. 'They offered me a church for a week's healing services if I ever returned to Nassau,' Mary said.

After the *Telegraph* story came a flurry of write-ups in the *Daily Mail, Evening Standard, Guardian, Brighton Evening Argus* and the in-group weekly, *Psychic News*, and I read them all with fascination. They told of her work with mongoloid children, old age pensioners and young drug addicts and there were several dramatic accounts of her healings. She re-told one of them in her own words :

'Elsie Meyer of Cobham, Surrey, dropped in with a friend who had a healing appointment. I looked at her and said, "My goodness, you have a big lump on your thyroid gland don't you." And she said yes, that her doctor described it as "big as a golf ball" and was removing it the next week. So I gave her treatment for five minutes. Soon after the operation she called me to say her surgeon demanded to know what she had done to the growth. And when she admitted going to a spiritual healer, he said, "Go tell your healer the golf ball had shrunk to the size of a pea and I took it out." ' (Mrs Meyer, when asked about the experience by the *Psychic News* reporter said, 'I want to tell everyone about this wonderful healing that is available. If they want proof they have only to look at me.')

One of the stories mentioned Mary's 'spirit doctor' Sir John Simon, and I asked her to tell me more about her belief that spirits direct the healing.

'He first attached himself to me about nine years ago,' Mary said, 'and introduced himself only as "Dr Simon". Then a few years ago when I was interviewed by Paul Cavanagh on BBC, he challenged me to find out what his earth identity was. So I asked him. "If you must know, I was *Sir* John Simon," he said, and gave me all his credentials. Cavanagh then looked him up in a medical history and found that everything matched. He was London's first Public Health Officer and the head of St Thomas Hospital and was also president of the Royal College of Surgeons and an expert on thyroid functions and abdominal ailments. He was not a society doctor but a man who really cared about the poor. He cleaned up the foul tenements and filth of London's East End and was knighted by Queen Victoria.'

I didn't know quite what to make of all this. At Mary's suggestion I had begun reading the books of Harry Edwards, the dean of Britain's spiritual healers, and he mentioned being guided in his healing by the spirits of Louis Pasteur and Sir William Lister! Then I came across a comment by Edgar Cayce in the *281 Series* on 'spirit communication' that helped clarify things. In reading number *281*-19, A-12, Cayce said in part:

> 'The Holy Spirit has been pointed out in its activity as designating an individual in the earth for a particular service in the earth; while the communication that may come from outside forces or entities—even though they may be sent as messengers—is as a relay. Just as the experiences of many of ye that are gathered here may receive through these channels that which will aid thee in awakening to the possibilities, the responsibilities, within thine own experience. But to experience that thou hast been awakened from within in thine own consciousness of being in closer walk with Him is more glorious still, and only known by those who experience same. Both are wonderful. One is as guided by the spirit of truth. The other as relayed to thine consciousness.'

This pronouncement of Cayce's, that being awakened from within by the Holy Spirit and receiving communication by relay from outside forces were 'both wonderful', helped me accept the strange concept of spirit doctors directing the healing. I was pleased when Mary said she felt an affinity for Cayce. A patient had brought her a copy of *The Sleeping Prophet,* she said. 'Now there is so much "ham" around, but Cayce's work and prophecy and stories of Atlantis are almost the same as I have received here. He's the greatest!'

Mary said that on April 26, 1969, right after the evening news, she made her television debut on 'Subject for Sunday' with Leslie Smith as moderator. The subject was 'divine healing' and she shared the programme with two clergymen, Archdeacon Lawrence and the Reverend Paul Peters, who explained the 'laying-on of hands' traditional in Christian churches and listened respectfully while she told about receiving the power of healing through the agency of spirit doctors. Also on the programme were two doctors who took opposite views, one believing that some humans do have the gift of divine healing and the other opposing the practice because 'there is too little known about it'.

After all this publicity in the press, radio and TV, Mary said she began getting patients from all over England. Then one day a man flew in from Iran who had heard about her and was healed instantly. Others came from The Netherlands and Germany. She now has patients in Canada, the West Indies, Thailand, Nigeria and thousands in America, a tidal wave of some 7,500 letters from all over the US having rushed in after the interview she gave the *Enquirer*.

She sent me a large packet of these letters and invited me to write to any or all of them to verify the results of her absent healing treatments, for use in the article. Among them was a letter from José Vazquez of Charleston, South Carolina, a barber who had been out of work a long time because of his shaky hands, a condition Sir John diagnosed as palsy:

'Dear Mrs Rogers,
 I write you a few lines to let you know that I am feeling much better . . . twenty-four days after receiving your letter, I went to work at the barber shop cutting hair. My hands are much better. Today I shave a gentleman and everything is going fine. I am feeling very good. People say I am looking much better . . . May God bless you all,
     Yours sincerely,
     (Signed) José Vazquez'

I followed up this and about a dozen similar letters. Not all replied. Mr Vazquez, a year after the above letter, reported to me that he was 'still in good shape'. One very old man in Brooklyn, New York, who had written Mary a Christmas card saying he was 'feeling better' refused rather angrily to let me use his name, and another woman who had been 'helped' declined use of her name because her husband, a local politician, might be embarrassed. Several, however, gave unequivocal endorsements. Mrs Caroline Richards, of Michigan City, Indiana, who had asked for help for three daughters—one with diabetes, another with asthma and a third with acne—wrote me to say, 'The tests of my children are now negative'.

Not a single letter that comes to her is left unread or unanswered, Mary said. 'The treatment begins when I open the ill person's letter. I never let anyone else open my mail because I get vibrations from each message and in that way make a link with the person. From that moment, the spirit helpers over there assist me with the cure.

She is grateful to have the devoted help of Hope Alexander, a retired barrister, who helps with her vast correspondence, typing up all the replies without pay. Mary hoped I'd not forget to note in the article that 'donations are more than welcome to cover postal expenses'.

After amassing all this information, and more, about the amazing Mary Rogers, and writing the article, I shot it off to *Life* magazine. But senior editor David E. Scherman would have none of her. He compared Mary with another 'far-out' Englishwoman, Rosemary Brown, who claims she receives the compositions of dead composers through spirit communication. He wrote:

> 'Dear Miss Hammond,
>   I really think we should not do anything about Mary Rogers. The whole thing reminds me of the rather cruel Krebiozen episode of a decade ago, when people got their hopes up falsely over an earnest and seemingly honest hoax. Fake music is one thing, a la Rosemary Brown, but fake life and death is another.
>   Best,
>   (Signed) David E. Scherman'

This totally negative reaction from a *Life* editor I respected highly was rather a jolt. But I began to realise that the real problem was the lack of information about the new gains made in psychic research. For some reason it has always been a subject the media shy away from. I decided to set aside the article about Mary Rogers and put together a presentation for a TV documentary to be called

'Psychic News', reporting all the latest developments on the psychic research frontier.

Teaming up with a friend from the ARE, Ed Rundquist, we spent the next six months digging up details of the latest experiments of parapsychologists and other researchers in the field and found there was an upsurge of activity going on that hadn't been reported. The Parapsychological Association had only in 1969 been admitted to the prestigious American Association for the Advancement of Science; and two of the most significant research breakthroughs were in the area of psychic healing!

We almost sold 'Psychic News' to NBC's 'Chronolog'. (A budget cut and pre-emption of the show by the coming political conventions were the reasons given us for turning it down after several months of negotiations.) But meanwhile Ed and I told the story of today's tremendously varied psychic research advances on educational TV in New York. We then took our presentation to Will Bradbury, science editor, and sold it as a picture story idea to *Life*!

At about this time an English healer arrived in New York bringing with him a bit of evidence that pointed up the more progressive attitude of the British toward matters psychic and the relative 'uptightness' of Americans, especially intellectuals. The healer, Arthur Kings, gave me a back issue of *Psychic News,* published in London, covered with pictures of a Whitsunday morning public demonstration of spiritual healing at the foot of Lord Nelson's Column in Trafalgar Square! And Monday's press coverage of it was reportedly 'fair and factual', according to *Psychic News.* (While in New York, Mr. Kings gave healing to my first mother-in-law, Anita Trope Ross, with excellent results.)

4. A Healing in the Garden

THE NEW YORK press was giving daily page one headlines to the extraordinary spectacle of the first old-time religious revival in Madison Square Garden, usually the scene of sweaty prizefights. Along with crowds of other observers sparked by curiosity, I dropped in to see the show. Thousands of hard-bitten New Yorkers—not just country folk—were going forward nightly vowing to love their neighbours and change their lives! Arriving near the end, I slipped into a high balcony seat where I could survey the scene and be comfortably distant from the fire-breathing evangelist who was known for his high-voltage style. At the climax, when people began responding to his exhortation to make a decision to follow Christ's example in their lives, I looked at their faces and their clothing, wondering what type of people they might be. Were they naïve? Merely susceptible to emotional appeals? Did they really intend to commit themselves for life?

The organ music trailed off and the crowd of decision-makers filed out in the direction of the meeting rooms downstairs, for counselling. I got up to leave and headed toward the nearest exit. As I walked alone down the corridor, lost in thoughts about the meaning of what I had seen, I began wondering how I, supposedly a believer, could justify walking away from such an invitation. And the thought struck me, who was I to be feeling so superior to all those people who had accepted the challenge? I felt a stab of remorse. Then, a strange thing began happening. My body was being gently wheeled about, seemingly by a force apart from my own will, and my footsteps were being propelled in a semi-circle, facing me in the opposite direction. I was walking willingly, even eagerly, toward the counselling room! I saw no vision and heard no voice. But I was overpowered by emotions I can't describe except with the inadequate words ebullient joy and a tremendous sense of well-being.

Soon I was in the presence of a kindly counsellor, whom I could barely see through tears, confessing all my errors of the past resolving to do better.

And so, in that dark, dusty corridor of the old Garden I was 'born again'—an experience of spiritual healing of the spirit, direct from the Source. Curiously enough it happened without my seeking it. Rather, I was like a runaway captured while trying to escape! But the sense of renewal has lasted to this day.

On this spiritual crest, I took to reading the Bible zestfully every morning over breakfast. And this led me to rediscover the early spiritual roots of psychic healing so familiar to my childhood.

Reading again about Christ's healing ministry was exciting enough in my new state of awareness, but when I came upon His charge to his disciples in Luke 9:2 ('And he sent them to preach the kingdom of God and to heal the sick') and later the Book of Acts recounting the healings performed by Peter and John, Philip and Paul, I was electrified. Here were ordinary humans using their spiritual gifts!

There was the incident at the Gate called Beautiful, where Peter and John healed the man lame from birth who sat there day after day begging for alms:

> 'And Peter, fastening his eyes on him with John, said, "Look on us." And he gave heed unto them expecting to receive something of them. Then Peter said, "Silver and gold have I none, but such as I have I give thee. In the name of Jesus Christ of Nazareth rise up and walk." And he took him by the right hand and lifted him up and immediately his feet and ankle bones received strength. And he leaping up stood, and walked, and entered with them into the temple, walking and leaping and praising God.' (Acts 3:4-8)

And coming to the healing performed by Paul, I felt a new affinity for the Apostle whose rebirth, somewhat more dramatic than mine, had blinded him for three days. With fascination I read the story in which Paul revived the young man who, having slumbered during one of his long sermons had fallen from a third storey loft and was 'taken up dead' :

> 'And Paul went down, and fell on him, and embracing him said, "Trouble not yourselves, for his life is in him !" And they brought the young man alive, and were not a little comforted.' (Acts 20 :9-12)

I had forgotten that Paul used his healing gift generously on the island of Melita where he was shipwrecked en route to Rome. Not only the father of Publius, chief of the island, 'who lay sick of a fever and a bloody flux to whom Paul entered in and prayed, and laid his hands on him and healed him' but 'others also which had diseases in the island, came, and were healed.' (Acts 28 :8-10)

I was mystified by what appeared to be an extraordinary psychic gift demonstrated by Paul in Acts 19 :11, 12 :

> 'And God wrought special miracles by the hands of Paul, so that from his body were brought unto the sick handkerchiefs or aprons, and the diseases departed from them . . .'

Most meaningful to would-be healers today, it seemed to me, is Paul's message on the diversity of spiritual gifts, among them the gift of healing. In I Corinthians 12, he clearly states that these gifts are innate in all humans and not uniquely bestowed on Christ's disciples and apostles.

> 'Now there are diversities of gifts, but the same Spirit. . . . But the manifestation of that Spirit is given to every man to profit withal.' (verses 4, 7)

Listing the spiritual gifts in this order—wisdom, knowledge, faith, healing, the working of miracles, prophecy, the discerning of spirits, diverse kinds of tongues and the interpretation of tongues—he then writes, 'But all these worketh that one and the selfsame Spirit, dividing to every man severally as he will . . . for by one Spirit are we all baptized into one body, whether we be Jews or Gentiles, whether we be bond or free, and have been all made to drink into one Spirit.' (I Corinthians 12 :11, 13)

If the phrase, 'dividing to every man severally' might suggest to some that only certain specially gifted people can be healers, that interpretation appears to be roundly contradicted by Paul's urging that the Corinthians 'covet earnestly the best spiritual gifts' in verse

31 of that same chapter and his exhortation at the beginning of Chapter 14 that they 'follow after charity and desire spiritual gifts'. The meaning comes clear in I Corinthians 14 : 12 :

> 'Forasmuch as ye are zealous of spiritual gifts, seek that ye may excel to the edifying of the church.'

Wasn't Paul saying that the gift of healing, and all the spiritual gifts, should be sought-after and developed by anyone desiring them?

I wondered why the established churches had virtually dropped such a potent element of early Christian teaching, especially when so many chronic illnesses remain incurable in the present state of medical science, and today's doctors' fees, in America at least, are beyond the reach of so many!

5.   The Psychic trail leads South

GRADUALLY THE IDEA crept into my mind of writing a book about spiritual healing, although I had never before had any such inclinations. Taking a year's leave from *The Post,* I started my research by heading South where I knew there were a number of outstanding healers and centres of healing activity. Ed Rundquist accompanied me in order to round up more research facts for the *Life* picture story.

Going first to ARE headquarters in Virginia Beach, I delved into the Cayce readings under the heading 'Spiritual Healing' and came across an extraordinary case of a woman who greatly reduced the size of a huge tumour by raising her spiritual consciousness resolutely, and by visualising herself being made whole by the corrective treatments being applied under Edgar Cayce's direction!

We were staying with my cousin, a retired Navy Commander, and it just happened that he underwent surgery for removal of a cancerous lung while we were there. Unable to find a spiritual healer to go to see him at the hospital, we put him on the ARE Healing Group's emergency list and his wife and I went to his bedside in the Intensive Care Unit of Portsmouth Naval Hospital. It was the morning after the operation and he was in acute pain.

My cousin said drily, 'Anything you want to do will be very much appreciated,' so we drew the curtain and, while his wife prayed fervently from the other side, I placed my hands where he hurt the most, hoping some healing power would flow through me to relieve him a little. Something must have happened, because he said he felt heat coursing through his body, and I saw a dazzling white light with my eyes closed! And several weeks later his wife told me the doctors thought his recovery was remarkable and 'all they could possibly want'. They expected complications because of an earlier operation which had removed a lobe from the lung. My cousin recalled that every time the doctors came in to examine him 'they just shook their heads in amazement that I looked so good'. (He did not believe in psychic healing to start with and I had to do a lot of persuading before he would take it at all seriously.)

Our next stop was Durham, North Carolina, where we visited Dr Helmut Schmidt, director of the Institute for Parapsychology, where Dr J. B. Rhine, the pioneer of telepathy testing, is still active as a consultant. Among other facts, Dr Schmidt told us about a test of psychic healing run there by Graham and Anita Watkins in which 'healing thoughts' were sent through glass by a healer to one of two anaesthetised mice. The 'healed' mouse awoke and frisked about sooner than the unhealed mouse, he said.

In Atlanta, which we christened the 'psychic city', we found a fast pace of healing activity at the Centre for Spiritual Healing and Enlightenment, 1625 Monroe Drive North East. Interviewing its attractive young founders, the Reverend Peter Calhoun and his wife Harriett, both practising healers, we learned about their group healing and psychic development classes where people have uncovered their healing gift. I was intrigued to hear Peter Calhoun, a former Episcopal minister, say that he is convinced that the ability to heal is inherent in everyone to some degree and can be strengthened. Then, in a lively interview with a gifted healer-teacher-psychic on the staff, Naunie Batchelder, she remarked casually that 'we are all healers', and I knew by a sudden rise in blood pressure that she had given me the title and direction of my book!

This new direction was enthusiastically recommended by several other healers and psychics I met in Atlanta who had developed their gifts by attending regular healing groups and classes at the Centre —Louvina Wuerster, Jo O'Shields, the Rev Robert Goodman, Ben Osborne and Bertin Leger—all remarkable people clearly on a high plane of spiritual awareness.

Up until that moment I'd planned to interview a dozen respected healers coast-to-coast and to try to verify their cures. I quickly saw that much more significant than the so-called 'occult revolution' was the wildfire growth of spiritual group healing in America and the training these groups give people like myself who want to develop their latent gift, as St Paul so clearly recommended.

And so, I decided on the spot to leave the verifying of healers' cures to Life Energies Research Inc, the Academy of Parapsychology and Medicine, and Edgar D. Mitchell's Institute of Noetic Sciences, three upcoming organisations with healing research at the top of their agendas.

I learned about Frances Farrelly, a healer living in Bimini, through Douglas Dean, a leading parapsychologist. Dean told me of Miss Farrelly's strong psychic abilities, which she used in diagnosing illnesses of people at a distance, and Ed Rundquist and I decided to make the short plane hop from Miami to interview her.

Now the statuesque, bare-foot woman who greeted us in an airy apartment overlooking sand and sea, answered my questions about her technique matter-of-factly, making the fantastic sound somehow logical. For the next couple of hours I was aware of being in the presence of a seasoned practitioner.

'Doctors send me blood samples, or handwriting, or urine, or hair from the patient,' she said, 'and using my psychic abilities I am able to tell what the trouble is.' She added that it is a bit more complicated than that. She makes out a chart and the doctor has to know how to interpret it.

Miss Farrelly also gives contact healing. I asked if she would outline her approach to the patient and she said:

'I guess you have to purify yourself, and reach a state of attunement. I give an affirmation, like, "Let only good pass through me to this person", or "Let the love of God flow through me to the patient". You put self aside, your mood is passive and receptive. You think of the power coming down through the top of your head and down through your hands.

'People say they feel heat come from my hands, or a tingling, waves, all kinds of weird things. I feel a sensation going from my head through my right hand, which feels hot. My left hand has no sense of warmth.'

'Do you put your hands on the patient?' I asked.

'No. I keep them at some distance, because I'm treating the aura of the spiritual body. I move them until I come into an area where I feel resistance from the patient. I'll put hands on either side of the area, with my right hand on top—I consider it more or less the sending hand.'

'Do you feel love and compassion for your patients?'

'Love, not necessarily, but concern, yes. The love factors may be important but it is not possible to love all people. Empathy, however, is needed. A healer should learn to shield himself from becoming emotionally involved with his patients through sympathy. You merely ask to be a channel of God's healing.'

'How do you feel physically after a healing?'

'In magnetic healing, in which you take deep breaths, forcing the healing out, the energy seems to come from the healer and leaves him spent. But when you think of yourself only as a channel the healing gives you a feeling of strength.'

'What basic attitudes are important for a healer?'

'I think you are limited by your basic beliefs. If a healer says he can do nothing with cancer, I ask him, "Are you doubting God or yourself?" You have to keep drumming into your mind that God is the healer and you are nothing but a tool. So, the minute you say you can't do anything about cancer, you're doubting your own ability and, indirectly, God's. The "I" factor is so big it's going to get in your way. So I feel people do limit themselves by the mental limitations they put on themselves. Clergymen have told me, "I tried to heal once and I failed". But I tell them, "Where in Christianity are we taught that living is a success and death is a failure?" '

'What is the best attitude for the patient?'

'They must make a very great effort to correct their errors, whether they be physical, mental or emotional. In most cases of healing, some kind of counselling is necessary, using a more or less non-directive psychological approach—you ask the questions and you let the patient tell you.'

'Do you think the healer should live according to any special rules?' I asked.

Miss Farrelly replied, 'If their state of health is not up to par they don't make a very good channel. I think a sensible diet is indicated and just plain common sense living. But I don't hold that the gastro-intestinal tract is connected with healing ability. You often see a healer who is not healed himself.'

I asked Frances Farrelly about her own background. It was impressively supportive of her present work. She studied for the ministry and majored in psychology at St Lawrence College in Canton, New York, then switched to the medical lab field, enrolling at Northwestern Institute in Minneapolis and becoming a medical technologist. She has since owned and directed medical labs, and holds a director's licence in Florida where she has also taught people to become lab assistants in the school system.

Dean had spoken of her research with the mysterious Radionics instrument, used by some healers as an aid to diagnosis and healing, and I asked her about it. She said she studied many years ago with Ruth Drown, one of the pioneers—with Abrams, de la Warr and others—in developing the instrument, which is described in a later chapter. Miss Farrelly said she had used it as a 'tool', but now relies on her psychic abilities in making diagnoses.

6. On the Spiritual Frontier

IN THE LATE SUMMER of '72, two conferences in the southern states offered workshops and lectures on various aspects of spiritual healing that struck me as irresistible since their sponsors put more emphasis on group healing and on developing the healing gift generally, than any other such organisations in America. I quickly signed up for both.

Luckily, the Spiritual Frontiers Fellowship's First Southeastern Retreat at Emory College, about thirty miles from Atlanta, and the Association for Research and Enlightenment's 'Week of Attunement' in Virginia Beach were scheduled end-to-end and I was able to fly conveniently from one to the other.

'How To Be A Healer' was the intriguing title of the workshop given top billing by the SFF in their announcement, and it was to be led by the Reverend Alex Holmes, a legendary healer and ordained Congregational minister, whose extensive healing ministry in the British Isles I had read about in the writings of Harry Edwards. I was delighted to see that Holmes was now healing and lecturing in the United States and settled in a Presbyterian pastorate in Caro, Michigan. Others were giving workshops in 'How To Lead Prayer Healing Groups' and on 'Meditation', the basis of healing.

En route to Atlanta I realised I was familiar with only part of SFF's programme, having joined them out of admiration for their uninhibited efforts to put spiritual healing back into the churches and to encourage group healing. Organised in 1956 by a visionary group of clergy and laity of major Christian denominations, among them the late minister-psychic Arthur Ford, their overall aim is 'to open the eyes of a materialistic and sceptical generation to man's intrinsic spiritual nature' through pioneering programmes for spiritual and psychic development. And they've challenged the church as a whole to take an open-minded look at the psychic phenomena modern researchers are studying scientifically, and relate it to the miracles and mysteries of biblical tradition. Very up-to-date in the field of psychic research, SFF has its own investigations going forward, and so I wasn't surprised to see a Scientific Research Workshop listed at which a Georgia Institute of Technology chemical engineering professor would report the effect on the growth rate of rye grass of a spiritual healer's prayers projected 600 miles!

Alighting at the Atlanta airport, I was met by my friend Lester Mers, an artist and former New York neighbour, who drove me in his low-slung sports-car to the tree-shaded college campus in Oxford. There I was greeted by several of the pleasant, stimulating people I'd met last spring in Atlanta, among them Jo O'Shields, a pretty, red-haired mother of three who was to be my room-mate in the modern dorm. Our ground floor quarters soon became a meeting place and park-your-tape-recorder depot by day and party lounge by night.

Across the hall and on either side were the rooms of several of the 'psychic consultants' whose role at the Retreat was to give spiritual guidance through their psychic gifts—clairvoyance, clairaudience, psychometry, clairsentience—or to lead workshops in 'spiritual and psychic development'. According to their bios, with which we were provided, they were people of substantial backgrounds and most had religious affiliations.

In the group were six women and four men, some colourful and striking in appearance and others indistinguishable from the Retreat participants, predominantly a middle-aged, comfortable-looking non-flamboyant crowd.

The ten consultants were: The Rev. Paul Neary, a well-known clairvoyant and lecturer who has worked with psychologists in Atlanta and in research projects at the American Society for Psychical Research in New York; Anita Josey, who has taught classes at Oglethorpe University on psychic and spiritual subjects; Marty Urban, associated with the Atlanta Centre for Spiritual Healing and Enlightenment; The Rev. Robert Goodman, a one-time Methodist minister and now an Atlanta businessman; The Rev.

LeRoy Zemke, the young and handsome pastor of the Temple of the Living God in St Petersburg, Florida; Phyllis Schlemmer, who runs the Psychic Centre in Orlando, Florida; Dorothy Moore, a former psychiatric nurse whose mentor was the late Arthur Ford; Jane Hudson, an ordained Spiritualist minister; Marlene Ferran, a National Spiritualist Association teacher who works with auric vibrations; and Donald Hudson, who for three years has given psychic readings at the annual festival-in-the-park in Charlotte, North Carolina.

Several of these people, I knew, had well-developed healing gifts along with their other talents. Among those with several gifts is Paul Neary, who left the Catholic priesthood to become a Pentecostal Spiritualist minister. He obligingly gave me these details of his practice and philosophy of healing:

'I was ten years old when I discovered that I had the ability to heal. People said they felt soothed and relaxed and a warm spiritual vibration when I was present. I developed this by continuous use and by concentrating on opening myself to the psychic flow of the healing power. It seemed to grow within me.

'I do the laying-on-of-hands and also place my hands three or four inches away from the body. I invoke the God-force through prayer, asking if it is the God-force's will for the person to be healed and, if so, for the betterment of the person.

'While healing I feel a sensation of energy flowing through my head and down through my hands. I am in an altered state, almost in a hypnotic trance. I am completely relaxed. My patients say they feel extreme heat, a flow of energy and vibrations.'

When I asked, 'How do you feel about your healing gift?' Neary replied, 'Awed, amazed and non-questioning.'

His mental and spiritual preparation involves prayer, and concentration on the energy flow from mind to hands. 'I ask if it is His will and for the soul evolvement of the person being healed, then let it be.

'I do not consider healing—physical—of the body as important as healing of the soul,' Neary continued, 'I believe most people are too interested in body, not soul, or better to say self-centred or obsessed with the now and not concerned with the why of it. They never question why they are ill. I think illness has a reason or cause. I would never think of healing body without consideration of soul and attitudes. I do not believe life is for long-suffering. Affirmations can heal almost all negative attitudes and illness.' (Affirmations, he explained, 'are spiritual truths that uplift the soul'.)

Neary added that at times he feels the presence of spirits while healing and he uses his psychic gifts of clairvoyance, clairaudience and trance abilities 'but not consciously'. He does not think his healing ability has developed to the fullest but feels it is developing naturally.

Several doctors have sent him their patients and he has treated doctors. Neary finds he is most successful in healing children and such illnesses as cancer, heart conditions, motor reflex disorders and emotional problems. His estimate of the percentage of patients healed is 80-85 per cent. 'All usually say they feel improved, but many say completely or slightly improved, progressively.'

In his opinion, belief in God is not a prerequisite to healing, but the person should be 'open-minded, receptive, and not expecting'. Even an atheist can be healed, he said, 'but if healed it will help him realise an awareness. It can be a way to God for non-believers'.

Summing up his philosophy of healing, Neary emphasised that it is more important to be healed in spirit than in body. 'It is that to which you must aspire', he said, adding that by accepting and coping with the challenge of ill health the soul evolves to a higher level than would be possible if the physical body were healed too quickly. I saw flashes of Cayce in his philosophy, but with differences, perhaps, of emphasis. His warning against superficial approaches to healing was certainly timely.

I asked Neary if he felt, as I did, that Cayce's life readings were a form of healing. He agreed they were, and said that a person's emotional and mental health is benefited when he knows who it is he has to work out problems with because of his failure to do it in a previous lifetime, and when he's helped to see 'the corollary between other lives and this one'. He added, however, that the problems we have in this life are not necessarily karmic and he may help people see that they are the result of present spiritual or physical relationships and the development of new karma.

In a few minutes, at the Rev. Alex Holmes' workshop on 'How To Be A Healer' I would be exposed to a totally different viewpoint, that of the spiritual frontiers of Presbyterianism! I hurried over to the Chapel and slipped into a front pew in order to be within close range of his famous well-known vibrations.

The atmosphere of the lovely modern chapel was serene and subdued. It was Quaker-plain except for a huge chandelier with thousands of sparkling prisms that would have done credit to an opera house, the gift of a wealthy alumnus no doubt! The arched windows were draped in beige, the floor claret-carpeted and the pews of form-fitting polished oak. A simple gold cross flanked by single gold candlesticks on a mahogany altar were the only adornments.

Arriving at the door, Mr Holmes, looking trim in a navy blue and white short-sleeved sports shirt, made his way through groups of admirers. Brisk, kindly, with reddish hair, blue eyes and ruddy colouring (he was born in Northern Ireland), he had a pleasantly informal manner. He avoided the platform and stood resting his hand on the front of the first row of pews.

As soon as the audience quieted, he sent up a brief but fervent prayer—a request for inspiration that was surely answered in the ensuing hour. It went something like this: 'Lord, speak to me that I may speak in living echoes of thy tone . . . that those who have come to hear thy word and thy truth may go away with thy word indwelling and thy truth revealed to them. Amen.'

He began by assuring us that 'anybody who can pray can send healing to others', as all of us must know through our membership in Spiritual Frontiers Fellowship.

Just as every doctor, nurse, dentist, osteopath, orthodontist and psychiatrist is a channel for God's healing power, we can be too, he said, for we can bring health and wholeness through our faith, our love, our prayers to those who seek our help.

But we will need to know the spiritual laws that are at the basis of healing if we are to become healers, and so he presented them to us, one by one, quoting liberally from the Gospels and then adding his own modern interpretations and spiritual insights.

Picking up a Bible, a New English Translation, he slowly read first of all the familiar passage in John 14 : 12; 'In truth, in very truth, I tell you, he who has faith in me will do what I am doing, and he will do greater things still because I am going to the Father. Indeed, anything you ask in my name I will do, so that the Father may be glorified in the Son.'

He paused to let the message sink in. Then he skipped ahead in time and told my favourite healing story from Acts 3, the astonishing healing of the lame beggar at the Gate Beautiful by Peter and John.

' "Whatever you ask in my name", said he, before he was tried, before he was put to death . . . Peter had forgotten all about it . . . but now he remembers. "In the name of Jesus Christ of Nazareth, stand up and walk!" And they took the man by the right hand, the hand of blessing.'

Holmes explained to us that in the Middle and Far East the left hand is the hand of filth, and so it was interesting for the story to specify that it was the right hand that was extended. 'Peter used a psychological approach in a way. The man *expected* a blessing because it was the right hand of blessing that was being offered him.'

The minister then shifted his emphasis from the quality of faith Peter and John used in the healing to the similar attitude on the part of the beggar.

'The man could have said, "Now wait a minute, brother. I've been born lame. I've never stood up in my life". But he didn't and the more he stood up, the more he was able to stand up, and the more he walked the more he was able to walk. And he walked and he leapt and he praised God.'

Having given us this double-pronged message, Holmes emphasised its significance : '*The more the man stood up the more he was able to stand up, and the more he walked the more he was able to walk.* For if beliefs are negative, they will materialise in discomfort and disease. But if they are positive good and whole-hearted, then they will materialise as comfort and healing. Be single-minded and within your single-mindedness, create what is good for yourself.'

Holmes gave a beautiful illustration of the psychic process through which an answer to prayer given in spirit is made real in matter. Had any of us had one of those lovely Finnish sauna baths where the heat is so dry that you can't see it although you can feel it? he asked. By lowering the vibrations a little it becomes heavy steam, and as they're lowered more it changes to wet steam, a liquid, and if you lower them still more it becomes solid ice, he said. 'What was there in the first place but couldn't be seen, you can now see, you can now touch, you can now taste, you can now handle.'

In prayer you 'put out the hand that is without doubt', he said, and as you do that you're 'lowering the vibrations' and bringing the answer to prayer that's already given in spirit into matter, where it can be seen. The analogy couldn't have been clearer!

Holmes thought God must be very frustrated when we ask repeatedly for things he has given us at first asking, prostrating ourselves before him as though he were an oriental potentate.

'I'm sure he feels like kicking us and saying, "Get up!" Because, you see, prayer is a two-way business, an asking and a receiving. You *believe* to *receive*. "Love thy neighbour as thyself. Love one another even as I have loved you" . . . And within the kingdom of right relationships, the kingdom of love, you can never ask for anything that is unworthy, but you *will* ask for what is legitimately yours—"Knock and it shall be opened up".'

Holmes now rounded up the laws we needed to know in order to become healers:

'So, now we have the law of the materialisation of belief. You put this into your prayer life, you perform within your prayer life and because you are asking as a child of God, you get an answer to your prayer.

'And the same laws apply to the subject who co-operates in his own healing. Remember the lame beggar at the Gate Beautiful—the more the man walked, the more he was able to walk; in other words, the more he claimed the more he got. As you let the living power of God flow through every part of your being, and you operate in the knowledge that the living power of God is at work within you bringing you healing and wholeness, healing of body, soul and mind, then you *will* be healed.'

In illustration Holmes raised his wrist. 'For instance, if this wrist of mine has arthritis and it's been locked for three years and I hold it and project my healing thoughts through it, asking for release and healing, and then claim what I've asked for, by gently moving the wrist, I'm claiming the healing that has already taken place, an answer to my prayer that has already been given in the realm of spirit. And I'm making it manifest in the realm of matter.'

(I realised while Holmes was speaking that I must have done this when acting on my own limited knowledge of self-healing. I had suffered painful dentistry just before coming to the Retreat and, rather than kill the pain with the codeine pills prescribed by the root canal specialist, I went into meditation, as I'd learned to do at the ARE. After about twenty minutes I felt a tingling in my left hand and was moved to place it on my cheek over the ache. About an hour later when I was preparing dinner, I suddenly realised the pain had disappeared! I had 'claimed' the healing by going about my chores, fully believing that the contact healing I had given myself would be effective. The dentist later told me he expected the pain to continue for 'about twenty-four hours'. I had suffered less than three hours.)

Part of the healer's role, Holmes said, was to help people claim their healing by placing the subjects' hands in such a way that they were encouraged to seek normal motion (if that was what was needed). Healings done in the formal manner at the communion rail —with a minister or priest putting his hand on the person's head and saying a healing prayer—were not as likely to succeed as when the subjects were helped to claim their healing in full view of the congregation. 'When they see the answer to prayer, the rest is easy— everybody becomes a healer to everybody else!'

I was delighted to hear him conclude : 'This, then, scotches the idea that to one man is given the gift of healing, to another wisdom, to another man this and to another that (referring to St Paul's discourse on spiritual gifts, I Corinthians : 12). 'There are varieties of gifts but the same Spirit who distributes them individually, as the individual wills to receive them.'

That afternoon, Alex Holmes met with a smaller, more intimate group in the quiet atmosphere of the modern library, surrounded by bookshelves. He began by gathering together the strands of his guidelines for healers, and after summing them up, said he would like to suggest some spiritual exercises that would help us develop our power of prayer.

First, however, he would help us to place Christ's power to heal in the context of the Trinity and the Creation as described in Genesis and in St John's Gospel ('In the beginning was the Word, and the Word was with God, and the Word was God. . . . . And the Word was made flesh and dwelt among us . . . full of grace and truth').

'You will remember that the actual creative principle in the story of the Creation is the projection of thought, that it was the logos quality or the thought quality that brought the material universe into being, that this thought quality became human in the person of Jesus of Nazareth.

'So he who created the material universe is able to recreate matter,' declared Holmes. 'He who created the material universe was able to bring healing to innumerable people when he walked the earth. He who created the material universe said, "He who believes on me, the works that I do shall he do also" and "Whatsoever you ask in my name, that will I do, that the Father might be glorified in the Son". If you ask me anything, I will do it! Still at work. Still creating matter! And for him there is nothing that's simple and nothing that's difficult. It's all the same.'

Holmes said he would like to erase from our thought the word 'difficult', and to let us see, as he himself tries to see, 'the Creator of the material universe in this situation, recreating matter and meeting a particular need as he said he would'.

Now he came to the exercises. He told us how he had worked them out when going through a barren period some twenty years ago, when God had seemed very far off and not listening, and he felt they had developed his own spiritual nature and made him more conscious of the reality of God and of God answering prayer.

'The first thing I did way back in those days when I tried to do something positive about my prayer life,' he recalled, 'was to remind myself of the nature of God. This could be a prayer of adoration or approach. And at that particular time I made my prayer of adoration or approach the 23rd Psalm. "The Lord is *mine*". I emphasise the personal pronoun. "*I* shall not want. He makes *me* to lie down in lush green pastures. He leads *me* beside the quiet, still, deep waters that are cool and easy to drink", and so on.

'Then, having reminded myself of the kind of God my God is, I'd want to say thank you to him for all his goodness to me, for the life that's in me, for the friends he gives me, for my family, for everything that comes my way.

'I would then want to tell him how sorry I am that I've let him down so often and I'd want to make my confession to him. Let us be specific in stating the particular sins we would like him to forgive. We ought to be able to mention one or two. And we should really examine ourselves . . . But our confession, in general, should be brief and to the point.

'Then, having done that, we will want to pray for other people, and this is the prayer of intercession. You think of the people in the hospital who need your prayers, the people who live down the street, all the people who need your prayers and you bring them to God in prayer.

'And, being good-mannered in prayer as in everything else, you put last your prayer of petition, bringing to God your own particular needs.

'So you have prayers of adoration, thanksgiving, confession, intercession and petition—and you who couldn't pray for two minutes find that you've been praying for fifteen or twenty minutes! And you keep this up. You become accustomed to talking to God, and this is very important, talking *aloud* to God.'

The listening-to-God stage was not yet. He wanted us to approach it with a 'deeper exercise in prayer', a kind of silent, thought-prayer that is somewhere in-between the vocal prayers he had just given us and mystical prayer. He roughly calls it meditation and yet it is not, he said.

'It involves first of all recollection—recalling to your mind a key sentence or phrase that is filled with meaning for you. It might be from a poem, a hymn, a passage of Scripture, from great prose. And it should be something you're very familiar with.'

The key phrase he most often uses, he said, is the prayer of Jesus on the cross : 'Father into thy hands I trust myself'. He recalls it to mind and then thinks of the phrase as a whole.

'Then I concentrate on it, or make it concentric to my entire being, and I bring it from mind right down into the centre of my being, here.' He indicated his diaphragm. 'Right into this main nerve centre. And I try to *feel* the sentence, every word of it, and because one can't avoid this, I also enter the situation which caused the sentence to be said. And then, having made it concentric, which is what concentrating is, bringing it to the middle of your being, the psychic centre. Having done that, I meditate upon it.

'Father. What do I mean by Father? What does this convey to me? Into thy hands. What are the hands of God? I. Who am I? Trust? What is the meaning of trust? What does it mean to you? As I meditate, as I chew it up, as I get all the juices from my key sentence, I let the whole lot just brood within me. This is contemplation—con-temple-ation—the body is the temple of the Holy Spirit—and as I do that I'm led forward into the realm of reality. New truth and new light is given me in and through the indwelling action of the Holy Spirit. And this is where I get my insights and the truths, many of which I project to you.'

And throughout the day, he went on, he sends out 'flash prayers', a habit with helpful results. For instance, when coming into a circle he is about to address, he'll say, 'God, give me the words to speak to these people' and when something disturbs him, 'God help me to be equal to this situation and show me insights and truth here. Help me love this person'. He felt that 'flash prayers' would be important for us, and that we, too, should develop this habit.

Our instructor then offered to demonstrate his ministering in healing prayer. He asked for a volunteer, and Virginia Weise, of Chicago, who was conveniently seated in a front chair, smilingly agreed to co-operate. As far as I know, he had never met her before and it was unlikely that he knew any details of her medical history.

'First, I would blend with the person and at the same time I would ask them what their particular need is,' Holmes began, after seating his 'patient' in a chair facing us.

He paused to explain that whatever a person thinks is his or her real need will be the need that is met, if the attitude to healing is sincere. An unmentioned need may not be met, but if the person simply failed to express it verbally but really desired it, that need may be met too.

'Let's say that she asks for healing for her spine. I would touch the top of her spine gently with my hand—using my right hand which, I think, is my healing hand—and I would blend, spirit to spirit, with her. Then I would follow my guidance, and it might very well be to ask her to just move forward, and as I move my hand gently down her spine I would ask her to let her body sink into her hips and then claim movement in the spine by stretching herself upward under my hand, claiming the healing and the release that has been asked for and has already come—but she has to claim it. Remember the taking and the receiving!

'Again, she might have a neck condition, so I would ask her then to put her chin on her chest and to claim movement and freedom in the neck this way.' He gently lifted her chin and tipped her head back a little. 'Now this is not manipulation, it is merely helping her to do this. Nine times out of ten she needs this help. Once out of ten she might do it herself, when I say, "Move your neck". But remember that she has been very aware of the fact that this neck has not moved freely for five years, maybe, so I will then move her neck and say, "Now you keep moving it". So she keeps moving it, and then the thought dawns on her that this neck that she is now moving easily and freely is something she hasn't been able to move like this for a number of years. So she has claimed the healing, and the more she claims it the more she will get. You see?'

Holmes then showed us how he would treat an arm, if that were the part afflicted. 'I would support the arm and project my healing thought from my right hand down the arm and then move it gently in this way (he lifted the arm slightly) then the elbow, I'd move it gently this way (he flexed the elbow joint slowly) and if it is completely free

I come down to the wrist, move it gently, then the fingers, smoothing away any arthritis that might be there, move the fingers and the thumb and then ask her to do it herself.

'Here,' he continued, 'if I'm going to minister to her legs, I'll concentrate healing prayer on the hip joint. I'll concentrate the healing thought where I've placed my fingers and then claim the movement slowly.

'Now suppose this knee is swollen and stiff with arthritis. I tenderly lift the knee and rest it, just like that (he supported it with his own knee) and then I would put my right hand very gently over the knee and I would ask for healing in the knee. Suppose the knee cap is frozen. I would make it loose in this way. Then, coming to the ankle, I concentrate healing on it and move it gently (he tilted her foot slowly up and down).

'Then, for the chest and indeed the body area in general, I will go to the psychic centre, which is the main nerve centre of the body—just where the ribs part, here—and I would concentrate here on healing for the lungs, the heart and the abdomen, all the while ministering in such a way that I'm helping the person claim the healing that has already been given.'

At that moment, Holmes noticed that his 'patient' actually had a condition that needed healing. He asked her to extend and straighten both legs. 'Would you care to come up?' he said, beckoning to a man in the front row. 'Do you see that?' The man verified Holmes' observation that one of her legs was considerably shorter than the other, after first checking to see if she was sitting straight with both hips touching the back of her chair. He asked the woman to bend her knees naturally but not to move, and she sat there looking a little puzzled as he continued his instruction, moving on to the subject of absent healing.

In his study in Caro, Michigan, letters asking for healing pile high on his 'prayer desk' and he works through them one by one, he said. 'I read a letter, I see what the need is, and I project the healing thought for this particular need. Then I'll put the letter aside. Then I come to the next one and I project the healing thought for this particular need, and put it aside. I do the same the following night and for six or seven nights. Then I answer the letter, and at the same time destroy the letter on my prayer desk.

'Now, if prayer is to continue to the person who wrote that letter and whose letter is now destroyed, and whose letter has now been answered, they must write me again and let me know, and in this way keep contact with me. By doing that, prayer is continuous for them.'

Not only continuous, but it is 'directive' to them, he said, 'I mean by directive prayer exactly what I've done right now. I've asked for healing for the woman's lower spine, and I've asked for this left leg to come into position.'

He asked her to straighten out her legs as they were before, but the woman wiggled in her chair as she did it and Holmes exclaimed disappointedly that she had spoiled the demonstration. 'The people here who are not going along with me are going to say, "Well, she moved. There's no way of telling".'

But when she stretched her legs out straight, they were very definitely even in length this time. 'You see? They're level.' Holmes said, smiling. 'This is what I was wanting to show you without her moving.' A 'miracle' before our eyes!

His patient then told him that she had suffered from a misalignment of the spine which had resulted in some shortening of one leg, but she had gone to a chiropractor and thought the adjustment had cleared it up.

Holmes had said earlier in his lecture that he felt so secure in bringing healing to spinal conditions that he would be willing to be challenged by any number of doctors. And if they brought two or three patients each with spinal conditions, he could assure them that two out of three would be healed or greatly helped as a result of his ministry to them. 'I had a lot of practice in this realm in my early days in Surrey,' he explained. 'The owner of a nature cure place was a member of my church and he asked if I would minister to two or three people with arthritic or spinal conditions each week. The experience was very helpful to me.'

The lecture ended, Holmes asked for questions. I asked him if he was in a state of 'attunement' when healing (the state Mary Rogers had said was necessary to permit the flow of healing energy). He said, 'Yes, with her and also I'm in attunement with my God. I'm the link man.'

Apparently, his spiritual vibrations are so high that he doesn't need to go into meditation to reach the state of attunement. He's attuned all day long!

In answer to a question about the healing of cancer, Holmes made the unusual comment that he couldn't believe cancer was evil because he couldn't believe God gave us anything evil. 'God gave man fire and until he learned how to control it and use it, it was evil. Then, when he controlled it, it became his ally and friend. If this cell is something good God has given us, perhaps we can make it our ally and friend? Perhaps we can learn to grow a finger that has been amputated!'

When asked the percentage of people who respond to spiritual healing, he said that in his ministry he found that about 85 per cent of those who come to him had been told that nothing further could be done for them medically. The remainder wanted his prayer ministry in conjunction with medical treatment. Of the 85 per cent, about 1 per cent received instantaneous, complete healing, he said, and 18-19 per cent were healed progressively and were completely cured. About 22 per cent were better but not healed completely and the remainder deteriorated physically and died.

'Can you send healing without the sick person knowing?' someone asked. 'Oh, yes,' he said. 'The healing is done in the realm of the spirit. A person can offer himself as a proxy for someone he knows and loves and is concerned about.'

'Do you feel virtue go out of you?' asked another, referring to the comment Jesus made in Luke 8 :46 after the woman who had had an issue of blood for twelve years touched the border of his garment. ('And Jesus said, "Somebody hath touched me for I perceive that virtue has gone out of me".') In reply, Holmes said, 'More often than not I'm stimulated. This feeling stays for about twenty minutes. Then I don't want to see anyone for an hour. I go flat.'

I asked if he believed in spirit doctors, and he said, 'Faith is always necessary. Belief is always necessary. It doesn't matter a great deal what your faith is in, but it matters in terms of your total ministry—and how much more effective it is when healing is done in and through Christian faith and prayer!'

The final question, 'What do you say to sceptics?' brought a jaunty reply. 'Sceptical people will always be sceptical,' he said. 'I've long since stopped worrying about them.'

The next evening, when the Rev. Alex Holmes conducted the Healing Service—noted in the programme as 'one of the highlights of the Retreat'—practically everyone attended, crowding the red-and-yellow brick church adjoining the campus. And he demonstrated from the platform a number of healings before our eyes.

The service began with a Schubert 'Intermezzo' that quickly

raised my spiritual vibrations, was followed by hearty singing of the familiar old hymn 'Nearer My God To Thee', a prayer, and a brief traditional sermon.

Then, in his vibrant, lilting accent, Holmes concluded : 'Although in a sense our worship is finished, we shall continue worshipping during the ministry of healing.' He said that a number of people had spoken to him about their healing needs and he asked them to present themselves during this service. And so, before giving the general laying-on-of-hands, which would come later, he was going to demonstrate healing with these few people because he wanted us to be able to see an answer to our prayers.

Before the service I had asked Holmes, out in the lobby, if I could send healing by proxy to my sister who was suffering from a serious bone condition and in considerable pain. Consequently, I was one of those invited to come forward. About a dozen of us stood on each side at ground level while he took two at a time, seating them in chairs facing the audience, one at each side of the platform.

Taking the first person at the head of each line, he invited two elderly men to sit in the chairs and he treated them alternately. 'The friend on my right,' he said, 'tells me that he has been unable to raise his right arm for about a year. The one on the left has had a continuous headache for eleven years. I want you to join with me in healing prayer as we concentrate on this man's shoulder and arm, asking in the name of Jesus Christ for healing.' There was a pause and, like a reflex, the man's arm shot straight up in the air. He looked stupefied. 'This arm has been unable to be raised for a year,' the minister said, calmly. 'Keep raising it, will you? Just move it up and down. Your prayer has been answered at this moment.

'And now join me in the name of Jesus Christ for healing for our friend here who has suffered a headache for eleven years. Remember the teaching of Jesus, when you pray, know that what you are asking for has already come and you shall have it! Put your chin on your chest and let your head come into my fingers as I help you claim the healing.' After a few moments, he went back to the first man. 'Put your arm up again,' he said. The man's arm went up easily. 'That's fine. That's good,' Holmes said. 'How does it feel?' 'Fine,' said the man.

Returning to the friend with the headache, he spoke privately to him, then turned to the audience and said, 'He has still got his headache, but he says it appears to be changed, perhaps lessened. I'm conveying to you what I've been told. So we're going to leave him for a few minutes . . .

'Healing can be instantaneous and complete,' Holmes explained, 'as it was here with our friend who was unable to move his arm, and it very often is progressive, as it is being with our other friend.'

A new patient took the other chair. Her complaint was a swelling and pain in her leg, and he asked for healing in the same manner, while gently touching the swollen area. 'I can move the knee cap. I couldn't do that before!' the woman said. A moment later, he turned to us to report. 'She tells me her leg is very much better. It's softer and not as tight as it was.'

After each patient had received healing he gave them the traditional blessing that's said every Sunday in thousands of churches: 'The Lord bless you and keep you. The Lord make his face to shine upon you. The Lord lift up the light of his countenance upon you and give you his peace,' and he added the words, 'and his continued healing.'

The next person had arthritis in both knees and both hands. She was an elderly woman who said she was in considerable pain and couldn't have stood much longer. Holmes said he was sorry he hadn't known, and kneeled as he placed his hands on her knees and held her hands while asking healing. In helping her claim easier movement in the knees, he said, 'Now, don't force it.' After working with her gently for several minutes as the crowd watched in hushed silence, he announced that 'both knees are now functioning freely and easily'. He drew the woman to a standing position and encouraged her to stamp her feet, and he informed us she could do it without pain.

A young black woman, one of about half a dozen attending the Retreat, stepped forward and told Holmes that she was deaf in her left ear. He asked her to remove her hearing aid and began his treatment. She had said she couldn't hear without the aid, but when Holmes asked her if she could hear him striking one finger nail against the other, she said, 'Yes.'

'I'd like all of you to write and let me know how you are because I'd like to continue praying for you,' the minister said.

A woman with a blind eye and poor sight in the other was given healing and was told that she would obtain increased sight in the better eye and no change in the blind one. 'This is a feeling I get,' he said. And another woman with painful bursitis and a pinched nerve in her right leg reported she had no pain at all when the treatment was finished.

Finally another woman, who wanted healing for her son, and I were invited on to the platform. 'These are two people who have asked for healing for two others,' Holmes announced, 'a mother for her son and a woman for her sister. They offer their own faith, their own love as proxy for sister and son. Will you join me in healing prayer?'

Then, turning his back to the congregation, he asked me in a low voice what was troubling my sister. I explained briefly, and he nodded. 'Try to visualise your sister as you would like to see her, as you would like her to be,' he said.

Moving behind me, he placed one hand on my forehead and the other on the back of my neck and I felt vibrations—slow, steady and almost as strong as an electric vibrator! 'In the name of Jesus Christ I ask for healing for your sister,' he said, and I tried to visualise her doing ballet kicks and laughing gaily. 'The Lord bless her and keep her. The Lord make his face to shine upon her and be gracious unto her. The Lord lift up the light of his countenance upon her and give her his peace and continued healing.' I felt a glow—by proxy!

When the other stand-in healing had been given, Holmes reminded the congregation once again that his purpose in acting as a channel for God's healing power, with us praying along with him, was to let us see that prayer is answered. He then asked the Rev. Gordon Melton to come forward with the people he had invited to share in administering the laying-on-of-hands. And he asked us to continue to pray, as we had been doing, for the people who would be kneeling at the altar rail, and to ask for healing.

Gordon Melton, the SFF's dark-haired, studious-looking young field director, stepped onto the dais alongside Holmes and was followed by about a dozen others, all experienced as healers. I recognised Bob Ericsson, SFF's executive director, and a few familiar faces of people I had never suspected were healers. And as each wave of people kneeled at the rail, Holmes and his assistants went down the line treating one by one.

In watching our workshop instructor closely, I saw that he used no set technique. Leaning over to speak to each one, he placed his hands on the heads of several, or he might place only his fingertips on a person's temples. And in a few cases, he kneeled too, the better to communicate. The other healers tended to do the simple laying-on-of-hands with prayer, and some held their hands a few inches above the head, not touching.

It seemed as though everyone in the church wanted healing and finally, after they had all returned to their seats, we sang a rousing hymn together, using a special songsheet that had been given us on arrival. It was someone's beautiful idea to link spiritual healing with world peace—just as I'd heard about it from George Rogers at the world federalist conference in the beginning.

'Let there be peace on earth,' went the words of the hymn, 'and let it begin with me.'

The healing service was the first public demonstration of spiritual healing I had ever witnessed, and it made me realise more acutely than ever that organised medicine must some day soon come to grips with the phenomenon.

Rather than continue to ignore the demonstrable and public fact that arthritic joints are unlocked and spines straightened when a mysterious energy that heals is invoked by prayer, shouldn't the American Medical Association be concerned, at least, with verifying whether such healings occur? Where, I wondered, was scientific research being done on prayer except under SFF auspices?

I hurried over to the Scientific Workshop in the old church where Dr Robert N. Miller was about to present his lecture on 'Scientific Evidence for the Effectiveness of Prayer', and I was pleased to find the place well-filled. Flanks of tape recorders were at the ready to take it all down verbatim.

I learned that Dr Miller is an industrial research scientist who directs research for the Atlanta Chapter of SFF. With an MS and PhD in chemical engineering from Ohio State University, he was formerly a professor at Georgia 'Tech', teaching courses and directing research in the fields of heat transfer, fluid flow, metallurgy, high polymers and corrosion. His professional affiliations include the American Chemical Society, National Society of Corrosion Engineers, and the Electro-Chemical Society. He's listed in American Men of Science, holds two patents and has written a score of scientific papers. In other words, a substantial scientist with impeccable credentials.

Tanned and fit-looking, with a gentle, benign manner, Miller conducted his workshop wearing shorts and sports shirt in the August afternoon heat.

He was challenged to put prayer under the microscope, he said, after reading the Rev. Franklin Loehr's book, *The Power of Prayer on Plants* describing experiments in which the growth rate of plants was speeded up to 20 per cent by the systematic prayer of individuals and groups of people. (Their prayers visualised the test plant thriving in an ideal setting.)

But while Loehr's experiments were seemingly evidential, they were clouded by the fact that the tests were not conducted by scientifically trained people, and the simple ruler used to measure the plant's growth could not be considered very precise. Consequently the findings had not been taken seriously.

'I knew if I could do it accurately, it would be a contribution,' said Miller.

Aiding his own efforts, he said, was the timely development by Dr H. H. Kleuter, of the US Department of Agriculture, of a highly accurate method of measuring plant growth. By using a rotary transducer hitched up to a strip chart recorder, Kleuter had been able to measure the growth rate of plants to an accuracy of a thousandth of an inch per hour!

Miller then designed his test of prayer-power or, as he called it, 'the effect of thought upon remotely located plant life', with the co-operation of two well-known and respected healers, Olga and Ambrose Worrall, of Baltimore.

He first took time to tell us more about the Worralls. In their 40 or more years as spiritual healers they had healed hundreds of people, many of their healings having been verified by medical doctors and recorded. And they have never taken money for their services. Olga has for many years been associate director of the New Life Clinic at the Mt Washington United Methodist Church in Baltimore, where she gives healing every Thursday morning at 11. Ambrose Worrall (he died in February, 1972) was for 41 years an aircraft engineer and executive with the Martin-Marietta Corporation. British-born, with a distinguished background as an expert in the field of aeronautics, he was also active in the United Methodist Church. Both Worralls had always been keenly interested in research efforts to investigate the phenomenon of healing and in turn, he said, had been studied by a number of scientists.

'I asked the Worralls if they would pray for a plant and they said they would be happy to do so.' Miller then described in cool, understated terms, the details of his experiment.

'The selection of a suitable plant was more of a problem than I'd expected. I first chose bean plants because they grow rapidly and are sturdy. But I found the instrument did not measure their growth rate because their new growth took place only at the tip of the plant, above the point where the transducer's lever arm was attached.' He finally hit upon rye grass seeds, after trying several others, having found that rye grass, also fast-growing and sturdy, does its growing from the bottom of its blades up.

Taking a Model 33-03 Brush Metripak Angular Position Transducer, he attached its long lever arm to a sprout of rye grass with a bit of tape. Connected to the Transducer was the strip chart recorder which translated the slightest motion of the lever arm into a deflection of the marker pen on the strip chart.

He put 10 rye grass seeds in a 25 millimetre plastic beaker full of fertile soil, planting them a quarter of an inch below the surface. They were watered every morning with five millimetres of water. After two days they began sprouting and in four days a blade was strong enough to permit attachment of the transducer, the counterbalanced lever arm of which extended over the beaker. The strip chart recorder was adjusted, he said, to a chart speed of one inch per hour and the amplifier set so that a pen tracing with a 45 degree slope represented a growth rate of 0.100 inch per hour.

'In preliminary tests we found that the grass grew faster under fluorescent lighting than it did in the dark,' Miller continued, 'varying between two thousandths and a tenth of an inch an hour. Constant conditions were then worked out so that there would be no variation in lighting, temperature or watering frequency.'

With all test conditions ready to go, Miller telephoned from Atlanta to Mr and Mrs Worrall in Baltimore and asked them to hold the seedling in their thoughts at their usual 9.00 p.m. prayer time that evening. They told him they would pray for the plant by visualising it as 'growing vigorously in a white light'.

Before Miller's call, the growth rate of the new sprouts of rye grass had stabilised at .00625 inch per hour and right up until 9 o'clock the strip chart recorder showed a sloping straight line, indicating a constant growth rate.

'The next morning I studied the strip chart tracing and found that at exactly 9 o'clock the trace began to deviate upward and by 8 o'clock in the morning the grass was growing .0525 inch per hour,' Miller said. 'That's an increase of 840 per cent. Instead of the one-sixteenth of an inch it would have grown at the previously stabilised rate, the grass had grown more than half an inch.' During the next 48 hours, he added, the growth rate slowed down a little but never fell back to the original pace.

Miller assured us that the door of the experiment room had been locked all night and the temperature kept a steady 70-72 degrees. The fluorescent lights were kept on and there was no apparent physical variable that could have caused any wide variation in the growth of the grass.

Underlining his results, Miller said that the eightfold increase in the growth rate of the rye grass which occurred while two spiritual healers 600 miles away were trying to make them grow more luxuriantly suggests that this same procedure might be used in further experiments in measuring the effect of mind over matter.

Ambrose Worrall, in one of his last interviews (for *Psychic* magazine, April, 1972) put forth a theory that seemed to explain the 'visualisation' process they had used in praying for the plants growth, and Miller had extra copies of the magazine to distribute. (It also included an account of his prayer-to-plant experiment.)

Said Ambrose Worrall, 'I believe that God creates by using the universal immutable laws. This involves selecting ideas and willing them into a composite form by picturing them in the mind, then holding the image and allowing it to be filled with the cosmic forces of universal substance, whatever it may be. This effort sets in motion the immutable laws of creation and eventually brings about manifestations at some level of density, either in the ethereal or in the material state . . .' A definition of the mechanics of creative prayer?

Dr Miller then informed us of the closely related experiments of two contemporary researchers, Dr Bernard Grad, the McGill University professor and biologist of Montreal, and Cleve Backster, the New York polygraph (lie-detector) expert.

Dr Grad enlisted the co-operation of a purported spiritual healer to measure the effectiveness of his healing treatment on animals, Miller said.

Since medical cures by such unorthodox treatments as the laying-on-of-hands are usually explained away as being due to the power of suggestion, it was Grad's idea to put that theory specifically to the test. If the healer produced visible healing effects in animals that are not suggestible, then that healer must be dispensing something other than suggestion !

Miller described Grad's experiment step by step and gave us a published copy of it in the researcher's own words, in case we wanted it for reference.

Forty-eight female mice, two to two-and-a-half months old and all from the same strain, were divided into three groups of sixteen each.

Group No. 1 were given a series of treatments by Mr Oskar Estebany, a one-time Hungarian Army colonel now living in Montreal who claimed to have observed healing in people and animals to whom he had given the laying on of hands. Group No. 2, the control group, were given no treatment by Estebany. Group No. 3 were not treated by Estebany but their cage was warmed up by an electrothermal tape to the same degree as the treatment cage when held between Estebany's hands. (The temperature measurements taken in the treatment cage reached 33 degrees Centigrade while Estebany was holding it.)

Careful controls were used so that all the mice participating were housed and trained identically at all times. When not being treated, all the mice were housed singly in stainless steel cages in a light-controlled windowless room, with the temperature kept at 26 to 27 degrees Centigrade. All were soothed and stroked to calm their nerves and handled gently, and they were fed as much Purina Fox Chow and water as they wanted.

The treatments by Mr Estebany were given in an adjoining room where the temperature ranged from 26 to 28 degrees Centigrade. The cage in which he treated the mice was of galvanised sheet iron divided by vertical metal dividers, with a mouse-size stall for each of the sixteen occupants. It had a sliding lid covered with galvanised wire mesh to keep the mice from leaping out.

When the time came for the test to begin, the mice were taken from their home cages, and in the same room, all were given small wounds on their backs in the following manner :

All 48 mice were anaesthetised with ether and hair removed from their backs in an area measuring about $\frac{1}{2}$ by $1\frac{1}{2}$ inches. Then an oval-shaped patch of skin about $\frac{1}{2}$ inch in diameter was removed with scissors. Each bit of skin removed was then weighed, and the wound area measured by placing a bit of transparent plastic over it and tracing its precise outlines with a grease pencil. The wound outline was then transferred to paper, to be cut out and carefully weighed.

The size of each mouse's wound was measured in this fashion on the first, the eleventh, and the fourteenth days after the test started, the mice being kept continually in the same room.

On the first day, the Group 1 mice were put into the treatment cage and held by Mr Estebany, who placed his left palm underneath and his right hand slightly above the lid. He held Group 1 this way for 15 minutes twice a day at intervals no closer than five hours, five days a week and once on Sundays.

The results of the test were clear within the two weeks and a statistical analysis was made of the paper projections of the wounds taken during that period.

On the eleventh and fourteenth days after the wounds were made, there was no significant difference in the size of the wounds between Group 2 and Group 3. But the wounds of the Group 1 mice, which were treated by Mr Estebany, were significantly smaller than those of the other two groups on the eleventh and fourteenth days. The wounds of the mice that had been given the laying-on of hands had clearly healed the fastest.

Dr Grad ran the test a second time and obtained similar results.

The discoveries of Cleve Backster, several of which Miller described in lively detail, applied in some aspects to healing research. The lie-detector expert found that plants respond to the energies released by thought, not only by growing faster, but by reacting emotionally, like humans. He believes this research, when elevated to human subjects, may shed new light on positive thought as a potent vehicle for healing, and negative thought as operative in psychosomatic illness.

(Backster sees thought as involving mind power translated into force fields, such as those studied within the electromagnetic spectrum, but points out that the thing that triggers the release of this mind energy has so far eluded science.)

He very soon suspected that this ability of plants to perceive— among other things—the thoughts of humans, which he calls 'primary perception', would some day be found in humans as well, when it began turning up in every living cell he tested, including the amoeba, the paramecium, and other single-cell organisms as well as in fresh fruits and vegetables, mould cultures, blood samples, non-incubated eggs, spermatazoa, and scrapings from the roof of the human mouth!

(He says this primary perception is the same thing parapsychologists call ESP, but he doesn't see it as *extra*-sensory, implying beyond our five senses, but rather as the psychic sense humans had first but turned off when they became less open and developed the five specialised senses for purposes of privacy—or intrigue. He believes the primary perception potential remains in all of us, in every cell of our bodies, and can be brought again to a useful level. For example, Backster had asked, 'If we consistently think kind thoughts toward people, the results may be astonishing.' And it might be added, if we sent healing thoughts consistently to everyone we knew that was ill, the results might be even more interesting.)

In the context of healing thought or prayer research, two of Backster's tests as outlined by Miller were particularly interesting. The original one, for example, showed that a plant will react to a clear, uncomplicated thought or intention but will ignore pretense. This is what happened:

Out of sheer curiosity, Backster connected a pair of polygraph electrodes to the leaf of a philodendron plant he had just watered to see if he could measure the time it took for the water to rise from roots to leaf.

Contrary to his expectation, the tracing on the chart showed a reaction pattern typical of a human experiencing a brief emotional stimulation.

'If this plant wants to give a people-like reaction, I'll use "people rules" on it,' Miller quoted Backster as saying. 'So he dipped the leaf in hot coffee, but didn't get much reaction. It was as though the plant were saying, "Is that the worst you can do?'

'Backster then decided to burn the leaf to see if a threat to its well-being might trigger a reaction, as it regularly does with human subjects. He was about ten feet away, and yet, at the very moment he *thought* of burning the leaf, the pen almost jumped off the top of the chart. It was as though the plant had read his mind! And later on, when he only pretended that he was going to burn the plant, absolutely nothing happened.'

Another experiment of Backster's showed the plant's ability to distinguish among several people the one capable of doing it harm, rather than good.

'Backster had six men enter a room in which there were two

philodendron plants on a table. One of the six men picked up one of the plants, pulled it up by the roots and stepped on it.

'He then connected the polygraph to the remaining plant and had the six men come back into the room—one at a time.

'When the "killer" entered the room, the plant that had witnessed the uprooting identified him instantly, sending the pen into a violent upward sweep on the graph.'

These two experiments, if raised to the human level, suggest that if a healer is to stimulate a response in a sick person, their thoughts or prayers should be clear and purposeful. And, on the other hand, if the sick person is to respond to another person's healing or prayers, they should be convinced of the healer's goodwill toward them.

Backster's tests showed also that 'primary perception' between plants and humans operates over long distances, just like the Worralls' prayers, and he has philosophised that if science has overlooked the 'vehicle' of thought involved here, it certainly could have overlooked the vehicle of prayer, and that the two may very well be the same vehicle. In using this kind of key, Backster says he has been able to remove many of the points of doubt he had concerning Christianity. He subsequently re-evaluated the spiritual teachings of both East and West and got an entirely new understanding of them. And if this can happen to him, he says, it can happen to other scientists.

Miller observed that Backster's discovery of 'feelings' in plants may be the greatest discovery of all time, since it suggests the existence of another universal field unique to life. 'In Backster's opinion, this primary perception is, in all probability, common to everything that's alive in the world. And he believes there's a communication link or life signal that is connecting all of God's Creation.'

Miller then told us about his own researches into the history of healing which evolved out of his dual interests as a research scientist and head of a prayer group. It has turned into one of the most stimulating assignments of his career, he said, 'and a pattern has emerged that seems to answer some of the questions that have been puzzling mankind for thousands of years'.

In studying the accounts of miracle healings in the New Testament, Miller said he was impressed by several that seemed to say that a form of energy passed between Jesus and the person wanting healing.

'Remember the story of the woman who was crippled for eighteen years? She was bent double, unable to straighten up, until Jesus saw her and said, "Arise". He placed his hand on her shoulder and immediately she straightened up and began to praise God!

'Well, looking at this from the scientific point of view,' Miller continued, 'the key seemed to be that when Jesus touched her she was healed. He didn't ask her if she had faith. He didn't tell her that her sins were forgiven. He simply put his hand on her and she was well.

'Then there was the woman who had a haemorrhage and unable to stop, who said if she could only touch Jesus she would become whole. And once she was finally successful in touching the hem of his garment, she was healed. And at the instant she touched his robe, he felt the virtue or the energy flowing out of him. Now, looking at this case objectively, she also came in contact with the source of energy.'

The many cases of absent healing, where there was no direct contact between healer and patient, Miller said, also indicated the presence of a mysterious healing energy, 'but all energy is mysterious before we discover the laws that govern it. Everything must happen according to law. I figured we just didn't understand the mechanism.'

Meanwhile, Miller said, he and his wife read hundreds of books on healing and prayer and they joined the Theosophical Society and the Spiritual Frontiers Fellowship to use their library resources on healing and continued going to church and praying with the rest of the congregation.

Going back thousands of years deeper into history, he found that healings and miracles were occurring in the time of the Pharaohs in the Third Dynasty of Egypt, where the tomb of Imhotep, chief physician to Zoser about 2980 BC, seems to have been the Lourdes of its day (had Imhotep returned as a spirit doctor?). And he found several references to miracle healings in the Old Testament. For example, the healing by the prophet Elisha of Naaman, Captain of the Syrian armies. ('Then went he down and dipped seven times in Jordan, according to the saying of the man of God, and his flesh came again like unto the flesh of a little child and he was clean.' II Kings, 5 : 14.)

'I also found that the ancient Chinese claimed that man is filled with a vital energy or a life force. They say that the universe, too, is filled with this energy and under the proper conditions man can attune to it . . . the Hindus, too, spoke of a similar energy. They call it prana. A Yoga breathing exercise emphasises the drawing of the prana into the physical body.'

In ending the part of his talk that dealt with healing research, Miller gave us some of his conclusions: 'Healing seems to come about where there's self-attunement to the Source of all healing power and energy. It seems to be a matter of raising one's vibrations to a state that enables one to receive the energy that is available to all. It is our task to discover the laws that govern this.'

He concluded with a cosmic speculation: 'It appears,' he said, 'that each of us is part of God and has some of His qualities whenever we are performing a creative act. By our thoughts, we are co-creators with Him—and every thought is a prayer.'

Later, I asked Dr Miller if he believed in the spirit doctor concept, and he said he did, but that all would not accept what, for him, is evidence. 'I've known mediums and psychics who have said they could see these people. The Worralls, for example, and they are old friends. Of course this isn't scientific, but it satisfies me.' And he added matter-of-factly, 'I think in five years, with all the evidence that is accumulating, we will have all the proof we need of spirit help in healing.'

The second session of the Scientific Workshop, entitled 'Research in Paranormal Phenomena' led by Robert H. Ashby, the personable young chairman of research for SFF, emphasised the organisation's educational programme.

'We will soon launch a programme to enable ourselves to educate the public in responsible and sound fashion about the psychic faculties and what they tell us,' announced Ashby, who has been headmaster of private schools in Tangier, Morocco and London and is the author of *A Guidebook To The Study of Psychical Research.*

Listing healing first among the four areas of research SFF is concerned with, along with prayer, survival and heightened sensitivity, Ashby said they had launched a nationwide survey of the practice of spiritual healing by clergymen in the churches of the nation, under the direction of the Rev. Gordon Melton.

'We're trying to find out how many clergymen in the United States do healing, and how often,' said Ashby. 'What is the reaction of church members? The vestry? This is the first study made in this area since 1955. Melton is also getting together a bibliography on spiritual healing.'

Ashby said that SFF also plans a 'meditation imagery' study and he urged any in the group who meditate regularly to share their experiences with Frank Tribbe, who heads the study. 'There seems to be no source of information that gives the student guidance in the type of imagery one may encounter at various levels of meditation,' he said. 'If everyone in this room would co-operate we'd have a very sizeable body of information.'

In the past, one of the greatest difficulties in pursuing psychic research has been the reluctance of people to report their paranormal experiences, and so thousands of them go unreported, Ashby continued, 'but as a group SFF has certain advantages here, because none of its members are either frightened by paranormal experiences or hesitant to tell about them, nor are they afraid of being called "kooks",' he said. 'We should be able to draw from our membership a steady stream of information of this kind. It's been estimated that perhaps one in ten has had a really striking psychic experience.'

As the workshop ended, Ashby passed out questionnaires on which we could list all the paranormal events in our lifetimes.

A few hours later, I buttonholed Gordon Melton and got a copy of the survey questionnaire for ministers who do healing in this country. The first six questions were concerned with background information, such as which church they serve and in what capacity, how many years in the ministry, and at what time did they become interested and begin participating in the healing ministry. They were then asked how often they do healing—regularly, frequently, daily, or occasionally— and to what source they trace their initial interest in the healing ministry—an organisation, a person, or through reading. Then the questions probe a little deeper :

7 What is your understanding of the process of spiritual healing or the healing ministry?

8 How do you understand your role in the healing ministry? Does it vary? If so, under what conditions or in what situations?

9 When is your healing ministry manifest? Check all that apply.
—Sunday morning worship.
—Mid-week service or prayer meeting.
—Personal counselling.
—In hospital visits.

—Prayer groups.
—Other (Specify).

10 The main motive in leading me to adopt a regular healing ministry was : (Check one)
—It was a natural part of my ministry from the beginning.
—I was enlightened to a Biblical imperative for it.
—I had felt a lack in my previous ministry which it filled.
—Laymen asked for it.
—I witnessed a healing 'miracle' and learned a new reality through it.
—Other (Specify).

11 Do you co-operate with doctors (MDs) in your work?
—No, because
—None are available or known.
—Yes. In which ways?

12 Have you developed any liturgical or worship orders which might be useful to others wishing to begin healing services?— If yes, would you enclose a copy with this form?

13 Can you detail *one* case of a particular noteworthy healing you witnessed or were involved in?

The recipients to which it was mailed, after a laborious effort to draw up a list through direct and indirect sources, were told in a covering letter that all the information gained would be for statistical purposes only and that their names would not be used with any published data. But, if they gave specific permission, their answers to Question 13 might be quoted.

Melton's workshop on 'How to Lead Healing Prayer Groups' was next on my agenda, and that afternoon I was sitting in an intimate circle in a corner of the campus Library hearing the 31-year-old United Methodist minister tell how he guides SFF study groups that want to become involved in healing.

A graduate, with honours, of Garrett Theological Seminary in Evanston, Illinois, Melton is now working on a doctorate in church history in Evanston before becoming a full-time field director on the spiritual frontier. Alabama-born, he has short dark hair, horn rims, a down-to-earth manner and wears a rough-hewn cross on a chain.

Our workshop leader began by recounting to us how the Healing

Prayer Groups had formed four years ago without concrete experience, and gradually evolved through trial, error and increased understanding to their present design.

Melton then came to a portion of the meeting that seemed to me to cover an area much needed and often lacking in healing groups —a study discipline in the growing literature of healing. He called it 'our lesson'.

'What this amounts to is that we take upon ourselves the discipline of covering a certain amount of material between meetings,' Melton said. 'But it's geared to the group. Some of them will read half a book between meetings and others only a few pages. But they'll read this material and we'll spend our lesson time discussing it.'

Happily, SFF study groups set up especially for healing are encouraged to concentrate on books in that field, our leader explained, and mentioned a few good examples: *The Healing Light* by Agnes Sanford ('a good *first* book'); then *Letters on the Healing Ministry* by Albert E. Day; *A Reporter Finds God Through Spiritual Healing* by Emily Gardiner Neal, and *An Outline of Spiritual Healing* by Gordon Turner (who was one of the main speakers at the Eastern Retreat of SFF earlier that summer).

After spending about a half hour on the lesson, he said, the final half-hour is devoted to healing, and it begins with another period of meditation.

'As a focal point of healing prayers and directed energies, a chair is placed in the centre of the circle, and when the leader asks, "Are there any requests for absent healing?" the names are slowly pronounced, one at a time—first names only, with no mention of ailments—and prayer is directed to them, as though they were sitting in the chair.

'When any member of the group desires healing for himself or wants to act as proxy for some special friend or relation, they may sit in the centre chair, and as the Spirit leads, members may involve themselves by giving their fellow-member healing prayers with the laying-on of hands.

'The chair is a useful aid,' he noted, 'because it's important that the power be focused, and it's not important *how*. The healing power is not related to time and space.'

Melton's talk then shifted to his healing experiences and how he teaches others. And the philosophy of healing he gave us as a background had an expansive quality which, it seemed to me, would appeal to non-Christians.

'Healing begins in the meditative silence, and this state of deep inner relaxation—known as the "alpha state", denoting the brain-waves of lowered frequency meditation produces—allows the healing to be channelled through me. The healing power is a gift of God, but it is not to be identified with Him. It is a natural power of the created order and its use is *not* related to the *theology* of the channel. The only gauge of a good healing channel is—do people get well?'

Melton said his first experience with healing occurred three years ago in a healing service when he joined the well-known psychic, Irene Hughes, whom he had met when studying religious cults as research director of the Institute for the Study of American Religion. Placing his hands uncertainly on the heads of people wanting the laying-on of hands, he began noticing that with about every third person his hands got very hot 'as hot as a heating pad turned up high' and terribly uncomfortable! And this heat seemed to bring healing to people.

Some months later, when visiting his home in Alabama, he took part in another healing service, and when a woman with painful arthritis came forward and called for prayers, his hands again became terrifically hot. In about 30 seconds the woman told him her pain was gone, he said.

As a beginning healer, he worked to develop his ability—which he believes to be inborn in all humans—through meditation and 'the healing work itself'. At his present stage he finds he can ease the pain of ulcers, but with chronic conditions the pain seems to be all he can affect.

What sensations does he feel when doing contact healing? Aside from the heat, he feels a magnetic pull sometimes, Melton said. 'Others say they feel an electric-like tingle or a coldness.'

But in the alpha state of altered consciousness he has experienced spontaneous clairvoyance—in the form of knowing just what is wrong with the patient and the internal effects of the healing they are receiving.

In Melton's opinion the healing is directed to the energy body, which he can feel but not see. He feels it as a 'barrier' about two inches away from the patient's skin and he works 'at the edge of the barrier'.

Any abnormality or pathology is felt as an irregularity in this barrier, he said, 'It will dip, become unbalanced, or vary in temperature'. He 'radiates' the healing power until the irregularity is dissipated. He rarely touches the patient he's healing.

He knows nothing of medicine or anatomy, nor does he require that knowledge of his pupils, because he feels 'a little knowledge is worse than no knowledge', and he adds, 'The healing intelligence can do its own work guided by any paranormal information received clairvoyantly.' He concedes, however, that a little basic knowledge of psychosomatic medicine is 'useful in creating a healing atmosphere'.

And what about those who don't respond? Melton had obviously studied this aspect, and had a long list of reasons, beginning with 'lack of maturity on the channel's part'. He also feels that people who are resigned to illness and hold such negative attitudes as a belief in karmic debt and in God's will that they should suffer, are probably not receptive to the healing power. Also inhibiting to healing are 'hidden guilt, lack of forgiveness, or stress on a patient; unwillingness to give up an unhealthy lifestyle and an unhealthy climate of faith among the patient's friends'.

Finally, giving advice to people wishing to develop their abilities to channel the healing force, Melton said they should begin to open their centres of psychic awareness through meditation 'and begin at once, while in the meditative state, to pray for others'. They should not wait until they begin feeling sensations in their hands or elsewhere.

'Working about two inches from the patient, a sensitivity to the energy body will develop in time,' he said. 'Avoid trying to feel in oneself the symptoms of the patient. This leads to unwanted symptoms in the channel. Sensitivity to the patient will come in the hands by feeling the barrier, and differences in temperature, or, in some cases, a partial trance.'

After he'd finished, he was peppered with questions. One listener wanted to know if healing had helped him in any way physically. 'Yes,' he said, 'I find my hands don't get cold any more. And some of the disciplines I've learned I apply to colds and headaches and stomach upsets. I've found that meditation is a much better way to get rid of these than medication.'

Another asked, 'Isn't it a good idea to start with little ailments when you're a new group?' 'Yes. Some have got started by healing headaches,' he said. 'But healing is also learning to have a healthy attitude and a proper diet.' In other words, healing can begin with *oneself*.

'Have you ever used a medium as a "sender"?' Melton was asked. 'For instance, we have him sit in the centre and we give him the name of the sick person. He concentrates and sends healing to them while we focus all our powers on him.'

Melton said it sounded like a fine idea and that he'd tried the technique of a 'double circle', where a group in the centre act as proxies for sick people and the others form a healing circle around them.

'Are addresses needed in absent healing?'

'Gordon Turner says it's not necessary,' Melton replied, speaking of the British healer whose workshop in Gettysburg he had just attended.

'What about multiple sclerosis? Can it be healed by the spiritual method?'

Melton answered by again quoting the famous Briton. 'Turner says in twenty-five years he's healed only three cases of MS. He says he finds it almost impossible to work with MS victims because their mental and emotional attitudes are so negative. They're apt to be hypochondriacs and resist anything you can do for them.'

As Melton wound up the session, he said he'd soon be travelling all over the country serving SFF's seventy area groups (membership is now more than 8,000) and running healing seminars which will combine lectures, workshops and services of worship.

He gave me a leaflet that was being distributed all over the country, which read in part :

'Spiritual Healing and You'
An Adventure Into the Paraphysical World

led by
Rev. J. Gordon Melton

The adventure begins with a talk entitled 'Spiritual Healing and You' which discusses the basic realities and phenomena surrounding spiritual healing. This talk is followed by one to five workshop sessions which lead the participants into a realisation of their own potentials for co-operation with God's healing spirit. Emphasis is placed on the emergence of latent and hidden powers through psychic attunement and spiritual disciplines.

Beside the emphasis upon the development of potentials, each workshop session would include a short input by Rev Melton covering the following topics:

'Understanding Spiritual Healing—dealing with the basic questions about its nature.

'The Story of Spiritual Healing'—a summary of the healing tradition in Western religion.

'How Jesus Healed'—a survey of Jesus' healing techniques and motives.

'Preventing Disease'—disciplines to stop un-health before it begins.

'Paraphysics—the Scientific Side of Spiritual Healing'—Relating current research in healing power, the aura and acupuncture.

While savouring all these different approaches to healing, I learned that at least three other workshops explored group-healing and self-healing techniques under a variety of headings. Above all, I was told, I should not miss the Prayer Workshop called 'Programme Your Life For Good' led by Dr William R. Parker, our Retreat Leader. A noted psychologist, lecturer and author, his latest book is *Prayer Can Change Your Life*.

The programme notes informed us that Parker works with doctors in LaHabra, California, in treating patients with psychosomatic disorders, which he considers basically spiritual problems. Using personality tests to uncover the hidden cause of the trouble, he helps the patient overcome it with prayer therapy.

A big friendly man with a warm smile, Parker started his workshop class by asking us to speak up if we had any symptoms that needed healing. He soon found we were a group of insomniacs and sufferers from stiff neck, post nasal drip, migraine, ringing-in-the-ears and other things more serious. The class grew hilarious when a woman said she had an ulcerated hernia, but was 'saving it for Rev. Alex Holmes' healing service' that night. When Parker answered benignly, 'Well then, you keep it', the laughter was so hearty that a man fell off his chair.

Parker went on to tell us the probable psychosomatic origin of most of our ills. My post nasal drip, he said, was due to 'anxiety about something that is important to you. You don't realise it except at a deep level'. Asthma is a 'stifled cry', and an ulcerated colon may be traceable to the sufferer's hatred of a parent of the opposite sex.

'Show me a male alcoholic and almost invariably there's a dominating mother in the background, and a passive father . . . Sinus trouble is due to a slight frustration about sex . . . a skin rash is due to irritation . . . You select these things—unconsciously. But you have to *realise* you select them,' he said.

For each ailment, Parker had a psychological explanation. It is his belief that we 'programme' most of our ailments and that they are 'displacements' for some attitude of mind. 'We'll show you how not to programme it,' he said confidently, 'through relaxation and meditation.'

But what about the serious chronic illnesses, like cancer? Parker saw this, too, as psychosomatic. 'Tests show that there are certain personality types that get it,' he said. 'Often they are individuals who have at a subconscious level a deep disappointment with life and would like to start over again. The new life is very much like an embryo.' Cancer and embryo cells even look alike and multiply at the same rate, said Parker.

'Cancer patients of this type must realise that they can't undo it. Life moves in one direction only and that's forward.'

Warning us against programming our ills any further, Parker cautioned us against taking such symptoms to a psychiatrist or a psychologist 'because the more you talk about your ailments the more you programme them. You talk about the past so long that you're lucky if you ever get well!'

Parker then carried us briefly back to our childhood to explain how it is we 'programme' ourselves.

'When you started school, we began programming you to read and write, first by having you write your name. We printed it out for you and you copied it. Then, after a while, we got this little child so he could copy his name very rapidly, because he'd programmed it.

'Almost always in the beginning,' Parker continued, 'what you learn as a child is visual, and so the programming takes place through the visual sense—hearing and touch come second and third—and as you go on through these development years you're being programmed through your senses, and most importantly through your visual sense.'

Parker emphasised that these sense impulses—essentially visual—are stored in your memory or your subconscious, and that is why the visual has to be stressed in the re-programming process.

The idea is to erase the wrong programmed impressions and substitute right ones, using the meditative or alpha brain wave state of mental relaxation which allows these visualised right impressions to sink in more deeply. (I had taken a Silva Mind Control course which prescribes similar visualisation methods while in the alpha state to promote self-healing, correct bad habits and solve problems. Comparing the two, Parker's technique does not extend to everyday problem-solving and, unlike José Silva's, is 'coupled to the divine'.)

But before telling us how to re-programme ourselves in meditation, our instructor took a little more time to build up our confidence in the technique. Giving us some examples of the kind of healings that can happen, he began with asthma. 'I deal with asthmatics all the time and get people over it very quickly. It's one of the easiest things I do,' he said.

Briefly outlining its cause, he drew a picture of the human lung full of thousands of air sacs and cells which in the normal, relaxed condition are open like a honeycomb, so the air can go in and out. But in the asthmatic, due to some activity of the autonomic nervous system, the ring of muscle around these lung cells is clamped down so that air is trapped in the lungs. The asthmatic has trouble breathing, not because he can't get air in but because he can't get it out. The reason for the wheeze, Parker said, was because the situation is like a blown-up balloon that's being stretched tight at the neck. Only when you loosen this tension can the air go out freely.

'Now we teach these people in meditation to relax, first of all, and then to visualise those cells open and to command those cells to stay open . . . We've had children who have been able to stop asthmatic attacks and do it without going into any panic at all.' He added that he taught the technique to a woman with asthma in his workshop yesterday and 'now she doesn't have asthma any more'.

He then gave us a lesson on headaches. A migraine is the exact opposite of a tension headache, he said, because instead of a clamping down of the blood vessels there's a dilation of them that's causing the pain. The greatest expansion takes place in the mid-brain, which controls the stomach, and that pressing-out causes nausea or 'sick headache'.

'Now you don't have to expand that blood vessel—you can absolutely control that blood vessel,' he said.

Parker reminded us that we were living in a New Age where there's much information coming in because of the biofeedback studies that have widened exploration of brainwave states. 'Now you can talk to the cells of your body and absolutely change their behaviour,' said Parker. 'We couldn't do this a few years ago.'

Asked how often and how long he would recommend 'this particular type' of meditation, Parker suggested twice a day, 'preferably in the morning to start the day and at bedtime when that which you are programming can sink into your subconscious. Ten to twenty minutes might be long enough, but the depth of feeling you get into it is more important'.

Our instructor then announced that he wanted us as a group to demonstrate the power of meditation for healing 'when two or three or more are gathered together'.

'I'm trying to tell you that every time you add another person to the healing group, it isn't arithmetic, like one, two, three. It's geometric. Three people here praying will be increased to the ninth power. So look how much power you have in this room!' (There were about fifty present.)

He invited Mr David Dodds, of Northbrook, Ill., to come forward. Dodd had spoken to him earlier about healing for an eye condition, which he now described as a deterioration of the maclea, the centre of sight, for which nothing more could be done medically. Parker had him sit in a chair at the front of the room and said encouragingly, 'This will do us all good, and we hope it will help you.'

'Thought,' Parker began, 'is a very, very powerful thing, especially when it is coupled with the divine which is within us and among us. . . . Let's not limit Spirit, for anything can happen. . . .

'Now we're going to do this together. We're going to be relaxed, and I will do the verbalising. If you will co-operate we will now generate the power to heal us. Is everybody ready?

'Will you put both feet on the floor and sit up straight without being stiff. We'll take a deep breath and hold it for a second. Let it way out. Take still one more deep breath, hold it and see how far out you can let it go. Then a third breath, and as you let it out just close your eyes and leave them closed until I let you know. This is to shut out distractions so that we can be of one mind and one accord, and also to enable us to go into the alpha state.

'Now will you relax the eyes and let that feeling go down the body. Relax the jaw muscle—it's the strongest muscle in the body of its size—now relax down the back of the neck and all the way down the spine—all you who have spinal difficulties can correct this as we go along. Just relax all the way down the spine and see it whole in a white light—now relax across the shoulders, going all way down your arms, and let the tensions go out of the fingers. Relax your chest. Relax your stomach. Let it rhythmically go in and out naturally as you breathe—the stomach is the sounding board of emotion.

'Now relax through your hips and down through your legs, past your knees and let the tensions go out through the soles of your feet. . . . Notice that you are acquiring bodily comfort from the top of your head to the tip of your toes. . . . You are now experiencing the ancient admonition, "Be still and know that I am God".' We sat in that deliciously relaxed state motionless and silent for a few moments, and then Parker continued, his voice gentle and soothing :

'Now, for good measure, in our imagination we're going to step on an escalator and and go down, while I count backwards, and every time I say a number will you allow yourself to become even more relaxed. And I say ten, nine, eight, seven, six, five, four, three, two, one, zero, and you step off. And you step across a hall into a lovely room, beautifully furnished, and you sit on a sofa, and directly across from you on the other side of the room is a lighted stage, and on the back of the stage is a movie screen.

'Now visualise yourself on this screen and see yourself happy. See yourself well. See yourself whole. See yourself turned on about life. Radiant, out-going, with a sense of humour, and being grateful just to be alive.

'And now we turn our thoughts here to David. We send all our healing energy to him and we couple it with love. We see him directing the healing energy through his eyes. We see them being made whole and healed. For the Spirit heals completely and wholly and beautifully, and we feel the power. We know that we will see his eyes perfectly normal and healthy and beautiful, and we say thank you, Father. Now we know that it is done, and so we step on the escalator and we start up and I say one, two, three, four, five, six, seven, eight, nine, ten. . . . We are joyful, for joy is the greatest single aspect outside of love for people. . . .

'So now I'm going to count to three, and on three you're going to open your eyes feeling rested and refreshed, with plenty of energy for the rest of the evening, knowing that all is well. And I say, one, two, coming up, three, open your eyes.'

It was like coming out of a vibrant dream full of action and images, and we all looked at David Dodds hoping to see some evidence of improvement. He walked to his seat looking a little embarrassed to be the focal point of attention. (I asked him later if he noticed any difference, and he said, 'Not yet'.)

Parker said he wanted to share with us an added technique he has been using in an experimental prayer group that has been showing particularly good results. 'This is what we do,' he said. 'We get quiet, as we did just now, and then we take these individuals who need healing and we see them surrounded by white light. It's like a film, and we seem them being enveloped by this whiteness and we allow it in our inner vision to grow thicker and thicker until the person is completely enveloped and disappears. We hold this for a few seconds and then we have him begin to emerge from the fog as it clears. We see him coming out radiant, happy, joyful. Completely healed.'

He explained the symbolism : the fog is spirit and the person emerging from it has died to the old and been born to the new.

Before graciously thanking us for our attentiveness, Parker suggested that we should not take meditation lightly, nor do it as a chore. 'I do it daily because I enjoy it. I wouldn't start the day without it,' he said. 'I'm very positive. I see people I love. I bless them. I wish them well. I know that they're safe. I know that they're happy. You can hold anybody in the light for whom you want something special, and in your meditation see them healed, and see them whole, see them well.'

The two other workshops that explored healing offered a fresh note—both were conducted by husband-and-wife teams; Mildred and Sheldon Blazier and Pat and Bud Hayes.

The Blaziers of Muncie, Indiana, are Quaker lay leaders with a non-traditional approach to Quakerism that includes imaginative meditational and spiritual healing techniques.

After a brief silence, or 'centring down', Mrs Blazier suggested that we visualise, with eyes closed, that we were surounded by healing energy. 'Let this energy come into your very being and feel it penetrate within you, and let it vibrate over you, under you and all around you,' she said. 'Let every cell of your body feel that it is being helped or healed.'

This was followed by a 'vibration-raising' song and deep-breathing exercises, accompanied by Mr Blazier's mental guidance : 'Breathe in more of this life force, this great power,' he intoned. 'Let it move up the vertebrae to the solar plexus, to the chest area, to your heart, to your lungs, until you are filled with Spirit, with the healing power within you.'

As the power moved down our arms and into our fingertips, Blazier said we would feel it pulsate there and were we to lay them on a sore place, it would help to alleviate that pain. (This was precisely the way I had been healed of my toothache.)

'Now,' he continued, 'you've raised your vibrations to where you can communicate with the Angels. All knowledge of past, present, and future ages is at your disposal. This is God's way of communicating it to you.'

In conclusion, Blazier said that we now had to use this blessed knowledge and power for ourselves and others as best we could.

Mrs Blazier then asked us to draw our chairs into a circle. 'We have all this beautiful healing energy around us, over us, in our hands,' she said, 'is there anyone who wants to sit for a healing for themselves or for someone else?'

Several people moved their chairs into the centre of the circle. Then everyone, in both inner and outer circles, was asked to stand and join hands.

Blazier brought our attention to some little red and white splotches on his hands and said this always indicated when the healing power was coming in and building up. 'They are not normally that way,' he said, 'Some of you will have this same experience.'

He asked us to send the healing power from left to right around the circle and to hold in our thoughts the names of the people who had asked for healing. 'Will you say their names aloud? We'll start with this lady here.'

Each person in the inner circle called out a name in turn and the rest of us tried to feel their vibrations. The name 'Ruth' was given first and we were told to concentrate on sending the power to her and to try to feel it actually going out to her. 'God is in our midst, in the presence of all of us,' our leader said. 'He is our light and our direction in all that we do. We thank him and are grateful for the healings that are taking place here and now.'

Mrs Blazier pointed out that the power we were directing was being multiplied by each one of us as we collected it from the person on our left, added our own to it and passed it on to the one on our right and then all directed it into the centre of the circle.

We continued this healing meditation in silence for several minutes. Then Mr Blazier ended the workshop by leading us in singing the Doxology ('Praise God from whom all blessings flow').

A four-column account in *Psychic News* in London first drew the Miami couple, Pat and Bud Hayes, before my line of vision. The Hayes, the story read, working together, had formed 1,000 SFF Development Groups in the United States. Their booklet, just out, described how others could start such groups, and reap the benefit of their ten years of trial-and-error experiment. A picture showed them as a handsome couple, and I was particularly fascinated by the fact that they were bringing up their five children to accept spiritual healing as a normal part of life.

So, on arriving at the SFF Retreat at Emory College near Atlanta, I had been delighted to see *Our First Thousand Groups* by Pat and Bud Hayes at the campus bookstore. I determined to read and digest it thoroughly before requesting a private interview and barraging them with questions about their methods (and those children).

Reading the sections entitled 'Healing Circle' at the end of each outlined weekly meeting, I found varied ideas for meditation, but the following is the guidance given for the simplified first session :

CLOSING MEDITATION

Meditation is the essential prerequisite in clearing the mind for the open reception of any spiritual experience which helps us identify with our inner selves.

(1) Turn the lights down low.
(2) Have group members close their eyes, take a few deep breaths and try to relax.
(3) Meditate on this sentence : 'May God's love and peace strengthen us now'.
(4) Allow yourself to be receptive and try to actually feel God's love and peace pouring into you and strengthening you (three to five minutes).

This is followed by the

HEALING CIRCLE

(1) Everybody stand and hold hands in a circle.
(2) Close the eyes, take a few deep breaths and relax.
(3) Visualise a white light filling the middle of the circle.
(4) Place the names of anybody that needs help physically, mentally or spiritually in the circle and visualise their faces as you say their names.

(5) Place your own name in the circle.
(6) Close with the Lord's Prayer.

In later meetings meditation may take the form of recognising faults and making resolutions to improve, in visualising and feeling 'oneness' with the universe, in mental imagery of colours in nature, in sending thoughts of individual and world peace, of healing and of love.

In several meetings the booklet proposes that anyone needing specific healing be seated in a chair inside the circle, and then, 'Have the group lift them up by bending down to the floor with hands cupped, making a lifting motion close to the person and bringing their hands slowly upward to the head. Then have them place their hands on the person and allow the healing energy to flow through them to the one in the chair'. Later on, each one does the laying-on of hands to the person on his right who sits in the centre, while the others send love and healing.

Discussion of Spiritual Healing is the focal point of the 17th Meeting, and suggested topics for discussion are : Why does healing sometimes succeed and other times fail? What happens during spiritual healing? How can we lift ourselves to this higher conscious-ness to be effective in spiritual healing? For this particular meeting, the group member is asked to practise meditating all the preceding week on his relationship with the Universal Mind 'of which you are but an atom', and then to visualise all life as one, and your soul or essence as being part of that oneness, receiving strength and wisdom.

When I was finally able to speak to Pat Hayes, my first question was, had their healing circles tried to cure serious illnesses?

The healing circle has several purposes,' Pat explained. 'There is much energy flowing in the circle following the meditation and all of it is being channelled to the centre of the circle where the names are placed, and *many* healings have occurred in this way, both serious and minor. But it is also for self-healing. With the flow of energy, many times while the members are sending healing to others their own problems have mysteriously vanished! I'm talking about such things as backaches and headaches. Furthermore, the circle leaves the members with such rapport and harmony flowing through them that they are literally charged when they leave, and love is able to flow in their lives more easily during the week.'

Pat added that more time is taken in case of a serious illness and the group concentrates for an extra five or ten minutes on that one name and sees the person's consciousness 'filled with the light of healing perfection'. She told this story :

'One of our group leaders found he had leukemia and we were informed of it at the group's Christmas party, so the members of all thirty-five of our groups in the city held a healing circle for him.

'The doctor said at the time he would not live through the night —but he did, and one month later was sent home, not cured but out of danger and responding to therapy.'

Then she told of the remarkable effects on her own little daughter.

'When we began our group work in 1963, our daughter Kelly, now 12, was told she'd have to have an operation for a birth defect, the replanting of a ureter. She would have fevers of 106 at least once a month and would have to be hospitalised. The operation was scheduled. . . .

'Then my husband and I decided to put her in the middle of the healing circle at the end of each meeting once a week to see if this would help. One month, two months went by with Kelly sitting in the middle of the circle each week. She never had another fever relating to her kidney problem and never had the operation! This was nine years ago and she's very healthy.'

Pat said that she and Bud are 'thrilled' with the healing circle because, as she puts it, 'each person in the circle is a healing channel and God's energy is being channelled through all of them at once. The light is that much brighter for healing to take place.'

About 1,500 groups are using their lesson-plan, Pat estimates, including some Silva Mind Control and Mind Dynamic graduates who use it to follow-up their alpha training. She and Bud are already swamped with requests for a new book they are writing for more advanced groups as a follow-up, although many graduates of their first series are already moving into 'specialty' groups to do healing, research or practise mediumship. None of their group leaders receive any remuneration, she said, and many have been doing it for years, for the sheer sense of fulfillment.

To my last question, Pat answered, 'Yes, our children are very much part of the work. Our oldest daughter, Kim, helps us with youth groups. She's 14. And Kelly is already using her healing potential. The psychic and all spiritual matters are very much a natural part of our lives.'

It was a revelation to hear how freely the average SFF member can talk about his or her psychic experiences and, indeed, how many have had them. I began jotting down these stories as they popped out spontaneously at what were known as 'rap-sessions', nightly gatherings for casual exchange between guest speakers, psychic consultants and the Retreat participants.

One interesting story emerged from Marty Urban's lively session, when about a dozen of us had gathered around her in a campus classroom. It was a hot August night and Marty, wearing one of her more exotic prints, started off by telling us about the form of mental discipline she's mastered, a form of deep meditation, by which she is able to separate mind from body, watch her body go to sleep and even hear herself snore! 'In terms of ecstasy,' said Marty, 'it's a pure, total joining with the Higher Forces.'

Don Hudson, a psychic consultant, spoke next of his extraordinary experience.

'I was in my service truck at about 11 o'clock in the morning. One of my customers, a lady, left a note for me saying she wouldn't be home that day because she had to be with her son who was in the hospital.

'Well, something hit me that I should stop and pray for the son. So I pulled the truck over to the kerb and prayed for his well-being.

'The next week when I stopped at her home, I asked, "How is your son?" And she said, "Something amazing happened last week. He was in hospital and on the verge of dying when all of a sudden—it was like a miracle of God—he began to change for the better." We checked our times and this happened at the hour I was praying, about 11 o'clock that same morning! You just learn to listen. . . .'

In another casual exchange, I heard of a more recent, but equally fascinating, experience. Wilbur Jones of Dothan, Alabama, was still aglow from an event the night before at the Rev. Holmes' healing service. He'd been sitting in the congregation and it was time for the general laying-on of hands, when suddenly one of the psychic counsellors, Miss Josey, came up to him excited and gasping, he said.

'She laid her hand on my shoulder and told me, "You should be doing healing" I was so overcome with emotion that I gripped her hands for at least four minutes before letting go. People were crowding up the aisle to the rail and she said, "You must go and assist with the healing". I said, "But they haven't asked me". She said, "I'm telling you—Go!"

'When I got up there I told Gordon Melton, "I've never done this

before, but I have this gift and I want to help in any way I can".
He welcomed me and I started in . . . It's just another demonstration of how God works in inexplicable ways!'

Isabel Hickey, author of *Astrology, A Cosmic Science*, a jolly,
expansive woman from Boston, was another intriguing source of
information.

Mrs Hickey said she started doing group healing forty years ago;
recalling two wonderful healings, she told of a man whose name
had been given to the group because he was to undergo lung surgery
in the morning, and when she had spoken his name she had felt a
knife slash across her back. 'I asked a nurse of my acquaintance how
they operate on lung cancer, and she said they cut across the back.
Well, the next morning when they opened the man they found no
cancer.

'Our first group healing was probably one of the most exciting,'
Mrs Hickey continued, 'because none of us knew anything about the
principles of healing. A friend of one of our people was having a leg
amputated the next morning. There wasn't time to call a meeting so
seven of us got together. Three in the group had never even prayed.
We got in a circle and each took hands. We said in our prayers,
"Father, we don't know what this is all about. We don't understand
how you work, but sincerely we're asking to be used as channels to
help this person".

'The next day the one in the group who had asked for our help
called very excitedly to say that very morning her friend's temperature dropped from 104 to normal. Instantaneously, she was healed!
We didn't know her, had never seen her before. It was such a thrill!
We were just neophytes and didn't know what we were doing.' She
added, 'It has nothing to do with intelligence or personality, it has
to do with the heart and caring . . . Love is the greatest healing force
in the universe.'

A few hours later I was reading on the central bulletin board an
interview with Mrs Barbara Wilson in the *Atlanta Constitution*.

Mrs Wilson, the Retreat chairman, is a charter member and chairman of Atlanta SFF. She is also a healer, and in the interview she
recounted more than one healing story. The first was the case of a
woman who had suffered a heart attack and was not expected to live.
To quote the *Constitution* interview :

'I prayed for her every morning and hoped that she would be
healed and made whole. On the third day of my praying for her,

attuning myself to her, sending her loving thoughts, a small voice within me urged me to go see her. I had the feeling I must go to the hospital and touch her.

'She was in intensive care and only her family could see her. When I got to the hospital the front door was locked, but I went in a side door and walked to intensive care. I had never been there, but I went straight to it.

'A nurse came out and told me the woman was in pain. She had had another heart attack. She asked me who I was and left. She came back a few minutes later and let me in.

'I talked to the woman and touched her chest. I didn't know what I was doing, but I touched her chest. Within twenty-four hours she was moved out of intensive care and in six weeks she was bowling.

'I wasn't going to tell her about the experience I had, but she brought it up at dinner one night. She told me that somehow the night I visited her something was different. Then I told her about the voice telling me to visit her and she believed me. I can't begin to explain what happened, but God used me.'

She then told me about the woman with terminal cancer, 'a massive tumour which involved the liver'. Doctors had opened her up and decided not to remove it and her days were numbered. Mrs Wilson saw this woman privately several times and then called together a healing study group to which the woman was invited.

'We sang, had scripture reading and then had the woman sit in the middle of our group, the interview continued. 'We all prayed, placed our hands on her shoulders and worked with her to help her understand spiritual healing. She had gone to church all her life, but she didn't know how to accept God's healing laws . . . After working with her six weeks she went back for a check-up. The tumour was smaller and the cancer had not spread. She was given more cobalt and encouraged to seek every avenue of healing—spiritual and medical.

'She heard about some success in curing cancer at a medical centre in Kansas. Arrangements were made for her to go there where doctors were able to remove the tumour. The cancer still had not spread and her liver had improved. Doctors are encouraged that she will be cured.

'Sceptics can say the cobalt did it. Perhaps she wasn't as sick as the doctors thought. Perhaps she had the type of cancer that doesn't spread. Maybe the sceptics are right, but when she told a doctor she was going to get well he told her not to kid herself.

'I am convinced more people die of cancer than need to because when they learn they have cancer they and their friends are negative in their thinking.

'This woman wanted to get well and she believed God wanted her well. She learned how to accept His love and His healing and I think this is why she is getting well.'

7. Tuning up with the ARE

At the ARE's 'Week of Attunement', on its home grounds, a huge, old-fashioned white clapboard building on a bluff overlooking the Atlantic Ocean in Virginia Beach, Virginia, the attraction was an impressive assemblage of youthful New Age doctors and health experts, all of them adept at applying the healing concepts of Edgar Cayce.

'Healing in the New Age' was the theme, and the accent was on the 'wholistic' or body-mind-spirit approach to healing. Prominently quoted in the announcement was this apropos saying of Cayce's:

'Each soul is the temple of the living God. Thus be more mindful of the body for the body's sake that it may be the better channel for the manifesting of spiritual truths.'

Rather than a proliferation of workshops, the ARE event was concentrated under one roof and lectures given three times a day. In-between, however, there was plenty of time for outdoor activities and individual appointments with the doctors. This unusual feature for those attending was outlined in advance:

'You can take advantage of this rare gathering of healers who have agreed to guide conferees toward the path of a fuller, healthier life. Private consultations and treatments will be available with your choice of healer. Moderate fees will be charged. This pioneering co-operative health experience is the forerunner of a planned healing/research centre at Virginia Beach . . .'

We were invited to list on our registration blanks any disease(s) for which we would like to have consultations so that facilities could be provided.

Arranging the medical programme, the first of its kind ever attempted by the ARE, was Dr Robert G. Brewer, chief of general surgery at Suburban Hospital in Bethesda, Maryland. Tall, strikingly handsome, Dr Brewer has incorporated many Cayce concepts of healing into orthodox medicine and is the mainspring of the proposed healing and health centre.

The doctors, medical professionals and other healers who addressed us beside Dr Brewer were : Dr Francis Woidich, a nutritionist; Dr Lindsay Jacob, a psychiatrist; Dr Genevieve Haller, a chiropractor; Dr Rex Conyers, an osteopath; Dr Harmon Bro, a psychologist and psychotherapist; Dr Rose Marie Hudson, a chiropractor who works with Dr Brewer and has patented a self-contained hydrotherapy apparatus; Doris Kendall, a masseuse; Joel Andrews, a music therapist; Harold J. Reilly, Edgar Cayce's favourite physiotherapist, and Robert O. Clapp, a herb expert.

When we weren't listening to these stimulating healers we were enjoying all the invigorating attractions of a health spa. As the sun rose every morning over the Atlantic we were out on the beach doing calisthenics under the snappy direction of Jeffrey Furst. And in the afternoon we were put through strenuous paces by Harold Reilly. At any time of day we could plunge into the waves or take a sunbath, and since Virginia Beach sand has a health-giving gold content, according to Cayce, we could follow his advice and bury ourselves in it up to our necks. Colonics and massages were also available.

The ARE's fare was organic, nutritious and often raw—even the sugar ! A typical breakfast menu was : figs, organic oatmeal cereal, cheese omelette, organic muffins, milk, butter, honey. Sometimes there were buckwheat cakes, homemade Yogurt and an item called 'Walnut Acres Organic Crunchy Cereal'.

For lunch we had such goodies as beansprout or lentil soup, celery sticks, slices of melon, blueberries, banana rolled in coconut, green salad, homemade bread and herb tea.

And for dinner, there was roast lamb, brown rice, Edgar Cayce carrot loaf, ambrosia, and, the final night, an oriental curry with sauces and garnishes of minced dried fruits and nuts.

All were served sit-down style in The Marshalls, the co-operating motel on the ocean-side where most of the conferees were quartered.

The ARE's opening panel, with Dr Brewer presiding, described an amazing team effort—using Cayce therapies—which brought back to health a young woman with 'incurable' rheumatoid arthritis in its advanced stages.

Introduced by Dr Brewer, Dr Rose Marie Hudson, a round-figured woman with a beautiful Grecian face, described the condition of the patient at the outset: 'There was limited motion, tenderness, lower extremities swollen to twice their size, pain acute in all joints, cervical area fixed, hands in tensed, flexed state, she couldn't hold a cup or toothbrush, atrophy in shoulder muscles . . . We put her on a diet recommended by Cayce and followed it to the letter, along with his physiotherapy, Castor Oil packs, thermal mittens and boots. She was taking huge amounts of bufferin, dexedrine and terramycin and she was withdrawn from these drugs gradually over six months.'

Dr Hudson said she told the story 'with a deep sense of humility' because it was an effort of so many who combined the whole spectrum of healing arts. And the patient accepted seventy-five per cent of the responsibility for her healing. 'In her desire to become completely well, she too was a link in the chain.'

Dr Hudson then gave a warm tribute to Dr Brewer, 'a healer with many years of dedication to his field'.

'In my association with Dr Brewer, attuning to the divine power to flow through us, I've been awakened to a higher state of consciousness. My strength has been renewed. I've been inspired by a rebirth,' she said.

'Love, understanding, the spiritual aspects of human beings, all came into it. The problem seemed insurmountable, but we used the tools of co-operation and belief and an elevation of the consciousness in meditation and helped the power of God to enter the body.' And she asked a rhetorical question: 'Are we to listen to our peers or to God?'

She then introduced the patient, Miss Shirley Askew, a blonde, wholesome-looking young woman who stood and smiled somewhat self-consciously.

Explaining the findings, Dr Brewer said that rheumatoid arthritis was a systemic disease, 'of the mortar not of the bricks', then it attacks the brick itself, and it tends to run in families. (He noted that in the Cayce readings it is described as 'a dysfunction of the life force finally exhibited in the physical body'.)

'Now Miss Askew can play golf,' he concluded, 'and has largely won her battle. All she needs is maintenance therapy. A truly remarkable case.'

Dr Woidich, a leader in his field, gave us daily talks on nutrition that were truly eye-opening. He began by informing us that 'every person in this room was once a single cell invisible to the naked eye', and the only difference between us and that single cell of yesteryear was the food, plus water and oxygen, supplied to that little cell since we were born.

In sharing with us some important tenets of good nutrition from his wealth of knowledge, Dr Woidich made frequent approving references to Cayce concepts of good diet, but added a warning against following indiscriminately every smallest bit of advice Cayce gave to others. 'The readings have some very interesting suggestions and insights,' he said, 'but some people have failed to maintain their mother wit in applying this informtion to themselves.'

For example, in the field of cancer prevention, Dr Woidich recalled that Cayce told one woman many years ago to eat three raw almonds a day and she would never get cancer, and a great many people concluded that if they ate three raw almonds a day *they* would never get cancer. 'And among them were two ladies who were longtime associates of Cayce. They took three almonds a day. I remember them offering some to me. They were very good. But I heard some years later both of those ladies died of cancer.' Dr Woidich said he suspected their 'misguided assumption', that what was good for one was good for all, had lulled them into a false sense of security and caused them to neglect the tests and check-ups that might have prevented their unhappy end.

Harold Reilly, a gruff, witty man who still looks youthful in his 80's, told us a moving story about a Vietnam veteran, paralysed from the waist down, who wrote him from California asking if he could come to Virginia Beach for treatment. Seven or eight vertebrae had been fractured with shrapnel and his spinal cord had been severed. 'I have hundreds of this type of letter', said Reilly, whose massage and exercise therapies were recommended hundreds of times in the Cayce readings.

The young soldier had been in a veteran's hospital for five months taking rehabilitation therapy. He had been in and out of bed and was driving a car. Apparently he was making no further progress and a girl friend had told him about Edgar Cayce and the treatments given by Harold Reilly.

'I told him if he had someone in the family who was very devoted I'd treat him as much as I can and teach that person the treatment,' Reilly said. He then read a testimonial letter from the veteran.

'My dear friend and room-mate quit his job to drive me over, knowing I'd have to have someone devoted to me to learn the treatments', he wrote in part. 'Mr Reilly began a massage treatment and taught my friend in nine sessions. I registered a slight amount of movement in my legs and some sensation. It was very little, but I hadn't had any improvement in three years. He told me about diet and food. I become a member of the ARE and requested the file of readings on paralysis.'

Reilly commented, 'He's a very self-sufficient man. He has motivation. I think we'll get results in this case. If they have any sensation at all it's a good sign.'

He then gave demonstration massages, showing us the smooth semi-circular motion he's perfected over his fifty years in the profession, and with his young assistant, Betty Billings, showed us how some of the stand-by Cayce remedies, such as the Glycothymoline pack, Castor Oil pack, spinal oil rub, are applied.

I was delighted to learn that a handkerchief dipped in warm Glycothymoline and folded over your sinuses is great for clearing up sinus congestion. And a man in the audience said he had tried it successfully with a cold. 'I had a very bad cold. I couldn't lie down and had to sit up all night otherwise I was unable to breathe. I put the handkerchief dipped in Glycothymoline over my nose for twenty minutes. My throat and nostrils drained and I was able to lie down and sleep for the rest of the night.'

The 'Glyco pack' is also very good for incipient colitis among other things, Reilly said, and is very beneficial when used in enemas and colonics—one tablespoon of Glyco to each gallon of water.

'One thing about the Cayce readings', said Miss Billings, 'if you don't get a lot of benefit from them at least they won't hurt you,' and Reilly added that we should look up in the readings to see if our condition is treated by these remedies. 'Do a little homework yourself. There are many ways of applying them.'

Dr Lindsay Jacob, a gentle, dark-haired man who is staff psychiatrist at the Home for Crippled Children in Pittsburgh and has a private practice, made some potent observations on the healing power of love. 'In psychiatry, when we make the learning of love a goal, things happen so much faster,' he said. 'Sometimes I feel like a preacher in a consulting room. Just as you are linked to what you desire, hate links you to the thing you hate just as strongly.'

Touching on a central Cayce concept, Dr Jacob said reincarnation is becoming more widely accepted, but still too few people are willing to commit themselves to it or use it. He, himself, didn't believe in it at first, but certain experiments and experiences in hypnotic regression into past lives had changed his mind.

'I now think we set up in each life a talent to learn or a wrong attitude to work out. If we're successful in this task it's a fairly successful lifetime, even if we fall short in other respects.'

(I asked Dr Jacob if he didn't think life readings—a psychic survey of past lives for experiences affecting the subject's present life, such as Cayce gave—were helpful in psychiatry. He agreed that they would be, but the difficulty was in finding someone as great as Cayce in this area, and someone who could be depended upon.)

Dr Jacob also gave us valuable guidance on the importance of relaxation in releasing obstructions from the body's natural forces. 'All healing works on the principle of trying to allow the forces of nature to be free to "do their thing",' he said. 'When inbalances occur, you have to find and unblock the thing that's being blocked.'

Pointing out that we can bring the physical body into balance by relaxing in meditation, he suggested the affirmation, 'Be still and know I am God', as a good preliminary, with emphasis on 'Be still'.

Dr Jacob explained that we can use our senses to enhance our physical health. We have not just five, but at least thirty senses, he said. For example, the senses that give you information on the chemical condition of your muscles, will 'tell you if you're eating too many beans and not enough steak, if you need rest and so forth, and if you continue to ignore them you will pay a price, sooner or later'.

The way to get around this is to 'get the body into a balanced situation. If you hurt, try to find out what your senses are telling you about what is physically going on. Scan your body for unusual sensations, for tingling, for tensions. Place your concentration on the particular area bothering you. If it's a headache, rub it gently, pay attention to the sensations rubbing produces. Use the conscious mind to enhance the re-balancing. A flow back and forth begins to happen. Energies are freed in the body so that the forces of nature can take their course.'

Dr Harmon Bro, who has taught religion and psychology at Syracuse University and Harvard and is the author of several books on various aspects of the Cayce readings, gave us an authoritative, unsentimental lecture on the inner spirit of the organisation.

'At first,' he said, 'the ARE was a society of people who were helped by Edgar Cayce. It became more and more clear that they had experienced an authentic growing from sometimes a crippling disability to greater freedom. It was the society of the saving secret. Now it has become known as a company of people who have helped each other. We've got a hospital run by the patients. People who were hurt come on the scene full of ideas and programmes. Often they're a bit unbalanced, but the joy is in watching all of us unbalanced people balance each other. We don't call it psychotherapy —we call it the working-through of karma. . . .

'The ARE, with its concern for ESP, has been a pioneer in practising psychic healing in group situations,' Dr Bro continued. 'People really do change. People really do get happy, if they use their heads and sit and meditate. We work at it believing in one another at the ARE. There's something in it that gives us encouragement. Somehow the other fellow starts looking better every day. That's the kind of therapy you find in the readings. Everybody grows and groans and grows in the process, and by discovering the mystery of grace, we find we don't have to make it all by ourselves. . . .'

Robert O. Clapp, in his talk about the use of herbs in healing, informed us that ragweed is very beneficial as an eliminative and that watermelon seed tea works fine for kidney problems, according to the readings. And he told us how to mix tender leaves of the plaintain weed with whipping cream to make a salve that heals boils and carbuncles!

Listing many of the old-fashioned herbs prescribed in the readings, he said, 'Our ancestors knew more about these than we do. We need to revive our knowledge, use it to help ourselves.' He ended by giving us the precise ingredients of a bracing potion Cayce recommended for co-ordinating the assimilations and the eliminations and correcting the balance of the body : To one quart of distilled water, add

2 oz wild cherry bark
1 oz sarsaparilla root
1 oz wild ginseng
$\frac{1}{2}$ oz Indian turnip
1 oz yellow dockroot
1 dram Baku leaves
15 grains mandrake root (May apple)

Reduce these by boiling down to one half or 16 oz. While warm, add 3 oz grain alcohol as a preservative and one dram of balsam of talu to make it palatable. Shake well and take one teaspoonful four times a day before meals and before retiring.

Joel Andrews brought us a message of healing through music. A concert harpist with an easy, friendly manner, he has for the past few years dedicated himself to the study of vibration and the healing of mankind through music and has improvised 'healing music'. 'It's too soon to give you the results,' he said, 'but I can say it's very rewarding.'

Andrews reminded us that Edgar Cayce spoke often of the healing power of music, together with colour, and he quoted the following from the readings :

'. . . Sounds, music and colours may have much to do with creating the proper vibrations about individuals that are mentally unbalanced, physically deficient or ill in body and mind; and may be used as helpful experiences.' (1334-1)

On another occasion, Cayce was quite specific in explaining how vibrations operate in healing :

'Every individual entity is on certain vibrations. Every disease or dis-ease is creating in the body the opposite or non-co-ordinant vibration with the conditions in a body-mind and spirit of the individual. If there are used certain vibrations there may be seen the response. In some it is necessary for counteraction, in some it is necessary for changes. The better way is first to develop in thine own consciousness, of thy associates or thy companion, that vibration which is in rhythm with the vibration of that body. Moods often change this vibration; yet by study, by practise, and by application, the vibration of the body may be ascertained.' (8161-12)

Applying these ideas to a concert situation, Andrews said that for the last few years he has been asking to be used as a channel of healing, before a concert, and 'to co-create with the highest co-creators'. He has had many beautiful experiences as a result. 'People have come up to me crying or saying they had some kind of illumination and that a healing has taken place,' he said.

Not only has he healed others with music, he has healed himself, said the harpist. 'Often I'll work so hard before a concert that I'll catch a cold. But if the concert goes well my cold will be gone. I'll have raised myself to a vibration where the cold couldn't exist and it has vanished like that!

'We can be healed, we can be lifted up, just by opening ourselves to co-create with God,' he said, adding that we are also healed by putting ourselves in harmony with and aligning our wills with God's.

'Music as a stimulant has fewer side effects than coffee,' Andrews said and, adding another Cayce quote: 'When illness and the like were to come about, soft music and the lighter shades or tones will quiet where medicine would fail.' Cayce also said that low music would assist diagnosis!

After hearing all this we were growing impatient for Joel Andrews to start pouring forth some healing music from the graceful gold-gilt harp that stood on the platform. He didn't disappoint us. Asking us all to send him 'thoughts of healing', he said he would give us an 'instant healing improvisation'. For the next five minutes glorious rippling sounds filled the auditorium and then, after sweeping us aloft on eddying swirls of music he changed to a calmer mood and a melody line of classical simplicity that was deeply moving.

Although she is a chiropractor and director of the chiropractic research division of the Edgar Cayce Foundation, Dr Genevieve Haller, a dynamic, dark-haired young woman who wore white slacks and a flamboyant shirt, spoke to us about the 'wholistic approach to healing' and, specifically, how we are healed through our senses at various levels of vibration.

There is no 'best way' to be healed, she said. People accept healing at different levels. 'But ideally we should be healed at *all* levels, mentally, spiritually, emotionally and physically. The minute we leave one out we're not going to have a complete healing.'

Dr Haller distributed a vibration chart drawn up by Roland Hunt which associates the seven senses with various levels of vibration, and relates the sense to the activity which will produce healing at that level, as follows:

Dense matter		Food, minerals	Taste
1st-3rd	Octave	Physical sound	Hearing
4th-15th	,,	Music; spoken word	
16th-20th	,,	(32,768 vib. per. sec.) ultra sound; electrical appliances	Touch
25th-35th	,,	Electricity; violet ray appliance	
40th-45th	,,	Unknown	
46th-48th	,,	Heat	
49th	,,	Colour Infra-red ray; 7 colours of spectrum; ultra-violet ray	Sight
50th	,,	Brain waves, chemical rays	6th Sense
51st-57th	,,	Perfumes; odours	Smell
58th-61st	,,	X-rays; radium	
62nd	,,	Unknown Cosmic rays White light	Spiritual Sense

Commenting on several of the healing activities at random, she said, 'Through our sense of taste we are healed by good nutrition; through our sense of hearing, by music. We know that plants are helped to grow by low vibrations, they seem to like low, heavy sounds . . . Some people can just look at certain colours and be immediately healed. Edgar Cayce prescribed red wine for blood building. Why didn't he say white wine? Because there is something in the vibration of red that was helpful for blood building . . .'

Explaining the heading 'electrical appliances' related to the sense of touch, she said it referred to the various types of electrical apparatus that are used for healing. This level also includes the vibration conveyed by massage and manipulation through the hands of a chiropractor to his patient.

The brain waves associated with the sixth sense are the alpha waves, she said. 'Many people can receive healing when they are relaxed at that particular vibratory rate.' As for odours, Dr Haller noted that Edgar Cayce prescribed many for healing, such as pine for fume baths, and eucalyptus and tincture of benzoine to be put in vaporisers and used in sinus conditions. 'Then there was the good old apple brandy keg which I wouldn't be without. It was through breathing these apple brandy fumes that Gertrude Cayce was brought out of TB when she was ready to die. It sounded like a weird idea but they tried it and it worked. I've used it for lung conditions, emphysema, bronchial problems, and it always seems to be helpful.'

It is possible to bypass all these levels and ask for healing through the seventh, or spiritual, sense where our vibrations are changed in attunement to the Christ Consciousness, she said. (Cayce defines the Christ Consciousness as the soul's awareness of its oneness with God.)

Summing it all up, Dr Haller asked us to consider on which level we accept healing most easily and on which the least, and 'see if you can't do something about accepting healing completely, with all of your senses'. She referred us to the suggestions in Hunt's vibration chart for combining perfumes, musical sounds and colours that blend well together.

During the morning 'juice break' I asked several of the doctors how they happened to become interested in the Cayce healing concepts.

Dr Rex Conyers, who was the osteopath on the panel, practises in the Denver suburb of Aurora. He is director of the osteopathic research division of the Edgar Cayce Foundation and active in enlisting the co-operation of other osteopaths in researching the results of Cayce therapies. So far 125 osteopaths in 33 states and three foreign countries are participating.

'I was going through a personal crisis and was all turned-on with self-pity,' Dr Conyers told me. 'I was a founding stockholder in a new hospital for osteopathy. It was a very good thing. Then a few men squeezed out the rest of us. What hurt was I couldn't understand how men could do this to other men.

'Then someone handed me a copy of *There Is A River* by Thomas Sugrue. It was a turning point, as though the Creator had put his hand on my shoulder and said, "You're going in the wrong direction". Maybe I had to do something about all that self-pity!' He was happy to say he had come to see that the tragedy was a blessing.

Dr Francis Woidich also got into the Cayce concepts by reading *There Is A River*. He was having 'a combination of troubles' back in 1948 and came down to Virginia Beach at a time when the ARE was poor and struggling. 'I wanted to see what it was all about,' said Dr Woidich,' and was indelibly impressed.'

Dr Lindsay Jacob told me he had become interested in the psychic before hearing about Cayce and had made some explorations in group sessions led by a man who was purported to be a 'sensitive'.

'Then a patient of mine brought in a replica of Cayce's Radio-active Appliance, which he recommended in so many readings. My patient wanted to know what I thought of it. I could tell right away by the feel, by the vibrations, that there was something to it. So I came down here in 1958 to see what the ARE was all about and I've been coming down ever since.'

A glowing highlight of the week was the Wednesday morning session presenting the legendary 'Glad Helpers' healing group. This was the continuation of the original group to whom Edgar Cayce gave step-by-step guidance in the *281 Series* beginning in 1931.

'We have a long and happy tradition, and I think the help the group has given is immeasurable,' said Meredith Puryear, its leader. What we do in healing is a process of attuning. Our basis of study is the *281 Series* which encompasses all the major readings on Medi-tation, on the *Book of Revelation* and on The Glands.

Mrs Puryear then encouraged each member of the group to express his insights freely. Here are a few samples of the ideas that came out more or less spontaneously :

'Belief that the healing is available to him is important to the patient's attunement. Cayce said, "If thou hast been prepared in thy mind, thy purpose, and thy ideal being correct, it is already thine" and he said the patient should be in a prayerful attitude and quiet when receiving healing.

'The patient should know what they're going to do once they get better. They have to have some ideal, something to fulfill before they will be healed. If one does manifest healing but there's no intent to change, it's very likely the illness will recur.'

'If attunement is difficult, start loving God as the first step. The easiest way to do that is to think of all His attributes, His goodness, His wisdom, His power, His divine providence and as you start loving God this increases your vibrations. Then you naturally give yourself wholeheartedly to Him and to His work.

'In the readings, people were advised to have a laying-on of hands repeatedly, over and over again. I emphasise this because I

think sometimes people look for a sudden, instantaneous healing . . .
I think more often it is a gradual process.'

There were eighteen in the 'Glad Helpers' healing prayer group,
ten women and eight men, of all ages and types, and they usually
have a healing list of 250 to 300, Mrs Puryear said. The group is
self-governing and they take turns being leader. They meet every
Wednesday morning from 10 to 12 o'clock in the room of the secretary, Ruth LeNoir, on the third floor of the ARE main building, and
visitors are welcome.

In his lecture, 'The Seven Wonders of the World', Dr Herbert
B. Puryear gave the essence of what the Cayce readings have to say
about the endocrine glands. The endocrine system is involved in
every psychic experience, and especially in the flow of energy from
healer to patient. It acts as transmitter, receiver and transducer
of that energy, he said.

A clinical psychologist with a Phd from Stanford, and Director
of Education for the ARE, Dr Puryear has as deep a knowledge of
the readings as anyone, and a knack for distilling masses of abstruse
information into understandable form.

When Dr Puryear gave the introductory message at the two
California symposiums on healing covered elsewhere in this book,
he spoke on Cayce's 'triune' approach to healing, the healing of body,
mind and spirit through 'a one-ness with the creative forces of nature
we call God'. He emphasised Cayce's basic message :

'The spirit is the life
Mind is the builder
The physical is the result.'

Dr Puryear then stated it another way : 'There is only one force.
There is a patterning of this force. What we see is the result.'

Explaining, he said, 'When the mind builds behaviour patterns
at variance to and not supportive of the life force, and the behaviour
pattern is not conducive to the life flow, then you cut off the life
flow and illness is the consequence.

'For example, an attitude of resentment will produce inflam-
mation. If it is deeply buried it can cause cancer. Hate, animosity,
hard sayings, weaken the body . . . Anger actually causes poisons to
be secreted from the adrenals and may result in diseases of the
liver if it is unable to flush out the poisons.'

Giving examples of 'behaviour patterns' that cut off the life flow, he added, 'the lack of exercise, wrong diet and exposing ourselves to certain kinds of stress'.

Summing up these ideas from the readings, Dr Puryear said, 'All illness comes from sin, whether of mind, body or soul, Cayce said. He was not being moralistic. He meant doing things we know we ought not to do that are not consistent with the life flow. He's talking about physical law.'

According to Cayce, no applications of medicinal properties or appliances can bring healing in themselves. They only help the body in its healing processes. All healing is from life and life is from God. 'Healing is allowing the life force to flow through, and its action is to stimulate and arouse and awaken each cell of the body to its proper activities.'

And this is where the endocrine glands come in. The endocrine system modifies the finer spiritual energy to an energy that is expressed in the hormonal secretions. These are carried in the bloodstream to every cell of the body, to instruct the body in its reproductive processes. 'Just by thought or an emotionally charged word you can awaken a response that will secrete this throughout the body,' said Dr Puryear, 'so it is by thought, by mental imagery that we can stimulate this powerful energy that flows through us at the atomic level.'

In conclusion, Dr Puryear added several more health pointers from the readings:

'Twenty minutes of meditation a day will give you a measurable effect which makes you stronger.

'By our thoughts we are either healing or destroying anything we may be in touch with.

'Don't try to get rid of symptoms too quickly. The idea is to change.

'Cayce recommended physical applications, osteopathy, colonics, but simply to awaken the natural responses of the body.

'To overcome bad habits, pray with the same consistence and persistence as the desire for indulgence and you'll find you bring strength.'

Dr Puryear ended his talk with a Cayce reading that emphasised the universality of the healing power:

'The forces which are manifest to bring the relief to physical force are not of a one faith, but a oneness in faith in the God-force manifest in the individual . . . Study, then, these truths, for they remain a oneness, whether Jewish, Gentile, Greek or heathen.' (136-12).

Hugh Lynn Cayce, eldest son of Edgar Cayce and managing director of the ARE, spoke to us of its growing role. He welcomed the strong participation of the doctors and predicted a useful function for the ARE 'as we move into and become part of and begin to expand consciousness in this New Age'. And he quoted that powerful, prophetic statement of Cayce's :

'For the time has arisen in the earth when men everywhere seek to know more of the mysteries of the mind, the soul, the soul's mind which man recognises as existent yet has seen little of the abilities of same . . .' (254-52).

'You and I are on the verge of moving into an age where man is discovering the new spiritual dimensions of himself,' said Hugh Lynn Cayce, 'and you and I want to be free of those blocks at the mental and physical and emotional levels to bring more balance into our lives that we may represent and fulfill God's purpose in this earth, his purpose for us. For you and I have no other excuse for being.'

PART TWO

England as a Laboratory

8. The National Federation of Spiritual Healers

IN THE LETTERS that flew backwards and forwards between Mary Rogers and me after I picked up her letter in the 14th Street subway, a clearer picture began to emerge of the practice of spiritual healing in England and the status and organisation of the healers themselves.

I could see Mary's standing as an unorthodox practitioner was several notches higher than merely 'respectable'—with MPS, opera singers, ballet dancers and the local police beating a path to her sanctuary. And although men high up in politics shied from acknowledging publicly that they resorted to spiritual healing, a prominent sugar magnate, John Lyle, had credited her with curing his arthritis, permitting his wife to tell it to the *Sunday Express.*

More important, I learned that Britain's healers had their own National Federation of Spiritual Healers, numbering several thousand members, and that they practised freely under their own rules, without interference from government or the medical profession.

'For spirit healing, it is free and easy here,' Mary Rogers had written in one of her letters. 'We're not penalised and we're not imprisoned. Some churches go along with it, some don't. The general attitude toward it is liberal-minded and tolerant.'

The stack of clippings she sent me from a fair cross-section of the British press and the books she recommended that I read by other English healers all seemed to concur with her point of view. The contrast with the United States became more and more striking. Rather than practise openly and confidently as in England, the gifted healers of America are widely scattered, hard to find, overworked and totally unorganised. In some states healers are forbidden by law to touch the patient, and some local medical societies have been repressive and hostile. Many healers are church-affiliated or have organised their own sect so they can be called 'Reverend' and avoid harassment. But with no substantial schools or accepted methods of training, most spiritual healing is done by relatively untrained groups of people or by a handful of charismatic evangelical healers, such as Kathryn Kuhlman or Oral Roberts, who have become TV or radio personalities.

It seemed to me as more and more Americans develop their gift of healing in the New Age of higher spiritual consciousness that England could serve as a 'research lab' not only guiding us into wise policies but helping us to avoid their mistakes.

In the English speaking world where but in England has the government enacted enlightened legislation to protect both healer and public without becoming repressive? And where else are healers organised professionally and able to demonstrate successfully healing in a Royal Festival Hall or a Trafalgar Square?

In the Spring of 1972 I went to Britain to see for myself what could be learned from their experience. What kind of training courses were available? Were there schools or centres where beginners could develop their abilities free or at low cost? What training techniques, if any, were considered the best?

Before leaving New York I went to see Dr Robert Laidlaw at his Park Avenue office to ask if he would look over my long questionnaire for healers, through which I hoped to get an in-depth picture of healing practice in England. I also wanted pointers on good information sources and the names of leading healers whose approach and philosophy would be of interest to Americans.

A leading investigator of psychic healing, and for eight years chairman of the Commission for the Study of Healing based at Wainwright House, Rye, New York, Dr Laidlaw is now secretary-treasurer of Life Energies Research, Inc., a solid group of professional people seeking scientific proof of psychic healing and other parapsychological phenomena. He is also a well-known psychiatrist and former head of the division of psychiatry at Roosevelt Hospital, New York. Consequently, I hoped he could shed some light on the 'spirit doctor' concept which I knew would soon confront me in

England if Mary Rogers' approach to healing was at all typical!

I was delighted when Dr Laidlaw said he had been to Aylesbury, England, to see George Chapman, the one-time fireman who is said to perform skillful psychic surgery while under the spirit control of a distinguished London eye surgeon named Dr William Lang who died in 1937.

'I believe that under certain circumstances communicating with entities who now exist on another plane following physical death is a reality,' said Dr Laidlaw, 'and that certain of these entities possess a desire and knowledge to help human beings, and then act as guides to certain individuals whose background and experience would in themselves make it completely impossible for them to achieve the healing results which they have demonstrated.'

Naming the late Brazilian psychic surgeon, Arigo, and Cayce, the psychic diagnostician, as two who were so guided, he added that when Dr Lang's elderly personality appeared to take over Chapman, he talked with 'Lang' and was very impressed with his authority. 'We had a doctor-to-doctor discussion for over an hour.

'If you want to call these spirit entities "the heavenly host", that's a perfectly good explanation that fits in with the dogma of the church,' he said.

I was later to find that these views coincided not only with those of Mary Rogers, but also of Harry Edwards, president of the National Federation of Spiritual Healers, Gilbert Anderson, its administrator, and a majority of its healer-members who, I later learned, fully accept this tenet of modern Spiritualism.

Dr Laidlaw also informed me that the NFSH offers a correspondence course in spiritual healing, and he gave me a copy of the prospectus. After suggesting the names of a few leading healers and having his research assistant, Miss Olive Freeman, give me the address and phone number of the new NFSH headquarters in Loughton, Essex—and approving my questionnaire without change —Dr Laidlaw graciously wished me success on my mission.

It was a sunny but cold day when I took the Underground at Tottenham Court Road to the prosperous-looking town of Loughton, and after stopping at a pub near the station for a cup of hot tea to warm me, I caught a bus that let me off atop Church Hill at the doorstep of 'Shortacres', the NFSH home base, a large brick-and-stucco house almost hidden by trees.

Mrs Gilbert Anderson welcomed me at the door, introduced me

to several busy women workers getting out a mailing, and took me upstairs to her husband's office.

A dapper, silver-haired man with the healthy glow of a country squire, Anderson rose from his desk and shook my hand hospitably. He told me that he combines his administrative work for the Federation with the practice of spiritual healing and teaching, returning often to his sanctuary in Norfolk at weekends, where there will usually be a queue of patients waiting.

Looking over my questionnaire, he offered to send it out in their next mailing to a sample 1,000 of their 4,000 healer-members. A great idea! I said, and offered to help with the filling and licking. We then sat back and, at my urging, he philosophised on the first question, which read: 'At what age and in what manner did you discover that you had the ability to heal?'

'I served as a flying instructor in the RAF during the war,' Anderson began, 'and firmly believe that flying brings one into a much closer awareness of the spiritual aspect of life . . . I was invalided out in 1945 with a spinal disease that was pronounced incurable by medical science and I experienced hell for two years with no pain relief whatever, day or night.

'I was reaching a state of anticipated suicide when I was inwardly compelled to try spiritual healing which I did for about eight weeks without any noticeable change. Then one morning I jumped out of bed—the first time such a thing had been possible in years. The pain and disability had completely gone during the night! I began investigating every avenue of psychic and spiritual experience to find out something of the power that had apparently healed me.

'I studied and developed trance mediumship in varying stages, including physical mediumship, and I thought I had completed my progression, but then, over a period of three months, a series of strange happenings led me in a new direction: I found everywhere I went—and I travelled the country extensively at that time on business—I was put in contact with desperately ill people who, for no explainable reason, would make a miraculous recovery without my even seeing them, just the fact that we were in the same house produced these staggering results!

'At first I could not accept that I had any part in this whatever, but after several weeks these incidents were far too numerous to be explained as coincidence. On inquiry, I was told that my subconscious mind was so convinced that such spiritual manifestations could never happen through me that this was the only way I could be convinced.'

I asked Anderson to describe a few of these remarkable healings, and he told about the three-year old child, very weak and sickly, unable to walk unaided, who had had twelve major operations and was due for another in three days. Her parents invited him to lunch when he was travelling alone one weekend in Scotland. 'We were talking in the living room and were interrupted by a door opening and the child tottering in. She came over to me, holding out her arms to be lifted on my knee. I did just this and saw a look of astonishment come over the faces of her parents. They told me she had never been able to stand, least of all to walk! We agreed that they would let me know the result of her visit to the hospital the next week. Their letter was waiting for me on my return. The surgeon would not believe it was the same child, they said. He called in three other specialists to examine her and could find nothing wrong. The last I heard she was sixteen and was a very healthy girl, free of illness since that day.

'Another case was that of an old friend whom I hadn't seen in years due to the war. I heard he was ill in a hospital some fifty miles away, but when I got there I was told he was too ill to be seen, that he'd been in a coma for the last three days. When I told the Ward Sister how far I had come, she let me go to his bedside. I sat there looking at him with a feeling of deep regret and my thoughts wandered back through the years to some of the hilarious times we had spent together—when suddenly his eyes opened and focused on me for a second or two. Then he raised himself onto an elbow and burst out laughing! My thoughts had been transmitted to him and we were both amused at the same thing! Three days later he was discharged and resumed his normal business activities.

'These were only a few of the many incidents which occurred at that time, and I began serving the Spiritualist Church as a medium and healer. Later I felt the need to widen my understanding and healing work, and opened my own sanctuary. After that my healing work grew rapidly. I joined the National Federation of Spiritual Healers shortly after it was formed and gradually found myself being drawn into administrative work through my chairmanship of various committees.'

After that amazing introduction, I asked Anderson to tell me of his religious background. He was Church of England, he said, but subscribed to the Spiritualist philosophy. I then urged him to expand on the 'spirit doctor' theory.

'We accept, generally speaking, that this is a divine power that is operating, but at the same time it needs someone of fairly high intelligence to direct it. If you've studied psychic forces at all you know just how powerful some of them are. They must be channelled with due knowledge and in correct degree. For argument's sake, if healing is focused on a malignant tumour, it will only affect that particular growth, and not any of the healthy tissue around it. This is not true of normal medical rays, of course, they not only destroy the malignancy but a lot of healthy tissue as well. So I think, generally speaking, we accept the fact that there are these spirit doctors, most of them having been doctors in their earth life. Because they pass into the next world they don't lose their desire to help humanity. They gain *more* desire to do it when they see the greater potentialities in spirit, and so they develop these new techniques and learn how to manipulate these healing rays or forces, call them what you will.'

'Would a beginning healer be able to attract a spirit doctor to work with him?' I asked.

'Yes, I would think so. Not necessarily someone who has practiced medicine on this earth. From my own experience of psychic things, we don't have just one helper in spirit, we have many. And it's inevitable, I think, that among several helpers, one would have some medical knowledge.'

'Is developing the psychic abilities of clairvoyance and clairaudience part of your spiritual healers' training?'

'No. It's not necessary. I've known some really first-class healers who don't have the slightest idea who their helpers are or what's happening. They just aren't aware at all. And yet there's some excellent healing manifest through them. We teach them to link up and attune with this healing force and if they're naturally drawn towards someone who's passed on well, fair enough, we'll encourage it and explain what's happening. If on the other hand it's someone with a very orthodox upbringing and they feel any power manifesting through them comes from God, then we'll not disillusion them.'

'Or that it comes from the Holy Spirit?'

'Yes, yes. You see, it depends, really, on how one envisions God to start with, doesn't it? I could never accept the idea that God is a human being sitting up on a cloud because visualising the whole of nature and of creation, I couldn't conceive that any one individual could be its creator. And so I could never see God as a person. To me, God is just a tremendous creative force that brings all good and all natural things into being. And when disease develops it is through our inability to live harmoniously with nature and natural law. I think of Christ as, shall we say, a wonderful teacher who came to show us what we could do if we were sufficiently linked with this divine force. I'm sure that was his purpose, to show us the way so we would try to follow as near as we could in his footsteps.'

Anderson said that the Federation is very actively engaged in research on healing and has its own Research Council. It sponsored a Parapsychology Research Symposium in May, 1971, attended by medical doctors, electronic experts, physicists and specialists in acupuncture, homeopathy, radionics and psychic healing. Right now it is launching a project on the psychosomatic cause of cancer.

'We have set a target of £20,000 to finance the first stage to be conducted via a questionnaire to cancer sufferers. We hope that a pattern will emerge from computerisation of this information that will determine the next stage of our research,' he said.

Unfortunately, the British Cancer Council was not interested in a co-operative effort, as proposed by Harry Edwards on behalf of the NFSH. Anderson gave me copies of the exchange of letters that discussed the matter, which put in sharp relief the points of divergence between spiritual healers and medical doctors.

In brief, BCC secretary Dr Graham Bennette accused Harry Edwards of being 'medically unsound' in saying Hodgkin's Disease is incurable. Edwards replied that every such case he had ever treated had been told their condition was incurable, but he was 'delighted' if an answer has now been found. Bennette claimed doctors fully cure 30,000 cancer patients a year in Britain and challenged spiritual healers to improve on that figure. Edwards countered that healers can't compete because (1) they are not given access to medical records and (2) they are usually asked to help terminal cases. Edwards then suggested the 30,000 figure be broken down to see how many were spontaneous cures that 'could well be credited to spirit healing'. He asked how many were 'suspected' cancer or 'wrongly diagnosed'.

'Whenever we have submitted a case of terminal cancer healing to doctors for their opinion,' wrote Edwards, 'the customary answer is that it was a "mistaken diagnosis, otherwise it would not have recovered".' He urged more co-operation between doctors and healers, but Bennette replied that their approaches and philosophies were so different that 'dialogue is scarcely feasible'.

Fortunately, all over England individual doctors co-operate with spiritual healers, Anderson said, and he added that many doctors come to him for treatment and many send him their patients!

Returning to the cancer research campaign, Anderson said they hoped to prove that cancer is caused by interference with the proper functioning of the genetic purpose of the cell or organ affected, and to show that spiritual healing removes the causative frustrations and substitutes new directions. They have a strong American medical voice on their side—Dr Gotthard Booth, of New York, a leading authority on the psychosomatic causes of disease, he said. Dr Booth addressed their annual Healers' Day Conference in April and told the members that current psychosomatic cancer research was 'in complete agreement' with their insights.

(Some weeks later Anderson sent me a copy of their cancer patients' questionnaire and their fund appeal brochure. It bore a message from Air Marshal Sir Victor Goddard. 'So much depends upon the success of this Appeal which ultimately can only be measured in terms of human happiness,' he wrote. 'I know you will give the best of your heart, mind, and, I hope, your support.' A long list of prior supporters included honourables, ladies, a princess, clergymen, several knights and high-ranking military officers and symphonic maestro Sir Adrian Boult, but not a single doctor!)

Anderson referred me to Marcus McCausland, their Research Council chairman, for more on their research activities, and said they kept abreast of developments all over the world, especially in Russia, the US, Germany and Japan.

A researcher himself, Anderson said he had just come back from the Philippines where he observed the work of the psychic surgeon Tony Agapoa on behalf of the NFSH. Standing at Agapoa's side through some 500 'psychic operations', he was able to assure the Federation that there was no sleight-of-hand.

Referring to Agapoa's reputed ability to open the body without pain or anaesthetic, Anderson said, 'To satisfy myself on this matter, I asked him to do my back which, after 30 years, was giving me a little trouble again, affecting the sciatic nerve. In two minutes he had rectified an ossified disc in my spine, restoring the disc to its normal state. And as I could not see this, I asked him to open my hip, and on another occasion, my leg, so that I could claim to have experienced the same as any other patient receiving treatment, and no pain or discomfort of any kind is experienced! We have had specimens of growths tested in a laboratory after removal from patients' bodies and they have proved to be not only human but also to match the blood group of the patient from whom it was removed.'

Anderson said he went to the Philippines with a German medical couple. Drs Edwin and Sigrun Seutemann, who brought fifty desperately ill or medically incurable patients to Agapoa for treatment. At his suggestion I wrote to Dr Seutemann and she quickly replied with a fascinating letter saying she had watched 2,000 operations by Agapoa and had seen many remarkable cures, including cancers and a migraine headache that had been unrelieved for twenty-five years! She herself had experienced the healing of an angioma of a cardiac valve which had given her pain and breathing difficulties for many years, she said. 'After Tony's treatment it all disappeared.'

Getting down to statistics, I asked Anderson how many members they had and he said 8,500, of which 4,000 are full healer-members. 'The remainder are either trainees or non-healers, many of whom are ex-patients who have benefited from spiritual healing and want to support us with their membership,' he said.

Describing the membership requirements, he noted that applicants must satisfy the membership committee as to their qualifications as healers and that they have been practising healing for a reasonable length of time. They must submit a minimum of four names and addresses of patients who have received treatment from them and benefited, whom the committee will check up on. Or, if they work within a church or healing group, and the church president or someone is prepared to guarantee they are what they purport to be, they will be accepted. But all are on probation for twelve months before becoming full members, and even then they have to satisfy the membership committee that they have the qualifications.

'A lot depends on the experience they get,' said Anderson 'We can teach them ethics, how to make a start, but most of the work has got to be done by themselves.'

All members, he emphasised, must take the Hippocratic Oath, just the same as medical doctors, when they attain full status.

One of the chief activities of the Federation and indeed its major aim is to raise the standards of spiritual healing practice, he continued, and to this end they offer evening classes and four Study Courses. He had his secretary bring a set of course books and I bought it on the spot. (The price : £7.10.)

Study Course No. 1 is entitled 'The Theory and Practice of Spiritual Healing' and is their trainees' course; No. 2, on 'Absent Healing' is designed for beginners; No. 3, 'The Science of Spirit Healing', is for members only and makes a deeper analysis of the processes involved; and No. 4 is on 'Anatomy and Physiology'.

Anderson gave me this tally of the number of people who have enrolled in each course :

No. 1—3,076
No. 2—2,079
No. 3— 436
No. 4—2,106

'Practically all of No. 1 have come back, it's been available now for five or six years,' he explained. 'The same with No. 2, and they are coming in every day. No. 3 is our latest one and No. 4 tends to stick a little bit because of all the complicated terminology.'

Their evening study courses are on much the same lines as courses 1 and 2, he said. A person can cover the beginners' course in eight weeks 'provided they do as we suggest, that is, make a daily habit of meditation and attunement' after which they should be able to link up with the spirit world or the Divine Power, whichever concept they prefer. Then they are ready for the eight-week trainees' course which introduces them to the physical contact—the laying-on of hands and the feeling of energy that may be transmitted through them. 'They are then brought in to the clinic we run here to work with qualified healers so they get practical experience under guidance,' Anderson said.

'One is able to teach them in the classes more quickly because the voice plays an important part,' Anderson observed. 'It brings them to a feeling of peace and tranquillity where they can make their attunement.' The average size class is 20, and the fee for each eight-week course is £2.

Courses three and four were not yet being given as classes, but he predicted they would be in the form of concentrated week-end refresher courses for 'the practising healer'.

Anderson and I then went into a huddle to make up a good representative list of healers for me to see in order to gain a well-rounded picture of the various approaches to healing to be found in England. At the top of my list, of course, was my old friend Mary Rogers and the names suggested by Dr Laidlaw. We made up a list of eight and, calling in his secretary, he asked her to look up their addresses and telephone numbers.

He also suggested that I visit the healing clinic and training classes at the Spiritualist Association of Great Britain (SAGB) headquarters in Belgrave Square, and look in on the College of Psychic Studies where they have an on-going programme of absent healing that is research-oriented.

As I picked up my papers, literature and study courses into a huge bundle, I was glad to hear Anderson stress the fact that the NFSH is non-denominational. He also wanted me to know that, as a result of their efforts to raise standards through training courses and other educational activities that emphasise such things as ethics, their healer-members are permitted to visit patients in 1,500 national hospitals, the patient's medical doctor agreeing. In many thousands of hospital visits, only once has it been reported that a doctor refused permission and this occurred in a mental hospital. 'We find both medical and nursing staff most co-operative as a general rule,' said Anderson, adding that this right of visitation was the outcome of the Federation's approach to the Ministry of Health, and the ruling was recently reconfirmed.

I asked, 'Would you say that the theories of healing expressed by your president, Harry Edwards, in his books express the general views of the Federation and of the Study Courses?'

'Generally speaking, yes', he said. 'But there are one or two points where, perhaps, Edwards is a little bit dogmatic. We don't always go along with everything, exactly.'

'On what kind of points would you differ?' I asked.

'As far as cancer research is concerned. He's of the opinion that all cancers are psychosomatic in their origin, but I wouldn't go along with that completely. Then there are minor differences on which we agree to disagree. But he's a very knowledgeable chap.'

9.   Harry Edwards

HAVING TAKEN the risk of arriving in England without an appointment secured in advance with Harry Edwards, Britain's most famous healer, I was tremendously relieved when Gilbert Anderson called to say he had arranged for me to interview the man and to observe his next clinic just two days hence. I was to call his assistant, Ray Branch, for travel instructions.

'Take any train from Waterloo that will deliver you to Guildford, Surrey, by two o'clock,' Mr Branch informed me. 'You will be met at the station by our small bus. This is the only trip it will make all afternoon to collect patients for the clinic, and it is a rather long way by taxi if you miss it.' I assured Mr Branch I would not miss the bus!

I took an early train that day and had ample time to reflect on the ideas and flavour of the six books by Harry Edwards I had crammed down the previous winter while acquiring background for my magazine article about Mary Rogers.

In general, they present spiritual healing as the common heritage of the entire human family irrespective of race and creed. Edwards emphasises that the marvellous healings recorded in the New Testament have been performed in other countries and cultures, for example, in the lamaseries of Tibet and by Mohammedan priests.

'The gift of healing is no more a prerequisite of Christianity than of any other religion,' Edwards writes in *A Guide to Spirit Healing*. At the same time his sanctuary's symbol gives due recognition to the healing tradition of Christ and his followers. A cross within a circle, it represents 'the whole of the human family and the influence of the Christ Spirit within it'.

To a die-hard World Federalist, Edwards' conviction that when spiritual healing is more widely practised it will bring about a sense of world brotherhood was an exciting new idea. By making humans more aware of their spiritual nature, he says, the divine purpose—that all people shall live in peace and harmony—will be brought closer to fulfillment.

Along with these broad-gauged views, Edwards relies on the Spiritualists' line of reasoning when postulating the psychic or spiritual healing process. In his opinion it provides 'the logical method of contact and development'. Outspoken without sounding dogmatic, he bases his conclusions on nearly forty years of research and experience. He summed them up in these terms when addressing the Anglican Church's Commission on Divine Healing which investigated the subject abortively beginning in 1953 :

'By a "spiritual or divine healing" I mean a healing that is brought about by a non-human agency. I define a healer as a person who is used as an instrument for healing by a non-human agency and that he (of himself) possesses no personal ability to heal . . .

'It is a simple truth that every change that takes place in the universe is the result of law-governed forces . . . Nothing takes place by chance . . . Our bodies are subject to definite laws that control our health from birth to death. Therefore a spiritual healing must also be the product of law-governed forces that have induced the change. Purposefully to bring about a state of change, intelligent direction is needed to apply the law-governed forces to the subject in the same way that man must direct the force of electricity to produce a given effect within the laws that control that force. Thus the administering of a healing force requires intelligent direction. Consider the diversity of human ills that can be healed through spiritual healing. They include all human ailments and range from sickness of the soul to cancer, from mental breakdown to cataract, from blue babies to arthritis. An intelligence must be behind the healing effort, one able to determine the correct character and strength of the healing force needed to remedy each given condition.

'I have tried to establish that the healing of an incurable disease requires a wiser intelligence than that of the human mind. If it is not incarnate, then it must be discarnate. What is this directing intelligence and what are its capabilities? Some believe that healings take place through the agency of prayer, establishing a personal contact with God who then, as a direct answer to that prayer, overrides the physical and metaphysical laws in a favourable discrimination for a named person.

'While it is true that we see instantaneous or "miracle" cures, the great majority of healings are a gradual process . . . Sometimes healings do not take place. Assuming that the power of prayer is equal in all cases, we have to account for the limitation of the divine effort by explaining why some healings are gradual, why others do not get well and why there is a special discrimination in favour of individual persons.

'The responsibility for answering these questions is not mine but belongs to those who subscribe to the view that divine healing comes directly from God alone. There is an alternative thesis that has a great mass of supporting evidence to substantiate it. This alternative rests on the truth that after the physical death our spiritual bodies live on in the spirit realm, able to acquire greater wisdom, retaining our individual characters, personalities and the potential for spiritual progression.

'This is not accepted by some Churchmen merely because it is termed "spiritualism" and must, therefore, be shunned. But prejudice is so often the negation of truth. It is either true or not true.

'A few years ago the then Archbishop of Canterbury (Dr Lang) appointed a commission of his own choosing to investigate the case for survival as you are now investigating divine healing. Their researches took a long time and were very exhaustive. The majority report found that the case for survival was proved and that communication with the spirit realm is effected.

'If it is true that communication can be effected, then we can accept the idea that good influences from spirit healing ministers can remove disharmony from the minds of patients. Mental stress is said to be responsible for more than half of our physical afflictions. It is an extension of this premise to see that the spirit doctors can transmit healing forces to heal sick bodies . . . We believe that spirit doctors are real, that the healings are proof of this, and a testimony to their wisdom and desire to carry out the divine purpose . . .

'The natural follow-on of this, as has been abundantly proved, is that those in spirit life who wish to are able to establish, through attunement, communication with those on earth. They are able to receive our requests and to transmit corrective thought and remedial forces for the healing of minds and bodies. The spirit healing ministers are able, in their advanced state of being, to acquire that greater knowledge of spiritual laws and forces which can be directed to heal the sick on earth. This is the only logical way to account for supernormal healings.

'At our sanctuary in Shere we have seen many, many thousands of sick people healed. The majority of these have been made well through what we call absent healing, which you might term "the power of prayer". The reason we see so many made well is obviously due to our possessing some additional quality. That quality may be summed up in the words "simplicity" and "attunement with the heavenly host". This attunement is a quality that can be developed when the purposeful effort is rightly made . . .

'I hold that the divine purpose behind the healing is not so much the healing of the sick but that through this healing the spiritual consciousness of the people will be aroused. They see themselves and their dear ones healed by spiritual means. This provides a demonstration of spiritual power that is so sorely needed in this scientific age. Restore the gift of healing to the Church and it will become a vital and living presence. I need not tell you how great is the need for this in our world of today.'

In this credo, Edwards made clear the areas in which he differs with the Anglican establishment in England—their refusal to recognise any spirit agency as directing the healing being the chief sticking point. Edwards writes that he was once offered a chapel of his own in an Anglican church where he could hold healing services. There was one stipulation, that he give up his belief in 'spirit doctors'.

It would have been harder for me, a non-Spiritualist, to cope with the spirit doctor concept if I had not read the healer's accounts of his methodical investigations of psychic phenomena in the '30s and '40s that grew out of his determination to prove or disprove to his own satisfaction the Spiritualists' belief in survival.

A printer by trade, and for a while a fiery Liberal Party politician, Edwards had no particular religious convictions when he first attended a Spiritualist church with friends in Ilford, Essex. His hobby was conjuring and he was confident he could see through any supernatural happening that might occur. Instead he was bowled over by a feat of clairvoyance. Attending a séance some years later at a Spiritualist church near his home, his interest was further whetted when told that certain spirit guides wanted to work with him.

He then began experimenting with enthusiasm, joining the church's 'development circle' to see if he could bring out any latent psychic abilities. There followed a series of experiences that were unearthly, to say the least. Edwards soon felt his faculties controlled by another intelligence who prompted him to give lectures in Spiritualist churches on topics he knew nothing about. And one day he felt himself hurled out of the way of a speeding truck by 'spirit intervention'. To the amazement of onlookers, he was simply tossed into the air and on to the kerb.

Edwards next began to feel a growing desire to heal, and upon hearing that a friend of one of the circle's members was in a hospital suffering from consumption with complications of haemorrhage and pleurisy, he tried sending him 'absent healing' as an experiment. Paul Miller, in his biography of Edwards (*Born to Heal,* Spiritualist Press 1962), relates the incident :

'As he settled to start his initial attempt at absent treatment, he had a vision of a hospital ward, and he reports that his attention was focused on a particular bed. He "saw" the patient clearly and told his friend, Mrs Layton, who had asked that healing be given, and she confirmed the vision in all its details . . .

'The healer was informed that on the night he began his absent treatment the victim of consumption began to improve, fever abated, haemorrhage stopped, and pleurisy ceased. In a week the patient was taken off the danger list and was sent to a sanatorium. Before the end of the year he was discharged as fit and was back at work.'

Edwards' World War I experiences (he's now 80) made him acutely sensitive to human suffering. Commissioned to direct relief supplies while serving with the Royal Sussex Battalion in Persia and Arabia, he had seen the starving and the dead lying in the streets and children threatened with cannibalism. And so, when he began discovering his ability to heal severely afflicted people, he threw himself energetically into his new calling.

At first, Edwards gave healing only when entranced by a spirit guide. But he gave that up in the belief that there might be 'spirit specialists' just as there are on earth and that he shouldn't limit himself to only one guide's wisdom.

He also discarded the traditional sweeping 'passes' and 'flinging away' gestures that were supposed to get rid of the disease vibrations, having satisfied himself by experimentation that only the simplest motions were necessary. And he decided that 'cleaning the aura' was nonsense since it reflects a patient's state and is not in itself a cause of illness,

An important aspect of Edwards' research was his intensive studies of two remarkably gifted physical mediums, Jack Webber and Arnold Clare, which began in 1938. In two books he described the striking phenomena he witnessed in hundreds of scientifically controlled séances in which the two mediums co-operated and which were on several occasions observed by members of the press who testified in print that they saw no evidence of fraud.

Both Webber and Clare allowed themselves to be securely bound to chairs from shoulders to ankles during these research sessions. The spirit guides also co-operated by demonstrating their powers in amazing ways, on one occasion walloping Webber, painlessly, on the head with a trumpet. *The Mediumship of Jack Webber* includes some unusual infra-red photographs of Webber's coat being removed by spirit means while he was in the roped-up state.

But the later experiments with Clare, whom Edwards met soon after Webber's unexpected death, provided the first direct, personal proof of survival he had so far witnessed. In a year-long series of sittings during German air raids in 1941, Clare's spirit guide, apparently using the medium's organs of speech, answered many of Edwards' questions concerning the materialisation process. Then, in a virtuoso performance one night, Clare materialised Jack Webber in a form unmistakable to his wife and all those present who knew him.

'I have seen many manifestations,' the healer wrote in his book about Clare's mediumship, 'but never before have I seen one so plainly. So much so that I am prepared to swear by all I hold sacred that it was our friend Jack Webber who stood before us. No finer or more absolute proof of the truth of survival could be given us than the return of Jack Webber to his own séance room, to his wife, members of his own circle and friends'.

Many non-Spiritualists and sceptics do not, of course, accept the postulates on which Edwards bases his healing. The results he obtains would seem to indicate, however, that his concepts are workable. Most spectacular have been his many large public demonstrations of healing in London's Royal Festival Hall and other major cities of England and abroad. (He has given demonstrations in Holland, Cyprus and South Africa, and in March, 1973 went again to South Africa and to Rhodesia at the invitation of the Rhodesian Healers' Association, where he reportedly packed Salisbury's largest hall.) On these occasions cripples paralysed since birth have been seen to walk off the stage and the locked joints and spines of arthritics have been freed.

Edwards' weekly post has been estimated at nine thousand letters and approaches half a million a year. The large majority, he says, are in the 'incurable' category—people who have been told that medical science can do no more for them. Among those making the pilgrimage to his sanctuary in the village of Shere near Guildford have been a famous conductor, peers, MPs, cabinet ministers, High Commissioners, Olympic athletes, and members of the Royal Family, although of these, only ones who have passed on can be publicly mentioned.

In recalling all these facts and impressions of Harry Edwards gleaned from his books, two particularly potent ideas stood out in my memory. First, his assertion that anyone able to sympathise with the distress of others who has a desire to 'render service to his fellows' can develop the ability to heal—the very thesis I was exploring— and, second, his prediction that as spiritual healing becomes more widely practised 'it will become part of family life' and recourse to it as general as the taking of present-day simple remedies. Did he still have the same beliefs, I wondered.

The ticket collector announced 'Guildford!' and I alighted at a quaint-looking painted brick railroad station. The country air was fresh and cool and a variety of homegrown flowers was being offered for sale by a flower-seller. In the neat ladies' room someone had thoughtfully placed a green glass vase full of garden flowers on the table!

On the street side, I saw a chic-looking elderly woman in a wheel-chair and asked if she was going to Mr Edwards' clinic. She was, and we exchanged pleasantries. She had been treated several times, she said, and had been helped considerably.

Others joined us as we waited for the bus to arrive—an antique, top-heavy vehicle that seated about a dozen. The driver helped each one of us aboard and lifted the wheelchair with ease, and soon we were trundling through the streets of Guildford and heading out through the countryside, shimmering and green in the June sunlight.

There were cows and sheep grazing in storybook meadows dotted with yellow wildflowers, and we wove through the narrow streets of a tiny village lined with thatch-roof cottages and a friendly-looking pub. Then, taking a sharp turn off the road, we went another mile or two and eventually wound up in a cobbled courtyard of an

imposing manor house with gables and exposed beams. It was
Burrows Lea, the remote estate that the Edwards had bought, reportedly at a good price, not long after their house in Balham was
struck by German V-1 bombs. A kind of world centre of healing,
it houses a small army of typists who transcribe the letters to patients,
which Edwards dictates on tape, and the editorial offices of the
Sanctuary's monthly magazine, *The Spiritual Healer.*

To our right in a low annexe was the Sanctuary, and we saw a
housewifely woman waiting for us at the doorway. She checked each
of our names against her reserved list of twenty and I was pleased
to be identified as 'Miss Hammond from America who will be
observing' even before I had a chance to give my name. She
motioned me toward a seat at the far end of the oblong room just
a few steps from the area where four chairs were placed, presumably
for Edwards and his associates. Facing them was an upholstered
stool, I supposed for the patient to sit on. For all the people attending
there were two rows of chairs on the right side of the room and I
was given the first chair in the front row!

The place was quite chilly, so most of us kept our coats on, and
during a wait of about twenty minutes I admired the solid simplicity of the room. There was natural wood panelling on the lower
part of the walls and the upper part and ceiling were cream-
coloured plaster. In the large window at the end of the room hung
the symbol, the cross within a circle. The only decoration I can
remember was a lithograph of Christ praying on the wall facing
me. The parquet floors were bare and the radiator firmly turned off.

Suddenly the door opened and Edwards strode in, followed by
his associates, Olive and George Burton and Ray Branch, whom
I recognised from pictures. All wore identical long white coats with
the insignia of the National Federation of Spiritual Healers on
the breast pocket. As they walked the length of the room I was
surprised that Edwards was not the tall fellow he appears to be in
his pictures. He is of medium height and quite portly with snow-
white hair, blue eyes and pink complexion. Olive Burton was fragile
and aristocratic-looking, her husband bespectacled and self-effacing,
and Branch, a man in his early '40s, handsome enough to be a film
actor. The demeanour of all three was serious but not sanctimonious.

After nodding pleasantly toward the waiting group, Edwards
and his helpers sat down and without further ceremony went into
a silent meditation. I watched Edwards carefully. He had sunk into

his chair and closed his eyes, with his right elbow on the chair arm and his face resting against his right hand. He began breathing heavily, his face becoming flushed. This continued for perhaps a minute. He then opened his eyes, sat up straight and taking a card from his pocket read the name of a woman. 'Is she here?' he asked. A pale, dark-haired woman who appeared to be in her 30s responded, and with the help of her husband walked with great difficulty to the patient's chair.

The woman's trouble was a large tumour in the lower abdominal area. Edwards gently placed his hands on either side of it and informed her that it had 'begun to yield' and showed improvement over her last visit. He looked into her face and smiled warmly, holding both her hands in his. He then put his hands over the tumour again and closed his eyes for a few moments as though meditating or praying. He asked the husband to help with the treatment, directing him to place his hands over the healer's. And he asked his patient to be more relaxed and to breathe deeply while imagining that she was 'breathing in strength, healing and oxygen' with every inhalation and, when exhaling, expelling the trouble and all impurities. When she was helped back to her seat her face looked much less strained, I thought.

The next patient called was a young boy of about nine, accompanied by his mother. He had difficulty in breathing, the mother explained, and had not been helped by medical treatment. Edwards diagnosed it as a spastic condition of the boy's chest muscles, and after applying massage and gently but firmly encouraging him to take several long, deep breaths he transferred the youngster to Burton, explaining to the mother that his associate was particularly effective with chest troubles. Mother and son went with Burton to a corner of the room where there were three chairs set out in readiness.

Then came the woman in the wheelchair with arthritis, the most generally shared affliction of the day. Edwards greeted her smilingly as though they were old friends and asked about her condition. He then began patiently and methodically to urge her to greater effort toward mobility and coaxed her to mentally direct activity to each stiffened joint. He massaged and flexed her limbs gently, assuring her she would feel no pain. 'Now you can do it yourself . . . You're a little bit afraid of motion . . . Do it while you're lying in bed every morning—but don't force anything.'

The next patient, another arthritic, asked the healer in a quavering voice if she would ever again be able to comb her own hair. She could only raise her arm a few inches, she said, because of the painful stiffness in her shoulder. After Edwards had worked with her for about ten minutes and cheered her on, she was able to rest her hand on her head, and she told him it didn't hurt at all! 'Now lift it up again,' he said. 'That's fine. You won't go back to the old style, will you now?' The woman laughed, her facial expression completely changed.

An old man shuffled forward on his wife's arm and dropped into the patient's seat. After a few minutes of gentle movement Edwards encouraged the man to lift one knee, then the other. 'Massage is very good for you. It will help the circulation,' he said. 'Stand up on your toes. Now, down. Get up nicely now. I think we'll be satisfied with that,' Edwards said, patting the man on his shoulder. Still teetering but with a visibly firmer step the man seemed to lean less heavily on his wife's arm as he returned to his seat.

Apparently Edwards was able to loosen knees, shoulders, elbows, backs without causing any anguish since even the most advanced arthritics did not cry nor gasp with pain. During each session Mr Branch worked in co-ordination, moving his hands up and down the patient's spine and across the back as though completing an electrical circuit. From my observations—and the impression was later confirmed by the healer himself—the treatment combined positive suggestion and encouragement of the patient to co-operate in his own healing with the application of the unseen healing energy through the hands of the healers.

When the last patient had been cared for, Edwards invited everyone in the sanctuary to have a cup of hot tea in the drawing room of Burrows Lea. I stepped forward quickly and introduced myself. He must have sensed that I yearned to have him apply healing to the tension in my neck because he said right away, 'Are you all right? Could we do anything to help you?' I accepted his offer gratefully and indicated my neck which had been troubling me for weeks. I was invited to sit on the patient's stool and while Ray Branch, standing behind me, co-ordinated his hand movements, Edwards gently manipulated and loosened the kinks in my neck, shoulder and back. He used no force and I felt no twinges.

After thanking them, I reminded Edwards that I had been promised an interview. He said, 'Come along then' and led the way to a secluded corner of the main house where we could sit facing each other on a cushioned window seat and enjoy a fine view of billowing meadows and flower gardens. I knew he must be tired and I was afraid he would be impatient to get our talk over quickly. Instead he graciously asked if I would like tea, called the house-keeper and ordered tea for two and settled down as though he expected to enjoy himself.

In his public healing demonstrations Edwards is often described as a man of imposing presence. His white hair, noble features and strong hands are widely admired. But in this informal moment what came across most strongly was a spiritual quality—open, giving, interested, are words that may explain it better—and there was no trace of self-importance. Someone had told me Edwards was a 'truly humble man' and I now knew what they meant. It worried me that he appeared even more tired than I had expected and that he was out of breath. His relaxed attitude betrayed no concern for himself, however, and I flipped on my tape recorder.

I began by reminding him of what he had said in one of his books about spiritual healing being practised some day in families and recourse to it as natural as taking simple remedies, and he predicted again that it will 'eventually' become the 'natural thing people will look to for help rather than running off right away to a doctor or a chemist'.

Could he expand on the idea he had expressed so often that anyone with the desire to help his fellow man could develop the ability to heal?

'I believe,' he said, 'that most people who have the desire to help someone who is in trouble, to take away pain and relieve sickness, have the healing gift that is inherent. It only needs a little time for development and the opportunity for expression.'

'In other words, even though the gift is inherent it probably can't be developed unless the person has the desire to heal? Is that what you mean?'

'That's what I mean,' Edwards replied. And when I asked what he thought of the title 'We Are All Healers' he said with a twinkle, 'Well, I think it would apply to everybody who buys your book, otherwise they wouldn't buy it!'

'And what about St Paul apportioning out "severally" the gifts of the spirit, among them the gift of healing?' I asked 'Do you think there is a contradiction?'

'No. I think some people have the ability or the gift to be better than others—like a good violinist. Some can fiddle while others can play.'

I thanked him for saying what I had hoped he would say, and asked if he thought his books had encouraged more people to become healers.

'Oh, undoubtedly, undoubtedly. There are so many, many people who now tell me they want to be healers! We are enrolling so many every day in our National Federation. Only this morning I had eight new members apply for membership.'

Edwards, who is its president, said he was Member No 1 when the National Federation of Spiritual Healers was founded nearly twenty years ago by the late John Britnell and Gordon Turner. Many others joined when he did, but he thought the great majority of its present membership were newcomers to the profession.

'Would a beginning healer have to find his own spirit doctor?' I asked. 'Or does the spirit doctor find him? Or perhaps there is an intermediate process?'

'You see', said Edwards, 'when a person has a desire to heal they sit for attunement, that is, attunement with Spirit—not necessarily with a spirit personality—but attunement with Spirit. That is the essential. And then, if there is an individual spirit guiding them, they will make contact.'

'Is this Spirit the same as the Holy Spirit we read about in the Scriptures?'

'Well, it's not so much the Holy Spirit they speak of in churches, which is part of the Trinity. We believe that the origin of healing is divine. It comes from God. But the operation of it is carried out by His ministers in Spirit, who are people who once lived like we're living today.'

'They are His agents?'

'Yes.'

'So, by Spirit, you mean an intermediary between God and man?'

'Yes, exactly.'

'And if someone wanted to call this the Holy Spirit?'

'It's the Holy Spirit running through it, yes. But we have to be careful of terms, otherwise people will read something wrong into it. If I said I was governed by the Holy Spirit they'd think I was God, you see . . .'

I asked Edwards what were some of the qualities needed to make a good healer and he listed 'generosity, willingness to give of yourself, and compassion and sympathy for those in need'.

'Well, that cuts out quite a few people, doesn't it,' I said. Edwards was more specific. 'People who won't do anything unless they get something out of it, they'll never heal. They're too selfish.'

'Do you still see a connection between healing and world peace?' I asked hopefully.

'Oh, definitely, definitely,' he said, 'because, you see, the tendency —the divine tendency—is against evil. The divine tendency is the progression of man's spiritual nature, and that will bring peace, not war. War is evil. Disease is evil. Those things are evil-minded where there's cruelty and persecution . . . Healing is a part of a spiritualisation process, the spiritualisation of mankind'.

'Then encouraging many people to heal can also be part of the spiritualisation process?'

'Yes. It is simply helping them to become better people!'

I asked Edwards if he saw any dangers or provisos in encouraging people to develop the gift of healing, and he said, 'No. I don't know of any. The unfortunate thing is that people are not content to be used as instruments of healing. They then want to do something themselves and they start bringing in gimmicks. So long as healing is simple there is no danger whatsoever.'

'And what about the fact that some are healed and some are not? Can you give reasons why some are not healed?'

'Yes, there must be a reason why people don't respond and there must be a reasoned process if people *do* respond. What governs healing is the laws that govern life. If I cut my finger off I won't grow another one, will I? It's against the law. And so it is with all things. And then if you maintain the cause of the trouble you maintain the effect. If a person is losing his eyesight because of working their eyes too hard, and he carries on doing it, the eyes will continue to get worse. The same with a person who has arthritis if they continue to sleep in a damp place. That is the main reason why healing can fail. Another reason can be that a person has mental troubles and the healing cannot get through into a mind that is obsessed with trouble.'

'Healing has to get into the mind,' Edwards continued. 'Every person must be treated singly to find out the reason why he or she does not respond.'

Just then the housekeeper burst into the room to say that the bus was about to leave. 'Doesn't Miss Hammond want to catch it? It is the last bus today,' she said. Reluctantly I turned off my recorder.

'If I send you one of my questionnaires will you promise to fill it out?' I asked Edwards as I packed up my things. He promised he would, and I spelled out my name to help him remember it. 'Oh, yes, I'll remember it,' he said, smiling, 'because we have a Celia Hammond in England who is a top model.' He walked with me to the door and, after thanking him for being so generous with his time after the long healing session I impulsively kissed him on the cheek. He looked a little flustered!

Crossing the courtyard to the bus I waved goodbye to a group on the doorstep and was the last to climb aboard.

While we bounced along the country roads to Guildford I jotted down the healing experience of two friendly women whom Edwards had treated at the clinic.

Mrs Irene Hawksworth of British Columbia told me she suffered from calcium deposits in the tendons and muscles joining the breast-bone to the arms. 'It's metabolic. I was born with the condition,' she said, 'but this trouble with the calcium deposits has become so painful the past five months that I couldn't sleep. Then one day a neighbour of mine, an eighty-seven-year-old lady who is a medium, told me about Harry Edwards.'

It wasn't clear whether Mrs Hawksworth came to England ex-pressly to see Edwards. In any case, she called him from London and asked for an appointment, confirming it in a letter in which she explained the chemical imbalance she had been told by her doctors was the cause. That was five weeks ago.

'He did absent healing until he could see me,' she said, 'and it's better. No question about it. I can move more and I don't have the pain at night. So now I think I'll keep this up.'

Mrs C. E. Reynolds of Mitcham, Surrey, said she had suffered from a slipped disc for ten years. 'The pain was so bad I thought it was cancer. Then one day a perfect stranger who saw me limping approached me and said, "Go to a healer". She said she'd been crippled with arthritis and was cured by a healer. So I got one of Harry Edwards' books out of the library. Just reading about his work made me feel better!

'I'd been to doctors and hospitals and had treatment and X-rays and all that. And the doctors as good as said I'd gone too far. I con-tacted Mr Edwards and he said absent healing would start right away. In two days I had a different outlook on life! And after a few months everyone began telling me I looked so much better.

'Mr Edwards tells me he's cured me, but to go steady while the weather is damp like this. He has me wear a surgical belt but tells me to leave it off more and more. He fixed my slipped disc—isn't that marvellous! I'm going to try to touch my toes when I next see my doctor, and I won't say a word . . . When I last saw him I couldn't even walk properly, and I would often fall.

'I feel now that I'm indebted to mankind and although I'm no longer young I intend to help the suffering,' Mrs Reynolds said, and her face looked radiant when she added, 'I've made that promise to myself. Even in small ways I'm going to help people who are in pain.' I felt like saying, 'Right on, Mrs Reynolds!'

When our bus swung into the station at Guildford, I thanked Mrs Hawksworth and Mrs Reynolds for sharing their experiences with me. Then, boarding the train for London, I curled up in a comfortable window seat and read the articles from *The Spiritual Healer* that Edwards had given me in reprints to supplement our all-too-brief interview.

Edwards' piece entitled, 'The Healing of Arthritis' gave interesting background to the treatment I had just witnessed. Pointing out that its cause is still unknown to medical science, he wrote, 'In our experience arthritis is often caused through mind disharmony and "sickness of the soul" . . . Doctors ought to be sufficiently interested to ask : "Why is it that arthritis is so often cured through spiritual healing?" Simply, the answer is that our spirit doctors are first able to ease and remove the inner unrest and from this the symptoms are quickly overcome.'

The healing of arthritis in its severe state is 'like a contest', he continued. 'The healing is fighting the encroachment of the disease and it is so helpful to the healing if the patient becomes its ally . . . Patients receiving spiritual healing should therefore always be on the lookout for looseness coming to all joints or, in the early stages, to one area such as the neck, back, shoulder, hands, legs, etc. *Easement should be looked for* and when noted should be encouraged. If in the morning there seems to have come renewed stiffness, a little time spent on easing the movements will quickly bring about the previous improvements with a little more added.

'At least once a day a general home rubbing or massage, using any oil or cream, will stimulate the circulation and help the bloodstream to carry away the adhesions from the joints and tissues . . . This is the physical way to help the spiritual healing which is not only engaged with removing the *cause* but with dispersing the adhesions in the joints, muscles and ligaments.'

In this article and the one on 'The Healing of Paralysis' Edwards stressed the need for the patient to seek movement in stiff joints and paralysed limbs by 'mental direction' which must be 'gentle and sustained'.

'If a patient has difficulty raising the knee upwards and can do this to a limited extent, the effort to raise it "just a little more" must be a sustained effort . . . If just a fractional increase of movement follows, it is good.'

He warned that any form of mental stress or 'gritting the teeth in a superhuman effort' was wasted energy. 'The purpose of the healing is to build upon what movement there is,' he said. 'The movement must be gently yet purposefully encouraged—seeking "just that little more".'

Other articles dealt with the healing of deafness and head noises, skin diseases, sleeplessness, spinal troubles and mental stresses caused by fears and frustrations. All were brimming with commonsense advice on ways the patient can cooperate with the spiritual healing process.

Undoubtedly, in his long experience as a healer Edwards had seen spiritual healing wasted or undone by people with bad health habits, and in these articles he often repeats the ABC's of hygiene. For example, he advises that badly decayed teeth be removed and constipation prevented by a suitable aperient. ('On retiring place a pillow under the knees and knead or massage the abdomen—this will often overcome any tendency to constipation.') Deep breathing habits should be cultivated with the conscious idea in mind that cosmic energy is being absorbed with each breath. He recommends drinking a glass of warm water morning and night 'to keep the body well flushed' and a good diet that includes fresh salads, sweet fruits and 'sun' foods. 'Enjoy the act of eating and drinking, having in mind "this will do me good". Of course if your disability needs a special diet then it should be followed.'

Edwards shows particular sensitivity to sufferers from mental stress, especially frustration, the causes of which are often 'emotional and sex problems, failure to attain one's ideals, and the desire of the inner self for expression that the existing way of life does not permit'.

For examples of the latter, he notes the person whose inner-self seeks expression in music but is fully occupied at something else, or someone who yearns to travel and loves open spaces but is held down to a humdrum factory job.

'Most mental disharmonies arise from frustrations that exist more in the inner mind or spirit-self of a person than in the physical consciousness. Because our inner spirit selves are on a mind plane similar to that of the spirit helpers and counsellors, they are able to give to the troubled mind calming and adjusting thoughts to overcome the basic causes of stress.'

To these mental stress sufferers—often lonely, apathetic and anxiety-ridden—Edwards gives a special set of self-help suggestions to make them more receptive to the inner upliftment of spiritual healing. His idea appears to be to change negative attitudes to positive. ('This is not merely psychological healing,' he insists, 'it is much more than this.') Some samples:

'Consider the daily tasks ahead with pleasurable anticipation of doing them easily and well. Look for happiness in the boiling of the kettle for the early morning cup of tea; in washing up; and enjoy walking to the station or the shops.

'Have a smile for all those you know, even the shop assistants or the ticket collector. More important, have a smile for yourself. Take care of your personal appearance, even if you are home all day; avoid dowdiness. Put on the radio and join in with a song and music.

'Get out of the mental rut. Go out for walks or to the pictures, theatre, or anything else that gives a change. A Sunday picnic when the weather is good, and so on.'

According to Edwards, 'as the happier temperament comes, so do headaches, neuralgia, tummy upsets, etc., go . . . In this way you assist the good healing influences to change your outlook'.

Other insights into Harry Edwards' philosophy and practise of spiritual healing came to me several weeks later. The questionnaire I had asked him to fill in was one of the first to reach me when I had returned to New York. The following is a brief summary of the added information it contained:

He was thirty-five years old when he began developing his healing gift, and he now does several kinds—laying-on of hands, prayer, magnetic and absent healing. While treating a patient he may feel either heat or cold in his hands. He also feels 'intuitive'. His patients say they feel such sensations as 'heat, cold, vibration, upliftment'.

In his view, it is 'helpful but not essential' if a patient is receptive, cooperative or expectant. He feels people can be healed even if they are atheists, have no belief whatever, are sceptical of the healing treatment and disbelieve in the probable effectiveness of spiritual healing!

He estimates that eighty per cent of those he treats report 'betterment' and thirty per cent say they are 'cured'. Those not helped might be twenty per cent, and those healed instantly, ten per cent. Perhaps fifteen per cent come to him too late for the healing treatment to be effective, but he is able to help such people die without pain.

'My attunement continues to deepen,' Edwards wrote in answer to Question 18 : 'Do you think your healing ability has been developed to the fullest?' And for those wanting to develop their gift of healing he recommended enrolling in the National Federation of Spiritual Healers' four courses and reading his book, *A Guide to Spirit Healing,* in that order.

His religious background was 'first, Church of England, then Rationalist, now Spiritualist'.

Asked to describe his mental and/or spiritual attitude while healing, he wrote, 'Attunement'. And in answer to the question, 'How do you feel about your healing gift?' He replied, 'Great'.

'I find all conditions will yield, some more easily,' Edwards said when asked if he had particular success with certain illnesses.

To the question, 'Should a healer live according to any particular rules and give up bad habits?' he suggested that they should 'live naturally' and not be 'artificially spiritual'.

He keeps records only of the 'supernormal healings'—presumably the ten per cent that are healed instantly. Doctors have come to him for spiritual healing and doctors have referred patients to him, he said. He is 'partially familiar' with medical terms.

He charges no fee but accepts donations.

Edwards wrote two large No's in answer to each of these questions : 'Do you believe in karma and reincarnation?' and 'Do you believe a patient's karma may effect his responsiveness to healing?' (the Law of Karma meaning that debts incurred in the flesh must be met in the flesh).

Does he feel aided by a spirit entity? Edwards wrote 'Yes'. But he does not use clairvoyance or clairaudience while healing.

He receives 9,000 letters a week from patients wanting absent healing, and he feels as good results can be obtained with it as with contact healing.

The final question had three parts : Are you overworked? 'No.' Able to treat all who ask for appointments? 'No. There are too many.' If not, how long must a would-be patient wait for an appointment? 'Normally five or six weeks.'

In a letter, Edwards gave me permission to quote from any of his books if I wished to and gave me up-to-date information on 'The Healing Minute'. I had seen the phrase in a small ad in *Psychic News,* the Spiritualist Weekly. Over the address of Edwards' sanctuary, it read, 'You are invited to enroll as an Observer of The Healing Minute every evening as the chimes of Big Ben are radioed from the BBC Home News at 10 p.m. There are no fees. Write for your evening tryst enrollment card and brochure to the Healing Minute Secretary.' In a separate letter, literature arrived explaining the purpose—to create a reservoir of Divine Power through prayer 'to extend the channel through which God's Light and Healing can reach us' not only for the healing of the sick, but 'to create a spiritual force for Peace that will overcome the threatened dangers of future wars'. (The observers of The Healing Minute throughout the world now number 76,586.)

10. Gordon Turner

I KNEW FROM reading his book, *An Outline of Spiritual Healing,* that Gordon Turner must also be an expansive type with a world view of the healing potential. Like Edwards, he sees spiritual healing as a 'teaching of brotherhood' that will heal the world's diseases and give all humanity hope for the future.

A reluctant recruit to Spiritualism, Turner sought proof of survival after a series of occurrences that pointed strongly in that direction. He had often seen shadowy forms in his bedroom as a child, and these visions came back to plague him as a youth in boarding school. Frightened and revolted, he tried to shut them out of his mind by convincing himself that he had a 'time kink' in his brain.

Turner's denial of his psychic senses might have continued if his brother—who had shared the visions of his childhood—had not died, promising in his last words to come back and prove that he was well and healthy. About a year later, Turner was driven to distraction by objects dropping off shelves unaccountably and strange tapping sounds in his bedroom. After many sleepless nights he decided his brother must have some urgent message to give him and he sought out a Spiritualist medium to settle the matter. He now defends Spiritualism against the 'totally unsubstantiated slander' so often aimed at it by orthodox religions.

I was soon to find out, however, that the healer has changed his thinking 'enormously' since writing his widely read *Outline* which sticks pretty much to Spiritualist concepts in explaining the spiritual healing process. We sat down and discussed some of the ideas which, he said, inspired his new book, *Journeys of the Mind.* In our interview. I also got a clear look at the two schools of thought that nearly split the healing movement in Great Britain, with Turner in the thick of it as protagonist, and it seemed to me that the same kind of contention might very well be anticipated—and hopefully avoided— as the movement becomes organised in the United States.

It was a rare sunny morning when I took a bright red bus out to Kensington and located Turner's house at 27 Warwick Gardens, a quiet side street lined with a row of large, comfortable dwellings, each with a blooming flower garden in front. At each side of the walk were dewy roses in delicate colours, accented by purple iris and geraniums. A leafy vine twirled its way about the iron handrail of the front staircase.

A housekeeper answered the bell, and upon being led into the living room I became immediately aware of the faces of royalty gazing down at me from all directions.

There was Queen Elizabeth on horseback, the Queen and Prince Philip in elegant formal dress, the Prince alone in a bemedalled uniform and the two in every variant of royal attitudes. While admiring the deftness of the artist, I marvelled at the intense patriotism of the Turners. Or were they just adoring admirers of their Royal Highnesses?

Another mystery intrigued me—a gilded harp loomed grandly in one corner of the room and ripples of harp music floated through the ceiling.

When Gordon Turner strode into the room and gave me a warm handshake, he quickly took care of my questions. 'Oh yes,' he said, 'my in-laws, the Bodens, are the Royal Portrait Painters. And my wife, Daphne, is a concert harpist.' With a note of pride, he added that she is not only professor of harp at the Royal College of Music, but is the first Briton to win the Premier Prix at Brussels.

One of Great Britain's busiest and most respected healers, Turner was a picture in himself. Tall, with an aquiline nose and a luxuriant sea captain's beard, his overpowering presence was softened by his ease of manner. He invited me to sit in an overstuffed chair under a romantic landscape painting and, at his signal, we were served hot coffee and biscuits. He wore corduroy slippers, a tan shirt and tweed sports jacket.

Taking a long look at my 'super-questionnaire' as he put it, he asked for mercy. 'Can't we just answer these now? I'm fighting for time, luv,' he said. 'I've got to take a complete book manuscript with me to America in about three weeks and I've had only ten weeks to do it! I'm here all day seeing my patients and I get about 400 letters a week asking for absent healing.' I was, of course, agreeable but soon gave up trying to hold him to fixed questions.

I started off by asking if he agreed with the people who have told me we're 'on the threshold of a great breakthrough' or at a 'cosmic moment'—the expression used by Dr Christopher Woodard, the well-known London medical doctor, healer and author—in recognising the potential of spiritual healing. 'These aren't romantic people using these terms,' I said. 'Do you feel that healing is about to come into its own?'

'Yes. But I don't see it as a sudden breakthrough. I think it will be a gradual evolution. It's happening now,' Turner said, speaking slowly and thoughtfully. 'I think that *science* is on the threshold of *religion*. Science and religion set out in the temple in the beginning, and then they went off in entirely different directions. Now they're meeting again. I don't think we're going to have a space ship come down from Venus with a new cosmic leader, or something of that sort, but I think it's going to be forced on all our realisations that the steps we've taken so far in science have led us to the beginning of a cosmic science that takes in the whole *nature* of man.

'What excites me in all this are things like Charles Tart's symposium at Berkeley on the altered states of consciousness and the tremendous EEG research being done with Eastern mystics. I've been in touch with the Chicago Sleep Laboratory for some time, and I've been in touch with the Russians in this research. Here again you've got a sort of breakthrough as to the *nature* of being.'

I said: 'I've been told the psychic healing ability is on a higher level than the other psychic abilities, involving a spiritual awakening or awareness. Would you comment on that?'

'Well—it would be very nice if it was tidy, but I don't think it is, because we've got to try to fit people like Rasputin into this. You'll find them all through history. Rasputin effected the most incredible cures both by contact healing and at the level we consider the highest developed spiritual level, absent or distant healing. Yet he was a libertine, a drunkard and perverted character indeed!

'When you study healers you wonder how far the different phenomena are related. There's George Chapman with his psychic operations and Ronald Beesley with his Eastern mysticism tied in with a form of Christianity and certainly a kind of osteopathy with great reliance on herbalism and homeopathy, and then Harry Edwards with his view that it is all done entirely from outside and comes through him, and he's influenced by Pasteur and Lister, and you find you're talking about widely divergent phenomena, which we group together and then say this is all spiritual healing.'

'But don't all healers have to do something mentally?'

'I think the common denominator is attunement. And if you then make that into at-one-ment, I think a healer is a person who has the ability to totally merge his personality, although his personality is dominant, with that of another person. Some people will call it mesmeric, hypnotic, the type of personality which can bend to encompass the personality of another. This is the one common factor I've found in my studies of healing with effective healers.

'Now it seems that I don't agree with Harry Edwards when he says that because things like cancer disappear in healing it means there's an intelligence greater than the human intelligence at work. But the computers of the human spirit can accomplish miracles by the minute which we never recognise. Every second the sugar balance of your body is adjusted, new cells are formed, the blood is changed, every single cell is more complex than the finest computer our scientists can build. I've seen incredible healing phenomena under hypnosis.'

'But where does the healing energy come from? Healing isn't only a matter of attunement to the patient or of body intelligence, is it?' I asked.

'Let's argue on . . . Let's talk for a moment about the instantaneous healing, which is what Edwards is talking about when he speaks of growths disappearing and no mind being capable of knowing how to do this. We have known of these things happening in slow motion. But when the healer intercedes this process is tremendously speeded up. The body has the capacity to heal its own sickness. It'll go on fighting and possibly lose. But healing speeds that process, changes the whole relationship of the healing of the body to time. I have seen a very, very bad burn wiped away like that. It's the most incredible thing I've ever seen in healing.

'A woman came to me who was an actress. She had cancer of the breast and the breast had been removed and a cancerous tumour had recurred on that side, under her arm. She had deep ray therapy but this had only burned it and it was a suppurating ulcer with pus running out of it. The poor woman had to have a pad of cotton wool and lint over it to stop this going over her clothes. She removed the pad and I treated this, and there was no obvious sign of anything happening at all. I left to get her some more cotton wool and lint and when I came back she was sitting by the fire—it was winter—and she was weeping. She lifted her hand and the entire area had totally new skin. The whole thing had healed completely. Now, you wouldn't think it the least miraculous if that had happened over a period of six months, which is the way healing usually occurs. Because the body, to our knowledge, has the capacity to do this. The point I'm trying to make is that a natural process is immensely speeded up.

'Now I believe the afterlife is a very real possibility and, this being the case, I would expect those who live on to be deeply concerned with our welfare and therefore our healing. But I don't believe spirits have the capacity to heal any more than we have the capacity to heal. I think the common factor first is this at-one-ment and this making available to us a complete changed perspective of inner healing, a totally different relationship with time and space.'

'Available to both healer and patient?'

'To both. I think what happens is that in every healing there is a changed level of consciousness, and that in an ordinary healing you step up one level and in another one you may step up two, but in this spontaneous healing they reach the level of satori, through meditation, and there's a complete breakthrough, in which a yogi or a fakir can pass a nail through his face and it heals straight up. It's exactly the same thing. The whole process of healing is speeded up, there's a totally different relationship between mind and body.'

'The mind of the healer and the body of the patient?' I asked.

'Yes,' Turner replied.

'But what about the patient's mind?'

'I've examined a lot of patients who have had instantaneous healing, and some of them speak of feeling a sudden physical blow, as with Kuhlman's healing in America. I've often had patients say it's like an electric shock. I think this is the mind jerking back to normal after the experience of at-one-ment.'

'Then the at-one-ment encompassing the mind of the healer and the body of the patient also is an at-one-ment of minds?'

Turner said : 'There's a total at-one-ment, I think, that takes place if only for a second between two people'.

'Then do you talk to the patient and try to tell him what he should try to attain?'

'No, I talk to them to take away the main barrier to healing, which is their tendency to turn into themselves. They're concerned with their symptoms and their sickness and not with their wholeness or health. I'll even chat away with a patient about trivialities until I think they're ready for healing.'

'In other words they should be open, or is "expectant" the key word here?'

'Yes, but expectancy also can be a barrier. I started by practising Zen meditation when I was very young and I've worked on meditation for twenty-five years and most of the problems which occur I find are problems of expectancy. Therefore I try to help the patient to a feeling of the presence of normality, first of all. Healing is an elusive thing, Sally. We don't understand it and it's probably going to be a long time before we do. Because we've got the whole of this outer strata of consciousness to explore. You see, I believe that we're not really in proper relationship *now*. I think that what we consider to be our normal state of consciousness is just a heavy, terribly limited thing. And I think reality is a form of realisation. I'm fumbling for words because there really aren't words for what I'm trying to say . . . I think we've gone along the wrong lines in our research in healing. I think we've tended too much to be concerned with the physical changes which take place in our patients, you know, the power passing through the healer and in asking where does the power come from? I don't think it comes from anywhere. It's *here*, the whole time. But we're shut off from it because we're locked in.

'I think all life is common to all. That tree there, and you, spring from the same life force. And that force permeates absolutely everything. You've only got to raise consciousness to a certain point and you achieve it more and more.

'About three years ago I was practising a new technique I had only just learned in Zen. I was alone in a rose garden of a lovely old house in Kent, and I lost all consciousness of time. When I came out of the state, the world was entirely different. I suppose it must be rather what mystical ecstasy is like to a religious—but I'm not a very religious man. The first thing I noticed was that all the colours were light as well as colour—of the roses, of the green leaves. I was walking on the grass and I was conscious not of a lawn but of every blade of grass, and I looked at a tree and at once I saw a tree as a whole, but I could see every leaf individually at the same time. It was

a totally different way of seeing. I was in this sort of exalted state
for several hours.'

'Your awareness was heightened?'

'That wasn't all of it. The whole consciousness was entirely different. I could smell wood burning somewhere, a tremendous distance away and it was, oh, thousands of smells sort of making up a
whole landscape.'

'What if you had done a healing in that state?'

'Goodness knows! This is a perceptual change of consciousness.
And after all consciousness, by definition, is of our senses. But I think
this is a changed state of being. It's in this sort of state that mystics
have healed. I think that in every single healing however slight and
however little the result there's a changed state of consciousness, a
changed state of being.'

'On the part of the healer?'

'Yes, and if he also achieves attunement then it happens right
away.'

'And what is it he's attuning to—only the patient?'

'You don't want me, you want a sage. But I think that we are
several things at the same time. You're Sally, which is the external
person which has shaped itself around the personality which you're
living. Beneath that there's a whole mass of other mental and
emotional activity of feeling and even beyond that there are things
of which you have no consciousness nor awareness which are developing and becoming at the same time. But you're more than this.
You're also a little baby who was first named Sally that turned into
a little girl, so that at every point of your life you're the culmination
of all your other beings. You're more than this. You're indestructible
essence as well. As a person, what we want to attune to, the simplest
answer is that it is a contact of spirit to spirit. But I can't tell you
what the word spirit means. So that what I've got to say is that one
essence becomes totally intermingled with another essence.'

'At-one-ment with the patient?'

'That is the at-one-ment.'

'But when I pinned you down and asked what you are attuned
to, I was expecting that you would expand it beyond just the patient.
It seemed to me there had to be something else. . . .'

'Well, that's difficult. You see, I don't believe, I *can't* believe in a
personal god. What I do believe in very strongly is that there is a
sense and there is a purpose, and that the purpose has being and that

we live through that being and in it, and that the sum of all this is the thing which we use the word God for, but that this is common to the whole universe. It's something so immense that it can't be understood by us. But when we centre our essence into that one being, as we do in meditation, then this creative power becomes manifest through us.'

'But now, how do we tie this into the lab tests with enzymes in which a healer's hands stepped up their activity? The healer said he was praying as he held them.'

'Well, prayer is one form of meditation, of attuning to God, or to this thing we refer to as God—I really am humble about my definition of God. I'm also, I think, a Universalist—but I feel that all other definitions are perfectly valid and I have tremendous sympathy with Catholics, with Buddhists, with the lot. . . .'

'One last question,' I asked, 'can you put into words what you experience when you are healing?'

'I think I'm so centred, because I've had to heal publicly so much, that I can talk whilst healing. I can hold one level of consciousness and exist on an entirely different one . . . There's also a sense of compassion. I do love people quite genuinely, I think.'

'That seems to be the vital ingredient when you come right down to it.'

'You can't have this at-one-ment without love.'

'Nor give your life to healing without love.'

'When I was about five years old I fell in love with life. I'm still in love with life and I'm still in love with people. I sit in buses and trains and chatter with everyone—I'm awfully un-British in this way—but I'm fascinated with people . . .'

We paused to enjoy our coffee for a minute (not that I needed any further stimulation!) and after a while our talk shifted to Turner's role in organising the National Federation of Spiritual Healers. He was a co-founder, he said, with the late John Britnell, and their idea was to hasten the formal recognition of spiritual healing in England and throughout the world by establishing a professional standard for healers.

'We quite realised that you can't turn a healer into just a purely professional person,' Turner explained, 'but we believed there were areas where one central body could bring about changes. For example, insurance coverage to protect them against suits for malpractice. We went to terrific pains and were successful in setting up an insurance system whereby British healers could be covered after £20,000.

'To do this we had to make sure they came up to some standard,' he continued. 'Now this was very difficult, because how do you examine a healer? What we tried to do was to insure that they were of good character, of any or no religion, but honest people who weren't going to con their patients or anything like that. This is not easy to do, but we checked up on their references, things of that sort. Next, we tried to find out if they were healers at all by examining case histories and records of their patients. It was on this basis that the Federation started.' (The NFSH was organised in 1955.)

About four years later, Britnell died and Turner became chairman. His first move was to try to raise professional standards further, to the level of a priest or doctor, by getting healers into Britain's hospitals. 'To my surprise, my scheme won,' Turner said.

He then got together with Harry Edwards to discuss a formal training scheme and they collaborated on the first study course used by British healers. 'It was fairly basic, put emphasis on ethics and gave a history and background of healing.'

The growing Federation set up a Parliamentary committee and Turner felt this body might pilot a bill through Parliament that would give professional status to 'a small hard core' of people who have reached university standards, including perhaps nurses, doctors and priests who are healers. Turner noted that many healers are psychologists and some are actually doctors. (He took a university diploma in psychology and a BSc in physiology and anatomy after deciding to become a healer.) 'I hoped this would lead to our getting a chair at one or another of the universities and we could gradually build on that,' he explained.

But he soon found out that the Federation was taking a different direction and that his ambitious plans for strengthening professionalism and formal training were not the urgent concern of the majority. 'The Federation was split almost down the middle,' he said.

Turner described the prevailing attitude with mock seriousness, exclaiming, 'The idea that healers should learn anything about healing! It's God-given and you are an instrument.' Subsequently both the insurance coverage for healer-members and the parliamentary committee were dropped, he said. And although he is still honorary life Vice-President of the Federation, he has given up his organisation work to devote full time to healing and writing.

Basically, what Turner had in mind, and would still like to see, is a system in which there were two general types of healers—those trained as healing counsellors who could do it on a voluntary basis for people who are lonely or in desperate trouble and need the uplift and comfort of spiritual healing, and those who would be trained to a high professional level and paid for their services.

Turner clarified his reasoning: some healers are good and others are not, and although the healing power itself can't hurt anyone, some of these less-developed healers may try to diagnose or advise. He has known cases of healers taking diabetics off insulin without medical advice, he says, and since healers tend to be individualists and may be vegetarians or whatever, they sometimes urge their own enthusiasms on to their patients.

Describing himself as a 'rebel', Turner sketched in the background that led him to advocate a two-level training system for healers, one for paid professionals, the other for volunteers.

'For years I worked for literally nothing. I put out a collection plate and if at the end of the week I received donations of ten or twelve pounds I felt very lucky. And this meant work. All the time I was saying, God, how am I going to pay the electric bill? I lived with it and it was really hell. And this went on for twenty years. I suddenly realised I was seeing more and more people and making myself ill trying to push up the collection enough to pay the bills! So I sat down one day and thought it out. What can people reasonably afford to pay and how much time would I like to be able to give each patient? And I worked out a system that is far better.

'What it means is that I'm not seeing patients for three or four minutes. And it's made a complete change of attitude on the part of my patients. Now that they have to pay they don't come to me just casually, because they've got a headache or want to be with other people. If you visit one of the SAGB clinics in Belgrave Square, you'll find people who have been going there for five to ten years, every week or two as a holiday. They know all the other people in the room! And if a healer has fifteen of these people, the number of people he can see whom he could really help is very small. So what has happened is that the people who come see me now want to be cured in one, two, three or four visits. I'm working at my absolute peak. There's no day when we're working that we don't sign off at least four or five people as cured! The cure rate has gone higher and higher and higher.'

Turner estimated that there are about six or eight professional healers in England who are getting a very high percentage of results, far higher than the non-professional healers, 'literally because the non-professional healers are mostly coping with the repetitive cases that go on and on and on'. The latter are filling a vital need, he says, but most of their cases could be adequately treated by volunteer 'healing counsellors'.

Turner would also like to see the Federation emphasise the need for cooperation between doctors and healers. 'Once the doctors know you're not going to use their names for publicity and you're not going to let them down, you'd be surprised at the degree to which they will cooperate,' he says, adding that over half his patients come to him from doctors or through doctors.

Indeed, the doctors themselves come to him for treatment of things they 'don't seem to have much luck with', such as slipped discs, arthritic and rheumatic ailments, sinusitis and cancer. 'In any one year I probably treat twenty or thirty doctors,' Turner said, and he chuckled to himself as he recalled the psychiatrist who came to him when he was healing at the SAGB's clinic in Belgrave Square. 'He was a wild-haired fellow who looked like a Marx Brothers film version of a psychiatrist.

'I advised him on his own essential problems, and about two weeks later he came back with three of his patients, and he said, "Can you give me some advice about them?" I saw them one after the other and then consulted with him. Well, the next week he was back with four more. This went on and on and there was no week that he wasn't at the clinic with a few more patients.

'On about the tenth week I said to one of the women, "I'm very interested in your case. I wonder if you'd like to pop back and see me in a couple of weeks so I can see how you're getting on?" "Well," she said, "I can't afford it." I said, "But there's only a collection plate outside, you know. There's nothing for you to afford, please, be my guest." She said, "But I can't afford the eight guineas." Well, I found this chap was charging these patients eight guineas to bring them up and be diagnosed by me! He was making about thirty quid a week out of it. I had him in for a talk, and I was absolutely furious. He said quite blandly, "Well, I come with them. They're not paying for your time, they're paying for mine."

'But that's a sort of rare thing. Most of the doctors I deal with are jolly nice.'

Reteurning to the Federation of Spiritual Healers and the areas of its work he'd like to see strengthened, Turner said he thought membership requirements were too 'slack'. The current requirement of four to six cases of people healed is 'too easy' and every applicant should be interviewed, even those living in outlying districts.

He would also like to see the summer courses he inaugurated and ran for ten summers return to the original idea of covering a wider area than just healing. One year, for example, he arranged a whole week of instruction on social service. 'We had a blind person come and tell us what it was like to be blind and talk about services for the blind, and a spastic boy come and tell us what it's like to be paralysed. We had the matron of an old people's home, films on first aid and Red Cross work and that sort of thing. All this is terribly useful education for healers.' He added that now the summer schools offer 'the same four or five people giving the same lectures'.

And although his *Outline* is used as a textbook for one of the Federation's study courses for healers, Turner feels that it's 'not healthy' that the basic training courses are now entirely written by Harry Edwards. 'I love Harry Edwards, I really do,' he said, 'basically the courses are the substance of his books. But I think they should take in a far wider field, for instance Beesley's, who's got a mass of brilliant ideas, and the evangelical healers like Brother Mandus. The courses should reflect everybody's approach not just one person's. This is causing the general public to talk not about a healers' federation but Harry Edwards' federation of healers, and that's not good.'

In concluding, Turner said that although England is looked upon as a mecca for healers because of the freedom they enjoy, England's healers are falling short of beginning to get a professional status for themselves. And he deplored the fact that they are currently giving priority to such things as fund-raising for research and for support of their headquarters.

When I asked if he planned to try to change things, he said no, that he'd made a mistake devoting so much time to organisational work and had given it up. He left the impression that the view prevailing in the NFSH is that healing, being a natural gift, can be developed by training, and should be allowed to flourish with a basic minimum of imposed regulations and concern about status, a view shared basically by its long-time president, Harry Edwards.

Some time after Gordon Turner waved goodbye to me from his doorway, I read through his fascinating report of 1969 entitled *Some Experiments in Healing*. It is an aspect of his work he touched on only lightly in his *Outline* and lacked time to cover in our interview. But his findings seem to be in advance of his times and well worth mentioning. Working with twenty-three 'staunch and dedicated' healers, some of them trained in medicine, physics, electronics and photography, he carried out many imaginative tests between 1958 and 1962, beginning with a study of the effect of the healing energy on large numbers of patients.

In the first experiment, of 353 patients, 180 felt heat, forty-seven felt electrical sensations and forty-four coldness. Some felt joints cracking or moving although the healers' hands were motionless. Many (seventy-three) saw colours mentally, forty-six reporting blue and eleven seeing red. Of the seventy-six who said they felt nothing at all, the majority were victims of mental illness. He found, however, that many who felt no physical sensation nonetheless responded to healing.

Several years before Kirlian photography came to the notice of the West, Turner and his team studied healing emanations using various types of photographic film in 'specially prepared packets' placed between healer and patient during treatment. Although done minus the Kirlians' sophisticated electronic equipment, the developed plate produced radiation patterns from the healers' hands, sometimes showing his palm and finger prints. Repeating the test ninety-three times, they produced fifty-seven marked plates. The percentage of success was increased by using infra-red and X-ray plates. At no time did the healers' hands touch them.

Several years before Dr Bernard Grad ran his healing experiments with plant seeds, Turner tested the effect of his healers' hands on ordinary grass seed. He found that when the seed and the potting mixture were treated before planting, the healed seeds popped up ten days before the unhealed control. And when only the water was treated, those sprinkled with treated water appeared six days ahead of the control. In another test, Turner found the life of cut flowers could be extended a third again as long as untreated flowers and that daily healing could keep a bouquet fresh for as long as fifty-five days!

Commenting on these tests, Turner writes that simple prayer might prove to be a far more effective fertiliser than many of today's high-priced and dangerous chemicals!

Having discovered that contact healing and absent healing seem to achieve a similar ratio of success (roughly between 55-70 per cent), Turner made a series of studies through a questionnaire to learn more about the mechanics of absent healing. One interesting finding—involving 197 patients—was that in a week-long test the number of 'sensory phenomena' reported during nightly absent healing sessions dipped sharply on the two days when severe thunderstorms raged round London, suggesting that the healers' 'transmitting station' might have been affected.

Turner's most important contribution to healing research may be his studies of healing failures and his experiments suggesting ways that 'stubborn' cases can be reached through improved techniques.

Concentrating on twelve patients who had failed to respond to healing, he tried strengthening the telepathic link between patient and healer. Patients were given an appointment time for linking-up and a pleasant picture to reflect upon, in this test a shepherd tending his flock. And they were asked to read aloud the first verse of the 23rd Psalm. At the same moment, the healers projected the same bucolic scene on the screen, read the same verse from the Psalm and then concentrated on a picture of the patient flashed on to the screen, continuing the 'healing link' for ten minutes. The results were striking: mental illness so improved that the sufferer could dispense with all drugs; a crippled child able to stand for the first time in years; nine others reporting definite improvement and only one feeling unchanged. Eight of the twelve reported continuing benefits.

Turner's report looks at the dispersal of growths in a healer's hand and relates the phenomenon to 'the transition of matter into radiation and radiation into matter, a well-observed phenomenon which has been photographically recorded in cloud chambers, bubble chambers and on sensitive emulsion'. And he refers to an experiment he instigated to confirm this under the auspices of the healing research committee of the Churches' Fellowship for Psychical and Spiritual Studies. Completed by Dr Michael Ashe, the experiment involved attaching plastic bags filled with certified pure water to the hands of the healer through which he treated an arthritic patient. Analysed later, the water was shown to contain calcic sediment.

Turner concludes that these 'pseudo-scientific' studies show that it is possible to apply orthodox research procedures to psychic science. He then adds that there are other aspects to be considered in understanding laws governing spiritual healing and he suggests that the cooperation of many healers throughout the world has enabled the 'spirit scientists' to advance their knowledge of the laws of healing. 'They are now able to achieve what was previously difficult or impossible' in helping to 'direct' the healing process.

And long before 'bioplasma' was reported this side of the Iron Curtain, Turner wrote that every living organism is constantly emanating patterns of energy, that they vary according to a person's health and age. 'Psychics see these emanations as an aura which is in fact a reflection of the physical, mental, and spiritual state of the organism,' he writes. 'When this fine balance is upset by undue emotion or disease, the loss of energy outbalances its replenishment.'

Turner adds that healing must meet the 'area of spiritual need' that exists in the patient, and he quotes the spirit teacher known as Silver Birch who defined the healer's role as 'touching souls'. He ends with an invitation to others to repeat 'our simple experiments' and a passage from the *Tibetan Book of the Dead*:

'Thine own Consciousness, shining void, and inseparable from the Great Body of Radiance, hath no birth, nor death, and is immutable light.'

'It could be added,' says Gordon Turner, 'Thus may man be healed!'

II.   Mary Rogers

SHORTLY AFTER my arrival in England I had my long-awaited meeting with Mary Rogers. She invited me to her home in Wivelsfield Green, Sussex, along with my friend Lady Suzanne Haire, and we were to meet at Victoria Station and make the trip together.

An Englishwoman and gifted writer now living in New York, Suzanne had flown to London for some magazine interviews and was looking forward to seeing Mary as eagerly as I. They were old friends, their husbands having been fellow MPs together before the late John Haire was made a life peer (I had looked up Suzanne in New York at Mary's suggestion).

Arriving at Haywards Heath, we were met by a pleasant gentleman who said he was Mary's guest and had come to fetch us. He drove us in his car past green meadows and through a pine wood to an imposing gabled house, 'High Pines' on Hundred Acre Lane. It was divided into three flats and Mary's was at the right end.

Mrs Rogers met us at the door and embraced us warmly. Buxom, pale-blonde, just like her pictures, she had blue eyes and a brisk manner, wore dark blue slacks and a flowered tunic. Soon we were gathered around an electrified hearth in the yellow-gold living room, sipping dry Spanish sherry. Dogs and cats padded in and out as we talked, and one large shaggy animal reposed at Mary's feet. The couple visiting were the Stevens, of Birmingham. Mrs Stevens, being treated for multiple sclerosis by Mary, gave her much credit for her improvement. She used to walk with a frame but no longer needs it. 'She is not yet fully cured, but I see no reason why she shouldn't be,' Mary said, and Mrs Stevens agreed she was getting better steadily.

Mary's extremely attractive married daughter, Shauna, served lunch in a dining room overlooking rose gardens, and the food couldn't have been more delicious—poached fresh salmon on garden lettuce with sweet English tomatoes and, for dessert, ripe sugared strawberries with heavy cream.

Later on, when we were able to talk about her work, she outlined her unusual method of treating young drug addicts:

'It's a matter of treating the soul-sickness that caused the addiction and then strengthening them physically,' she said. 'I have a motherly way about me, I suppose, and they listen.

'Now, the escapism of drugs is only a way of leaving this world, which is what they want to do. So I catch their interest by informing them that their souls will survive this life and have the potential for progressing to a higher spiritual plane in the next, and therefore there's a reason for living.

'To give them evidence of survival, I bring back people who belonged to them—a devoted grandmother, perhaps, who's passed on—and I'll be able to give her name. I never have any trouble providing proof and I find that young people are open-minded and want to believe.

'Then I send up a prayer asking that the power shall be given to me, and I tune in with the spirit intelligences. I am the medium, the go-between, between them and the patient.

'In a few minutes I'll hear a voice—it's usually Sir John— although I have four spirit doctors altogether. Sometimes two or three appear and they'll be discussing the case. Usually they will begin by diagnosing the illness, but in drug addiction they tell me why the sufferer resorted to drugs in the first place, pin-pointing the reason as part of the healing treatment. I repeat this to the patient: 'I know why you're taking drugs. You are doing it because...' I face them with it and it's rather like a shock. I find the great majority of these children were hooked because of an inferiority complex or parents who don't understand—they can't help it, poor things—or they may have become hooked at a party. Some are merely weak, and in such cases I give them a strong pep talk: "Stop or else..." and I warn them that by taking drugs they are endangering not only their bodies but their immortal souls as well.'

I asked Mary if she knew in what way their souls were endangered. Isn't the soul fairly indestructible? She knew only that a spirit message had come to her urging her to 'tell the children who take drugs that they're in danger of losing their immortal souls and will, if they persist, actually lose them'. She has found this information 'a great deterrent' to youngsters who usually are very afraid of annihilating their souls, she said.

'I'm not saying this as a bogyman. This drug addiction is really like taking your own life, you know.'

I then asked Mary how she administers the actual treatment. This is what she says she does :

'I place my hands on the head, and if other parts of the body are affected, my hands, which seem to have a life of their own, place themselves at the seat of the disease or pain.

'Now there is this great eternal force, call it God, call it what you like. I have learned to open myself to it and to pass it through. And so this healing power seems to flow through me from the spirit intelligences and then through the bodies of my patients.'

In treating addicts, the healing power seems to have the effect of a 'fix', giving them a sense of exhilaration, she said. 'It does something to the brain and nervous system, I think, because in treating nervous diseases and paralysis it does stimulate parts of the body in which the motor nerves have died.'

In extreme cases of addiction, she applies the healing power daily, she said, allowing them some drug at first but, as the craving grows less, spins it out until they don't need it any more, reinforcing the process with much absent healing. She added that her patients do not need to be committed and that her recovery rate is about seven out of ten—a much higher rate than most addict programmes are claiming.

She is sometimes able to buoy up the confidence of young addicts, particularly, by giving them a precognitive glimpse into the future, Mary continued. She gave as an example, a young girl who had run away from home and met with near-tragedy.

'She had taken up with man on the Continent. He had put her on heroin and she was pregnant. Thank God her mother brought her to me! Before treating her I had a vision of the girl happily married and living abroad, and I told her about it. This happened about a year ago. After having an abortion she came to my sanctuary for healing about a dozen times, and I also gave her absent healing. About six months ago her mother told me she's engaged to a good man—so it's starting. Today she's absolutely fine and able to start life over again.'

She would give no names because she promises her drug addicts complete anonymity. 'I have records of all my other cases, but not of the drug addicts. I promise them that if they will give it up and take the cure they can be completely whole again and nobody will know. Their records are all locked up in here,' she said, touching her heart, 'they're forgotten and done with. I think if they've given up drugs they've achieved something so fantastic that they have a right to remain anonymous. They're so deeply ashamed of it, they're happy to know that once they're cured it's definite.

'It's not like going to a clinic,' she continued. 'I prefer to work with them privately, and to give them some hope. "Now if you stop doing this your future is so-and-so". I can see into the future, you see. I tell them if they stop doing this, this is what is there for them, what they can achieve, nice little carrots, if you like, held out, but it works, and it's a harmless way of working. I've had parents bring me beautiful girls who are addicted, the most horrible stories. . . .'

'Are any of your healings the instantaneous kind?' I asked.

'In recent months the power has become more easy to direct,' she said. 'A man with broken bones in his foot came in yesterday. He was limping and wearing carpet slippers and in great pain every time he put his foot to the ground. I just stroked the foot and said "Let it be healed", and it was. I couldn't do that a year ago! I used to give very long healings.' She remarked that he was a very high-powered business man who had never had anything to do with healing and had come to her with the idea of having her to see his wife who was in the advanced stages of cancer. . . .

'I apply the rays, which I can see, you know. They are different colours, coming from the hands,' Mary Rogers went on matter-of-factly. 'So it's definitely a force, you see. It's not a magnetic force—there are magnetic healers who direct their own magnetism and magnetic forces around them towards a patient. But it isn't that kind of thing. It is most definitely a force with colours in it.'

In healing the eyes the ray is violet, she said, and for cancer and arthritis it is deep red, magenta; for nervous diseases, gold and green. 'So there you are. It is a force from God that can be seen and felt. It isn't just a spiritual force like faith and prayer.' She added that the 'love vibration' certainly helps, and she finds herself really loving most of her patients. 'Then someone will come along and I'll think, oh, no, I can't love him—and he still gets healed!' She laughed.

'Can anyone wanting to heal be trained to do it?' I asked.

'Yes, I believe so,' Mary said, and she quoted the famous passage from St Paul's letter to the Corinthians about the spiritual gifts. 'Latent within most of us, I feel, is some little spark of the healing gift.' And she told the story of a nine-year-old boy who died of Hodgkin's Disease in spite of all her efforts and whose father, rather than bewail the loss of his son, had taken up healing. 'I told the father, "The only thing you can do is use the latent healing power within you", and he did. He isn't a great spectacular healer but he does, in fact, give me healing when I need it and is helping quite a number of people.' She added that if people will sit in circles and meditate, 'their psychic consciousness or awareness becomes greater and deeper and gradually their talent unfolds'.

'What do medical doctors think of your work?'

'There are two coming to me for treatment right now,' Mary said lightly. 'One has familial palsy of his right hand and was finding it difficult to give injections. He's improved a great deal. The other is coming to see me for a nervous trouble and also to learn more about psychic medicine.' She emphasised that she never speaks against the medical profession and that it's 'ridiculous' for anyone to think medical doctors are not needed.

'I work in *conjunction* with doctors, but if it's something they can't do then I take over with an easy mind and get going on it,' Mary Rogers said, adding that at least seven doctors, some of them Harley Street specialists, send her people suffering from hardening of the arteries, cancer, asthma, heart disease, arthritis, hiatus hernia, diverticulitis . . . 'I've helped six out of ten alcoholics recover and I've healed diabetics, although it takes time. I've also had success with cataracts and glaucoma, but I'm not very good with detached retina, and I've never healed anyone who was born blind.'

(Mary said she never mentions the names of the referring doctors because it might get them in trouble with the British Medical Association. But an osteopath in Liphook, Hampshire, Norman Sanderson, had praised her in a *Psychic News* story so I called him and asked if he would comment on Mrs Rogers' treatment for my book. He said she had 'worked miracles' with his patients and that people with slipped discs had responded 'within hours'. He hadn't the faintest idea how she did it, Sanderson said. 'When we find cases baffling and can't get anywhere with them, we always say there's just one last place we can send them—to Mary Rogers. She's our last hope, you know.')

The sceptical type of doctor doesn't worry her in the least, judging from the anecdote she told us with gusto:

'One of my patients, Ruth Plant, arranged dinner at the Danish Club in London for a friendly give-and-take, inviting me and some doctor friends of hers who wanted to ask me questions. Among them was a Harley Street specialist who didn't believe in spirit healing. I'd never seen him nor his wife before in my life. But I told the group that while this doctor's wife looked very healthy, she had arthritis of the spine in three places and the end of her spine, or coccyx, was bent. This doctor told his medical friends, "Do you know, she's right! I have all that on X-rays." I think they'll agree I shook 'em rigid.' She laughed.

Mary estimated that her overall cure rate is a modest forty per cent, but she reminded us that most people come to her as a last resort when told by their doctors they would have to 'learn to live with it'. She thought some failures were due to karmic laws, or that it was a person's time to go.

I asked how many cancer cures she claims, and she thought perhaps a dozen. They usually come to her when they have only a few weeks to live, she said, but she can extend their lives about three years and help them die without pain.

'If they have healing, they never have any pain, which is the most terrible thing about cancer,' Mary said with feeling. 'Who cares about dying, anyway? But to die in pain is nasty.'

Recalling a dramatic instance of healing, she told about the gradual recovery over two years of a teenage youth who had been operated on for brain cancer:

'His mother confided to me that the surgeon had been unable to remove all the malignancy. The poor lad had fourfold vision and was unable to speak, and he had to walk sideways like a crab does. I began treating him regularly, and after two years he was able to work as a joiner's apprentice. He could also skate and ride a bike! His vision is quite normal and he's able to talk. He has been going to night school for retarded people and learning to read and write again.'

Could she tell us about a few of the well-known theatre people she had healed?

Unlike the politicians, they are not at all secretive about frequenting the sanctuary of a spiritual healer, Mary said, and she told about healing the famous operatic tenor, David Hughes, who sang with the Sadler's Wells company. 'He had three slipped discs and a prolonged sciatica which made him limp badly, and in three treatments, he was healed,' she said.

(I called up Hughes, who sang a fine Don José in 'Carmen', and asked if he would comment on Mrs Rogers' treatments, and he related a grim series of events that preceded his recourse to spiritual healing : 'I first went to a chiropractor for a bad lower back, but he overdid it so much that I was limping badly. I know Mary put it right for me, but if you speak to him he'll say, "No, I put it right". And if I were to give you his name and say he gave me a limp, he might sue me for defamation of character! I next let two osteopaths have a go at it, but it didn't get any better. Unfortunately none of them are available to verify this because one of them has died and the other has gone to Spain.' Hughes volunteered the information that Mrs Rogers had helped him emotionally to overcome negative feelings about his artistic ability and to help him 'fit into this mad world we live in'. He said she had brought him encouraging messages from the late great tenor John McCormack and the conductor Sir John Barbirolli, now deceased, 'who said he believed in me and would help me'. Continuing, Hughes said, 'Barbirolli told Mary that I would sing a great Verdi "Requiem" some day. Well, a few months ago when I sang the "Requiem" I clearly saw him in the hall, and I sang my bloomin' head off ! I've never sung so well in my life'.)

Mary then mentioned Shirley Bishop and Joan Blakeney, two of the many dancers in the Royal Ballet who have come to her for healing. 'Shirley had a very bad back and had been told by Ninette de Valois she'd never dance again, a verdict that was confirmed by X-rays at Wembley Hospital. But after a dozen healing treatments she danced nine years! I cured Joan of a cracked pelvis and a very bad foot. Both girls went on to open their own ballet schools—Shirley in Pinner, Middlesex, and Joan in South Africa.'

Finally, I asked Mary what sort of relationship she has with the Anglican church. She explained that they frown on the idea of spirit doctors, but that individual Anglican priests have come and blessed her sanctuary. Then, just a year ago, she had been invited to do her first healing in an Anglican church—St Laud's in Sherington, with three priests assisting. Later, she gave me a clipping from *Psychic*

News of July 10, 1971, headlined : 'PACKED CONGREGATION SEES TWO INSTANT CURES'. The front page story related the incident almost matter-of-factly :

> 'People travelled long distances to listen to the rector and Mary, and to be healed. There were several remarkable results, including two which were spontaneous. Mrs Chibnall of Bedford had been told by her surgeon she would never bend her back again, after the removal of two discs from her spine. Following Mary's treatment she stood before the congregation if only for one minute and touched her toes. She volunteered that numbness in one foot was also completely cured. Mrs Margaret Brown, also of Bedford, received treatment for a large goitre. This was seen to diminish rapidly.'

Mary asked Suzanne and me if we would like to see her sanctuary, and we eagerly followed her through the kitchen to a small 'el' on the other side of a heavy door. It was a small white room about ten feet square, with red carpeting and a large hassock for her patients. There was an altar with a lace-edged scarf and a crucifix on the wall. Illuminated from below was the beautiful painting of Christ she had told me about in her letters. It was painted by a very fine artist from a vision Mary had that lasted twenty minutes! A young man, bearded, he had a gentle, loving expression in his eyes.

Mary gave Suzanne a healing and then asked me to sit on the patient's seat. After giving me the laying-on of hands, she said, 'There's something wrong with your feet'. Coming around, she kneeled at my feet and began stroking the arches. 'Too many barefoot sandals as a child, or too many miles as a newspaper reporter,' I suggested. She flexed each foot and it felt really marvellous! I wished I could have had before-and-after footprints taken, but it seemed to me that I felt more strength in my arches.

Suzanne and I asked Mary if she expected to come soon to the States and I offered to help arrange some kind of demonstration of healing in New York. She said she hoped to and that her spirit guides had told her she had much work to do in America.

As we were leaving, regretfully, and taking a short last-minute stroll through her rose garden, I asked Mary how she feels about her generous share of the 'gifts of the spirit'.

'I've always said throughout my life, "Why me?" I'm so ordinary, you know. I cook, I brought up my children, I carry on absolutely normally. Whatever it is I'm a perfectly ordinary soul. Happily, people believe me. I haven't told a lie yet about clairvoyance or healing. I would be afraid to because it would be misleading and that is something I mustn't do,' Mary said.

'I feel the world must know about it, that we must get the word out that God's power can be used to heal humanity—if people will only avail themselves of it. And the world never stood more in need of healing than it does today.'

12.   Ronald Beesley

RONALD BEESLEY has been called a 'practitioner of the future' because of the trail-blazing quality of his therapies and teachings. A veteran healer of forty years, he kept right on healing and lecturing about it while bombs rained down on his London centre during the war. Now principal of the College of Psycho-therapeutics (meaning 'soul healing') in rural Kent, he teaches students from all over the world what must be some of the more exciting New Age courses being given anywhere.

For, in training them to help people overcome illnesses that originate in the spirit, Beesley has his students immerse themselves in a wide variety of studies ranging from anatomy to spiritual healing and including chakra and auric healing, natural medicine and psychic attunement, to name a few.

Above all, his students are encouraged to aspire to the level of 'soul power' demonstrated by the life of Christ in preparing themselves to become effective healers. They are also taught to be humble and tolerant and how to heal themselves.

An authority on reading the aura to diagnose illness, Beesley was invited to give his views at an important Life Energies Research, Inc. conference on healing at Wainwright House, Rye, New York, in 1968.

His book on the aura, *The Robe of Many Colours,* is evidence of his virtuosity. Analysing the components and colour of each level of the auric structure, it offers a sample 'auric diagnosis' drawn and presented in twenty-three minutes that proved correct in most details. And in his foreword, Reginald Lester also gives Beesley a high score for the auric reading he requested.

Not only did Beesley detect a pre-natal incident that was confirmed by Lester's mother, but he pin-pointed breaks in the aura at the ages of three, fourteen, sixteen and fifty-two, each one a year of crisis for Lester!

At the end of the book, a student had this to say after Beesley drew his aura on the blackboard and analysed it before the class: 'Not only was my life unrolled before me, my weaknesses, illnesses, operations, birth of children and so on, but the pattern of my emotional, intellectual, astral and spiritual bodies were all "seen" by our tutor's X-ray sight.'

A newer specialty is Beesley's chakra system of therapy, dealing with psychic maladjustments and the body's emotional centres. And in 1969, after years of inconclusive experiments, he made a breakthrough in his research with colour therapy. Travelling to India on a study tour, he discovered what appears to be the key for which he was searching while investigating the healing methods of Tibetan exiles on the Himalayan frontier. Visiting a dispensary, he was intrigued when a healing Lama diagnosed the condition of a sick person far up in the mountains by holding the pulse of a relative who was sent as a proxy!

Returning to his lab in England, Beesley applied the proxy idea to healing by colour therapy. He had an artist draw the outline of a human form on a large projection screen and then worked out a method of diagnosing and programming the colour. He then had the sick person's name called while colour energy was transmitted to the area of need by a kind of 'spiritual photography'. The results, he says, were 'extraordinary'.

The process is described vividly by Beesley's associate, Cicely Allan, in the December, 1971, issue of the College magazine, *The Psycho-therapist*:

'When the name is spoken here in the Colour Room, then also is the name called in the heavens, the great Cosmic Computer swings into action and the relevant history of the recipient is made available. It then needs only the power of attraction of the light wave to translate this incident of history thrown upon the screen of life that it may be revealed for its healing ... The light speeds down the earth beam we have created to burst upon the recipients, a glowing prism of colour, aglow with an atmosphere not of this world, raising the quality of the body, helping to reinstate the blueprint within their lives, reminding the consciousness of what needs to be done ...'

And so, an interview with Ronald Beesley promised a mind-blowing glimpse far into the future and a chance to learn more about his College of Psycho-therapeutics, which seemed to be just the kind of higher training school for healers we would soon be needing in the United States.

Having made an appointment by mail and phone, I took a train on Sunday afternoon from Charing Cross station and soon alighted at Tunbridge Wells where a taxi took me the rest of the way over the hilly Kentish countryside. We veered and scooted as though on a roller coaster past green fields dotted with yellow wildflowers and grazing cows to the village of Speldhurst and 'White Lodge', the imposing three-storey red brick main building of the College.

A few minutes later, Mr Beesley and I were face to face in comfortable living room chairs before a large picture window with a ravishing view of rose gardens and meadows stretching off into the distance. A lovely place for teaching healing through spiritual upliftment and right living!

I almost expected him to be wearing a space suit, but he was disarmingly gentle and gracious and wore country tweeds. He asked for tea to be brought in—the never-failing English ritual that warmed every one of my interviews—and began chatting about his heavy schedule lecturing on soul therapy.

He had just returned from Germany and would soon be dashing off to Chichester, Newcastle and then to Sweden. After that he'd have a week's grace before starting off a new students' course. An engineer by training, he now works harder than he ever did. 'The demand for this knowledge is so heavy,' he said.

Groups of twenty-five to thirty students, 'a nice tidy number', come to White Lodge from many countries to work intensively for two weeks, he said. Then they'll take twelve months to write a thesis and do field work and return for the 'associate course'. Next comes the 'fellowship course'. The fourth, further advanced, is still in the planning stage.

'Although we have guidelines, to me each course is a happening. Different students bring out and require certain types of approach,' Beesley said as he handed me the curriculum for the student course Part One. It began with 'General Anatomy—as viewed in conjunction with spiritual psychotherapy' and next came 'The Emotional and Desire Body'. Other subjects were 'Mental Body Processes', 'Auric Patterns and Radiations', and 'Chakras and Psychic Structures', followed by 'Mental Sensitivity and Psychic Attunement', 'Diagnosis' and 'Spiritual Healing—its approach and transmission' and, finally, 'Manipulative, Magnetic, Psychic and Nature Healing'.

'Will these courses develop the healing ability in anyone who desires it?' I asked.

'We believe that the ability to *help* people is inherent in everyone,' Beesley said. 'Our job is to train people to *help* people. Then they must equip themselves with spiritual knowledge in tune with physical knowledge in order to become healers.'

Amusingly, he chose a musical simile much like the one Harry Edwards used to answer my question more fully :

'Training healers is very much like training pianists. Here and there you will get a concert pianist. The others will do quite a nice job and will entertain a lot of people, but they won't get to what I call "teacher quality",' he said. 'And to become a substantial healer a student needs more than just the desire. A healer must have dedication, discipline, and a complete belief in his ability.'

I asked if he taught his students any particular technique of attunement and his answer was surprisingly free-and-easy. 'Not really,' he said. 'You give them guidelines and each one will develop his own. You see, you can't produce a lot of people who imitate the teacher! Originality in spiritual work is very important, and if you produce people who work from a book of rules, as far as I'm concerned that's bad teaching.'

Expanding on his teaching philosophy, Beesley said he found years ago that he couldn't run a healing programme without a teaching programme that applied to the patient just as much as to the prospective healer. For that reason he lectures once a month at Caxton Hall in London and has been doing so for the past twenty-five years. He has made available one of his instructional lectures on meditation which was recorded live on one of those occasions. (Obtaining a copy, I found it the best meditation record I'd ever heard. It lucidly guides the listener through three stages—physical relaxation, mental attunement to deeper knowledge, and spiritual soaring—for the purpose of self instruction and self-healing. The spiritual wisdom is expressed poetically without becoming flowery.)

'You see, you can't put a back right and then leave the patient in the middle of the misery which caused the backache,' Beesley continued. 'You've got to work within the patient's consciousness and then the disorder will look after itself. But the healer doesn't do the work, he only helps by showing the patient how to do it.'

He gave as an example the strong photographic subconscious images a person collects in his youth that come home to him in old age. 'If the person's consciousness can be helped to work within itself, these images can be released and with them the illness,' said Beesley. 'But the healer is only the activator. He should be neither judge nor jury.'

I began to see that soul-therapy demanded as much work on the part of the patient as the healer, and I asked Beesley if it meant the patient must have a spiritual awakening. He said this was 'very essential', but it also involved his spiritual and mental attitudes and his physical preparation, by which I assume he meant improved diet and living habits.

I then asked if the healer isn't often able to stimulate his patient's bodily self-healing mechanism whether the patient co-operates or not.

'Yes,' he said, 'but we believe that when the *spirit* is active within the body, self-healing is always good. And if for any reason this vital force becomes depleted, then the health pattern breaks down. But once you provide the essential spiritual energy, like giving a car petrol, it will go. But it won't run without any fuel!'

Continuing, Beesley said the healer can't 'dictate' the healing because he's dealing with 'a good deal of karmic and pre-existent life'. So he subtly puts himself 'within the feeling' of the person's requirements, because what they ought to get may be very different from what they want.

'The patient may have a big programme of personality development to carry out within his consciousness,' Beesley explained. 'Some of this is painful. Like making a piece of steel that must go into the fire a lot of times. Often what people think of as pain is evolution working through the consciousness. And so it isn't the illness you have got to help. It's the person!

'We've all experienced many life structures,' Beesley philosophised. 'The spirit must pass through great valleys and shadows.'

Karma and reincarnation! Beesley sounded very much like Edgar Cayce in relating these tenets of Eastern mysticism to healing, but he seemed to go a few strides farther.

'Soul therapy is really a way of walking into the deep waters of the consciousness,' he observed understandingly. 'You're not fishing in the shallow end, you know.'

Beesley said he preferred the term 'continuity of incarnation' to reincarnation because the consciousness flows in and out of the various periods of our growth. We immerse ourselves into earth-consciousness for a short time and just dip in and out, in and out. 'Just think of a flow line,' he said.

'While we go through a short experience here, we're going through other experiences somewhere else because total personality is not incarnated,' Beesley raced on. 'The total you is not here. It would suffer too much. It would be damaged.'

I asked Beesley for some of the sources of his concepts, and he said they were based on the old Essene teachings, the ageless wisdom and the adjusted consciousness. Elaborating on the latter, he said truth must evolve, otherwise we have a medieval religion in a highly technical society.

'What Christ would say today would be very different from what he said in Palestine because the whole concept of consciousness has changed,' he said. 'There you had an agrarian society, so you had to use grapes and sheep and ears of corn for education. Now we should be able spiritually to see the superconsciousness of the cosmic region in a new light rather than in an agricultural sense!'

To provide balance, Beesley said the College programme includes prayer and fasting, yoga and meditation. 'We are also homeopathic, we are herbal, we are biochemic, and we believe anything that is natural is good.'

His prospective healers are trained to be 'wise as serpents and harmless as doves', he said. 'They do sensible work and at least we stop them from trying to be prophets. We teach them a little holy respect and a bit of homage to the Almighty.'

Amazingly, the school is run by a full-time staff of four, his assistants being trained therapists. It is non-profit. Good students are financed and helped with scholarships. 'We do all we can to foster good work,' said the principal, 'and we will not have any of this low-grade psychic stuff.'

I asked Beesley if there were similar training schools in other countries, or if the College of Psycho-therapeutics was unique.

'That's the problem. England is one of the few countries where you can practise spiritual healing,' he said. 'In practically every other country in the world, especially those with a strong Catholic background, it's legally impossible to treat. Even in New York I felt healers were saddled with this terrible medical authority, this idea that medical doctors are *supreme,* that they are God. But they're holding their hand out for a colossal amount of money while they're acting God! I can tell you that far from being able to train healers, you'd be illegal in many countries even to tell a person to take an aspirin!

'It's a closed shop all over the world, even in Poland and France,' Beesley continued, heatedly. 'People all over the world must be helped to realise that no particular school, whether medical or metaphysical, should have the right of monopoly.'

What is needed, he said, is an 'international zone' for healing. He's been working on that idea when lecturing abroad on the 'esoteric and spiritual side' of healing work, and was encouraged when his listeners at two big conferences in Frankfurt were agreeably surprised that his approach of working within the consciousness is in harmony with any religion or school. 'It hasn't got an "ism" and therefore we can be friends of all and enemies of none,' he said.

The idea of an international zone where healing could be practised and demonstrated seemed to me a solid idea. What better way to educate the public and generate the forces necessary to bring about change?

Shifting the direction of the interview to Beesley himself, I asked how he first discovered his healing ability. He was a boy of five when his pet dog, suffering from canker of the ear, nuzzled his hands and tried to place her head between them, he said. The ear healed! 'Even at that age she seemed to sense something.'

When he tried to find out more about healing as a young man he met much 'nonsense and religious confusion' among the larger denominations, and he recalled his investigations among the smaller groups, beginning with the Christian Scientists. 'I studied them and I quite liked them,' he said, 'then I went to the Theosophists and quite liked them. And the Spiritualists—I quite liked them. But my leanings were more toward the Quakers because of their quietness and humility. To me the Quakers seemed the healthiest and most balanced of all the religious groups.' He didn't join them officially, however. And today if he had to put a name on it, he'd call himself a Universalist.

He deplored the fact that most churches have fallen short of the 'therapeutic side' of their teachings—even the Quakers, whose founder, George Fox, was a spiritual healer. And he feels that Christianity worships the shadow of Christ not realising that the shadow is very much alive.

'To me, I cannot bear to think that a public execution is going to save the world,' Beesley said with feeling. 'To me, Christ is the spirit of the Cosmic Arisen working within the consciousness of you and me.' He wished 'so-called religion' would stop worshipping its past and get on with its future.

I asked Beesley what advice he'd give people wanting to be healers, and he said they should find a good teacher who is a natural healer and work with him until they find a better one. Each teacher will add something to their total knowledge, he suggested, but they should also reach out into their own higher consciousness and it will feed back much they need to know.

'Once they get into group work of the highest order, they can bring all the resources of the soul group to bear on a case—and they are very, very efficient.'

'Are you talking about spirit entities working in groups?' I asked.

'Yes, but we should try to think of them as Higher Beings or the Luminous Ones,' Beesley said. 'They are not ghosts. They are more real than we are. We are the ghosts. They are the reals.'

'Don't you call them spirit doctors?' I asked.

'Not necessarily. You must realise that three parts of illness is not medical at all, so your teachers and philosophers—the teaching groups—are much more in demand than the doctor groups,' he said.

I asked what provisos or pitfalls healers should watch out for, and he said diagnosing should be approached with caution. Many healers make sweeping statements about a patient's condition when it would be better if they held their peace, he said. And a person should not consider himself a healer unless he's had proper training.

'There are people who go into what they call "psychic development" and then put on a white coat and think they are Solomon in all his glory. They haven't even started!' said Beesley.

He told a grim story about a woman who came to him saying she had been told by a psychic that she would die in six months. She had given away her money and her clothes. He stopped her and advised quick surgery. 'She went through the operation and is now fitter than she's ever been—after being in darkness six months! Just because a silly little psychic came up to her in church one day and diagnosed her condition.

'This is why we need training schemes for healers. The public must be protected and so must the healers. The status of spiritual healing is very high now in England, but we need only a few untrained people like this making diagnoses to undercut all our good work,' he said.

When I asked if more healers might learn to diagnose by reading the aura, Beesley said that after working on it thirty years 'we have now gone past the aura'. He explained he has found that the consciousness of an individual can be felt and seen sometimes far more accurately, although he still uses both methods.

He added a warning against going into healing for the wrong reasons. 'A lot of people do it for the glory, the romance, the religious glamour. The ego can get very inflated. The temptation to become a personality is very strong.'

'But can they still heal, with inflated egos?' I asked.

'Yes, they can, but the point is they're just repeating. They are not evolving. Everything must evolve . . .'

Just then my taxi driver knocked at the door, ending our interview abruptly. But my host persuaded the young man to wait a minute while he took me on a brief tour of the grounds. Before leaving the house he gave me a peek into the Colour Room with its human form outlined on a screen. There was no time, unfortunately, for a demonstration. Instead he supplied me with literature on it and I bought two of his books.

We walked through a rose garden to 'The Galilee', the beautiful sanctuary for meditation that is obviously Beesley's pride and joy. 'The idea for this was conceived on the shore of the Sea of Galilee on one of my pilgrimages to the Holy Land,' he said. He placed a small white folder in my hand that interpreted and gave the background of its spiritual symbols, but I had to linger a moment on the first page. In Old English type was one simple phrase: 'This Place of Meditation is Dedicated to all Peoples and Nations that we may join in Unity to God and the Brotherhood of Man'. I pondered the thought that spiritual healers have a way of breathing life into such expressions.

We took off our shoes, exchanging them for grass slippers and entered the peaceful, cool sanctuary, and Beesley pointed out one by one the Copper Panel from the artist's colony at Safud in the Holy Land, the World Cross suspended in space, 'a reminder that we are not earthbound', the Solar Window, the old print of Asclepius healing in his temple, the Chakra Sun Window, its design based on man's 'centres of being' and the Tree of Knowledge Window, the branches symbolising 'the soul's way to realisation or the higher dimension of consciousness'. Tasteful and understated, the designs and decorations represented a myriad of cultures and religions.

As we left, I signed the guest book and saw several names in it from New York and others from Spain, Holland, Bangkok.

The final touch was a drink from the outdoor spring. I've never tasted water so delicious. And as he escorted me to the taxi and its impatient driver, Beesley pointed out the new construction under-way—a new dormitory, treatment rooms and a clinic being made out of an old stable. The College of Psycho-therapeutics with its teachings of the New Age was obviously a going concern and growing!

When I found time to read Ronald Beesley's latest book, *Service of the Race,* I came across an intriguing chapter on healing entitled 'The Soul of the Universe'.

Explaining that this great Universal Soul is the sum total of the soul essence that exists in every atom, he says by attuning one's own soul essence to it, an energy is transmitted that will heal and energise other earth souls needing replenishment.

In performing his miracles, Christ changed the frequency of disease in sick people by using this same great power of the universe, Beesley writes, and what God can do, we can do. 'This may sound like blasphemy or heresy, but it is not.'

The first step is for us to recognise that the power is there and ours to use, since we are part of God and his 'working-partners'.

Then, he continues, 'detach yourself entirely from all sense of earthly bondage. Feel yourself in tune with the great reservoir of waiting energy, and when you speak to or touch anyone, when you bless anyone, feel it, and know that you are blessing that person, healing him, helping him with the very Soul of the Universe behind you', and he adds, 'If you do this, and the other person has enough receptive faith to share this experience with you, you can literally see the transformation taking place. I have seen it on rare occasions, and I hope to see it again.'

This great soul energy is a source God created for us to use 'unstintingly, unselfishly and constantly', the author writes, and he proposes this meditation :

'Visualise the sun and all its planets and movements and begin to feel yourself as a sun radiating light, heat, warmth and life to every other form of life that is around you. Become a light of the world.'

13. Dr Christopher Woodard

DR CHRISTOPHER WOODARD is in a secure niche all of his own. Although a qualified medical doctor with a masters' degree in psychology from Cambridge, he prefers to be known simply as a 'faith healer'. A craggy individualist if there ever was one, he declares that he gets excellent results with prayer and meditation in his healing practice and prescribes drugs and surgery only rarely.

The author of a flock of books on medical technical subjects, including *Treatment of Sports Injuries,* a classic in its field—he's an Olympic consultant and looks after young athletes at the Olympic games—Woodard is much better known for his trio of books based on his special brand of Christian faith healing—all of them best-sellers. *A Doctor Heals by Faith* went into nine editions the first year and was serialised in the national press. The others are *A Doctor's Faith Holds Fast* and *A Doctor's Faith is Challenged.*

Years ago I had read of Dr Woodard in Emily Gardiner Neal's book, *A Reporter Finds God Through Spiritual Healing,* in which she tells of the time his son was gravely ill with spinal meningitis and not expected to live. Rather than call in his eminent Harley Street colleagues, Dr Woodard called an Anglican priest, whom he knew to be a healer, and asked him to send up prayers for his son. Then, calling up several more churches, he generated the prayer power of hundreds of people. The boy made an astonishing recovery!

In another account I learned that Dr Woodard first became aware of his own curative powers when at the age of twelve he was able to heal sick animals. And during the war when he was chief surgeon for a flotilla of minesweepers a number of 'miracle' cures took place under his hands. (The same story emphasised that, although guided by faith, he does not reject other forms of treatment.)

A fervent Christian, Dr Woodard has said that in faith healing it makes no difference whether healer and patient are Buddhist, Jewish, Muslim or any religion, and he has made pilgrimages to the East to discuss spiritual matters with sages and gurus of non-Christian faiths.

Our meeting was not in a sanctuary or quiet town house but in his busy doctor's office, between patients, on Devonshire Place—just a stone's throw from Mme Tussaud's. As we talked, roaring waves of London traffic ground past the office window.

Brisk, talkative, a stocky man in a dark business suit, with iron convictions and an audacious sense of humour, Dr Woodard glanced at the Questionnaire for Healers I proposed to leave with him and said he, too, was writing a book on spiritual healing. Reaching into a drawer, he gave me a sheaf of pamphlets entitled, *The Ministry of Caring for the Sick and Suffering* and suggested they 'might be a guide' to me.

They are published, he said, by the Fellowship of Christian Healing Trust, 'a very, very large trust I've built up over twenty-five years', and express the beliefs that underlie his healing practice. I slipped them in my bag for later reading.

'It's a cosmic moment. We're coming into our own very soon,' Dr Woodard began, setting a fast clip for our interview. 'You see, allopathic medicine is in its Dark Age with drug addiction, its use of frightful methods of healing, and disasters like one thalidomide tragedy liable to happen at any time. So now I go around the world speaking on the subject, "The Recovery of Health Through God and Nature", that's my theme! Nature cure is away ahead of allopathic medicine in its answer to the problems of sickness.

'I'm also associated with a terrific undertaking, largely medical, that's developing on the Costa del Sol in Spain where they are building up a whole village settlement surrounding a nature cure clinic. They've asked me to co-operate by teaching all these wealthy Americans and others how to relax and meditate.

'I plan to give them a meditation technique that will be perhaps two steps better than the transcendental meditation of Maharishi Yoga,' Woodard rushed on. 'Two years ago I met him and discovered that he was potentially very good, but there's a lot more to it. You see, we are only now able to measure the *degree* to which a person knows how to relax and meditate.

'I have here this amazing machine produced by the Medical Research Laboratories which is called an Alpha Sensor,' he said, drawing forward on his desk a black, box-like object. 'Now, normally one is producing beta waves on the electro-encephalograph, and we've known for years that if you have a tumour or migraine or epileptic fits or even asthma, those waves change. But what wasn't known until quite recently—and we were largely helped with this by the Americans—is that if you go very, very still and meditate or relax, your beta waves change into alpha waves.

'Now some people, of course, can put on this degree of relaxation. The average old duchess who thinks she's paying for something will sort of pretend just to satisfy herself and you. But there's not an alpha wave on the horizon, let alone anywhere near! It varies, you see, from one person to another, but we can identify the alpha waves, and this is a tremendous step forward because in our classes in meditation we can now separate people into advanced, medial and beginners groups by the amount of alpha they are producing.

'We are scientists, you see. We don't just presume these things or tell them to people just to boost their ego. We have to establish it scientifically. Now, you'll find that these people in the National Federation of Spiritual Healers make the most unholy claims at times, God bless them! And they are actually advised against the scientific analysis of what they are doing.'

Dr Woodard explained that the Alpha Sensor reveals how many alpha waves the subject is producing by sounding a 'bleep'. 'I haven't time to demonstrate it to you this morning although I'm more than willing to later,' he said, 'but you get a bleep that increases in frequency as you relax. In other words, alpha waves are bleeping and nothing else comes through because it's confined purely to alpha distribution.' He added that its cost is high, unfortunately, and only a few are available.

I asked the doctor what happens physically and mentally when producing high alpha, in other words, why meditate?

'Well, the scientists will call them relaxation waves and leave it at that, but we go further. How do you identify them? They give you a lovely feeling of warmth in your muscles, in your glands, in your joints, in your tummy, in your lungs, they alter your breathing, they give you a feeling of peace and any expert in the field of medical diagnosis will tell you they produce benefit with regard to all sorts of complicated things. They produce a feeling of well-being which can be reflected in the whole of your cosmos.'

'Is it true that in producing more alpha the psychic sense is stimulated or awakened?'

'There's no shadow of a doubt that it's a psychic thing at that stage,' he said, and he sermonised for a moment on the gifts that are realised at various levels of meditation, with the psychic at the lower level, 'a much lower level than spiritual healing'.

'Now the psychic gifts are the intuitive, like clairvoyance, telepathy, magnetism, water divining, all sorts of charismatic things, and these can be developed intellectually, or even with the aid of machinery.

'On the other hand, with the spiritual gifts—any guru will tell you this—you reach a certain point of involvement in meditation where you can't of your own accord go any further. Contemplation reveals it! You contemplate in silence, in stillness, and there suddenly comes a point where you're given a direct gift from God!

'Now Paul referred to this in I Corinthians. He said the spiritual gifts are direct gifts to you and me. You can't buy them, you can't develop them *intellectually,* but we can lay ourselves open to God, let go and let God just pour his spirit on us. The gifts of the spirit are true wisdom, true knowledge, true faith, true healing—that means whole-making, as Christ did it—true discernment, true gift of tongues, true interpretation of tongues.

'Now the *fruits* of the spirit are a stage further. The fruits of the spiritual gifts are joy, peace, purity, confidence, trust, fulfilment—the complete integration. You can't get as far as that without committing your consciousness to Christ and completely submitting to God, you see. A humble obedience to God, that's how it's done. And you say, "What about Buddhists and the Hindus and so on?" Well they, oddly enough, have learned to use silence much better than we have—we so-called Christians. But they can only go so far with it. The rest is a gift of God and it's not anything they anticipate, and thus don't receive.'

'Isn't Buddha the same for them as Christ is to us?' I asked.

'Oh yes, because we talk in terms of the Universal Christ. Our Christ bears very little resemblance to the traditional "churchianity" Christ which is about as backward as you could imagine! I mean, the traditional Christian church is the most restricting of the major religions, it's utterly prejudiced by dogma, theology, ritual, all sorts of nonsense, you see.

'Now the Cosmic Christ is represented in Buddhism and Mohammedanism and all of them but, in my opinion, the only perfect manifestation of the Cosmic Christ was in Jesus Christ. Of course other people don't hold that view. But in talking to His Holiness the Dalai Lama it's fascinating to say to him, "What is the significance of reincarnation and karma?" and to hear him say, "It's taught by the Lord Buddha and of course it all has essential meaning, but what is much more important is to recognise what he said about *now*, and what the Lord Jesus Christ said about *now*." This is the Dalai Lama speaking . . . He says "Recognise your potential now, don't get restricted by karma or the thought of reincarnation and being able to come back and do better next time."

'Jesus said, these things I do—heal all manner of sickness, raise the dead—and these things you can do *now*. The main thing is to recognise your potential *now*. I can do all things through Christ. I can. And I will claim them because of my ultimate faith in him.

'What occupies a lot of my thought now is the need to respect and recognise what these other great religions have to offer us, which is enormous. You've no idea how much value there is to a study of Buddhist relaxation in silence. It's *essential*. I don't know of any Christian church in this country or in the world for that matter where they begin to recognise the essential meaning of silence.'

'Except the Quakers! I'm a Quaker, and I know what you mean about the importance of silence.'

'Oh, yes, yes, the Quakers. Well, they are fairly good but they're not as silent as George Fox meant them to be! But here's another interesting observation. When you go into a church and receive the sacrament, the priest, in *talking*, is only producing beta waves. He's making it jolly difficult for himself to produce more spiritual waves! When you sing a hymn there's not an alpha wave in the place, and yet . . . Well, we can prove it now at last, you cannot really receive the gift of the Spirit in what Christ meant to institute with the breaking of the bread and wine—without silence!

'Have you discovered the value of fasting?' Dr Woodard asked, abruptly changing his line of thought. I had to admit that I hadn't, although I knew there was value in it.

'Well, there's no such thing as an evolved alpha producer who hasn't learned the disciplines! Most peoples' trouble is they're so totally undisciplined, either food-wise, or smoking, or in their thoughts. Thoughts are the most appallingly destructive things to most people, and the Holy Spirit never uses the negative. This Spirit we're talking about never says don't, can't, mustn't. You have to wait until it says "Speak with boldness" or shut up, got it? Be still and *know.*'

Would he give me his opinion of the Spiritualists? I asked.

'Well, all right. I love everybody, so Spiritualists are particularly in my prayers because they can so easily get off-track . . . It's a crankish thing to take up a particular aspect or factor and try and develop it out of proportion to the rest. I don't know a disciplined Spiritualist, and the crowd in this country are the most mixed-up in the lot. They're even more mixed up than psychiatrists!' he laughed.

'It was a spirit doctor who told me that I should try to find a medical man who also practises spiritual healing.'

'Well, splendid!'

'Do you know Mary Rogers, the healer, who is the wife of George Rogers who was in Parliament?'

'I haven't met them, but I do have the greatest admiration for them.' The doorbell of his office buzzed, and Dr Woodard left the room for a moment. When he returned his mood had suddenly changed to almost beatific.

'I went out of this room to the most supremely evolved human being,' he explained, 'a youngster, only eighteen and yet absolutely Christ-centred. He's just arrived from India where he spent two months to be with these very advanced types. Do you know Sai Baba? He's a very famous guru in Bombay . . .

'I hope you've got some material there that will help you,' Dr Woodard said as he saw me to the door.

That night I read through all nine of his pamphlets. They were written with directness as though speaking personally to the reader and included frequent touching references to the faith of children. The doctor's brash humour was all but invisible. Curiously enough, there was little mention of the Eastern philosophy that so intrigues him.

Pamphlets 1 and 6 were particularly interesting because of the way they complemented each other.

In the first, he proposes a 'Prayer of Faith for Healing' that must be firmly based on the certainty that it is God's will to heal and that our complete healing has therefore been promised. 'It is morally and psychologically wrong to approach this prayer in any spirit of doubt or hesitancy,' writes Woodard, so we are to imagine and expect and anticipate the best with the attitude that 'all things are possible to them that believe.' But the prayer also includes a request for grace to accept whatever happens, 'however difficult it is to understand' without 'jibing' or turning our backs on God. This sort of prayer, he says, does not command God what to do. Instead, we put ourselves or the people we have prayed for unconditionally into His hands.

In Pamphlet 6, he squarely faces the situation where the concerted prayers of many seem unavailing and the person prayed for dies. Woodard saw part of the answer in the words of a poet : 'We come from God; we return to God. We can, if we will, know, feel and identify with God now'.

14. Gwen Murray

THE NEXT HEALER on my list was Gwen Murray, and I was soon to discover, when we sat down to talk in her sanctuary, that she had come into healing from a different direction than the others.

Mrs Murray's house on Finchley Lane, in a London suburb, is an attractive brick and stucco house, with a clipped privet hedge and a small but colourful garden. She had greeted me at the door with cordiality, a woman of strong yet kindly presence, perhaps in her middle 60s, with short greying hair, glasses attached to a ribbon about her neck and the confident air of a schoolteacher.

The sanctuary to which she then led me must once have been the front parlour. It looked like a small chapel; the curved street-lined windows were of stained glass, there were rows of chairs, an upright piano and a pulpit. Colourful sky-blue walls blended with purple carpeting and a portrait of Christ hung over an altar of natural wood.

When I asked what the chairs were set out for, she explained that part of her healing work is lecturing on psychology 'but much more on the spiritual side'.

'I came into healing through psychology over forty years ago because my own father was so very ill,' she said. 'He was dying of pernicious anaemia and doctors had said no more could be done for him. My dear mother went to lectures at the International New Thought Alliance in search of something that might help.' A young girl then, she had gone along with her mother to hear every speaker and was soon 'heart and soul' in New Thought activities.

She found the lectures of the psychologist Harry Gaze so stimulating that she took them down in shorthand, and later sat by her father's bedside and referring to her notes, re-delivered the lecture, hoping the psychologist's teachings about the workings of the subconscious, the conscious and the superconscious minds, with a spiritual content added, would help him.

Then, knowing that her father, a very thrifty man who had worked hard all his life, would not want to see a season ticket to Mr Gaze's lectures series go to waste, she bought him a ticket. 'That did it,' she said. Her father not only got up and about but took the bus and tube right up to Aeolian Hall!

She began helping out at New Thought Alliance headquarters and one day heard an American lecturer who held her 'spellbound'. He was Walter Lanyon, whose inspirational teachings emphasised healing through belief in Christ and attaining a higher spiritual level. She attended his succeeding lectures. 'Then one evening after a lecture he said he saw me "bathed in light" and he knew I had to be a speaker and a healer.'

Returning after a speaking tour of the Continent, Walter Lanyon offered further guidance—she was to open a healing sanctuary in her home. 'I did,' said Mrs Murray, 'and this is it, and I've carried on ever since!

'Everything has just unfolded, I've no training whatsoever, but I do spend a great deal of time in prayer and meditation. I do my healing by the laying-on of hands and I feel the power going through me and through my hands. Subjects say they feel terrific heat going through their bodies.'

What does she experience when she meditates? 'I begin,' she said, 'by holding some spiritual thought, perhaps a text from the Bible, then I just drift off and get completely lost from this sphere.'

I asked Mrs Murray if she could describe any healings of children and she recalled the Jewish couple who came to her with a child they thought was deficient. She found him only backward, but he was in such a nervous state that she couldn't do anything for him while he was awake.

'He was on the go the whole time,' she recalled. 'So I said, "The only way is for me to treat him after he's asleep at night. If you are willing, I will come once a week and I will put him on my absent healing list." "Oh, anything," the father said, "I'll come and fetch you and take you back home." I did that for months. Sometimes I'd get there and the child would still be awake. Well, never mind, I'd say, and I used to sit and talk with the parents until he'd go to sleep. Then I would go up and be alone with him in the room.

'I never touched the child for fear of awakening him. I just put my hands as close to his body as I could. I knew the healing had to be done at the back of the head and the spine, and it was a remarkable thing—that child was always lying asleep facing the wall, and his back was always where I could treat it. I thought, well, this is really marvellous. I knew there was a power right beyond that was taking care of things! Never once did he turn facing me or lie on his back. I shall never forget that. After a while he got into a special school and began to go ahead, so they put him in a regular school and he's perfectly normal today.'

She has had cripples unable to walk come into her sanctuary and walk out perfectly all right, she said.

'There are instant miracles, but they are not in the majority,' Mrs Murray emphasised, 'and they are not always permanent. Because, you see, I think one has to be educated to it. There's got to be a change of mind, in thought, in attitude, in living habits. The Master said when he healed, "Now, go and sin no more". Well, he simply meant not to continue to behave in the same way you have been behaving.

'I know that ailing bodies need attention,' Mrs Murray continued, 'but I always go for their minds. I give them teaching. It's not just a question of come in, sit down and I'll put my hands on and that's that! No, I give teaching.

'But first of all I let them talk, and that lets me understand where they are, their attitudes toward family, their frame of mind, I see if there's any tension, resentment or hatred. It has to go, I'll say. You don't expect to get your healing until that's gone. I'm dealing with that first.'

The teaching she gives in her lectures is 'more on the spiritual side than pure psychology', Gwen Murray said. 'I take a passage from the Bible and then give it an interpretation in a way that will help us live our lives.'

15. Brigadier Firebrace

TOWARD THE END of my spiritual healing survey of England I had the good fortune to meet Brigadier Roy Charles Firebrace, a grand old man of psychic research, and a healer. Weeks later I was to hear him praised by the Reverend Alex Holmes for the 'tremendous job' he did some years ago as self-appointed watchdog for Britain's psychic and spiritualist societies in exposing fraudulent mediums, an effort that greatly benefited bona fide healers as well as honest mediums.

Now, sitting at his office desk in London, a mellowed but dignified old gentleman of eighty-three wearing a jaunty bow-tie, the Brigadier took a realistic glimpse of the psychic healing scene in his country, adding a few sidelights from his own experience.

But first I inquired about his Army career and learned that he had been a military attaché in Latvia, Estonia, Lithuania and Finland before the war. Then, having learned to speak Russian fluently, he served three years of the war in the British Embassy in Moscow. 'I handled all the Russians in England and interpreted between Molotov and Churchill, saw old Winston in action—a marvellous experience,' he said.

His research in the psychic field generally began forty-two years ago, Firebrace informed me, and he has practised healing mainly in the field of radionics, which he considers a form of mental healing with a spiritual power behind it.

'I'm a great believer in mind over matter and I believe that most, if not all, diseases are of the mind or soul and that spiritual healing works more on the mind, by changing the mind, than it does direct on the body,' he said.

'Can the ability to heal be developed by anyone with a deep desire to do it?' I asked.

'You could develop it to a limited extent, yes,' said the Brigadier. 'I believe the healing power of God can flow through us if we are willing to use it. I also believe that the purer the channel, the more effective and the more miraculous, if you like, will be the healing.

'We have the example of Christ who was able to tune into the highest level and therefore produce instantaneous cures. Few reach that height. Some reach it for just a moment or so, or on certain occasions.'

'Then you believe there are several "levels" of healing?'

'Yes. The famous healers have the higher gift naturally. It comes out at a certain age in their life. They may not know they possess it. Many sort of run into it! I think spiritual healing on the high level is an inborn gift, given you for this life. I am an astrologer, and I would expect it to be shown in the horoscope. The magnetic healing on the lower level of development can be effective, but it is not what I call true spiritual healing.'

'Do you think those less gifted, working at the lower levels, as you say, should not try to tackle difficult cases?'

'Perhaps, although if they are honest, and most of them are, it is all right for them to try because you can't always tell whether you're going to help the person or not.

'I'm going to be quite frank and say there are many people in England who want to heal, who are quite honest, but who have not got the gift for healing at the higher levels. And I don't think these psychic societies and healing groups are, on the whole, very effective . . . But I don't think for a moment that healing is easy! It is not. We can all get better at it, and I think we shall get better. If it were easy there would be more healing of the higher nature than there is,' he said.

The Brigadier noted that instantaneous, permanent healings happen all too rarely, perhaps occasionally at religious gatherings such as a Welsh revivalist meeting. And, recalling a visit to Lourdes fifteen years ago when he spoke to the doctor in charge who had to certify to miracles, he said at that time there were only thirty-three recorded.

'Although "Heal the sick" was one of the commands of Christ, healing has been neglected by the church,' he commented, 'because, I suppose, they have not found it very effective. That's the only reason I can think of.' He questioned whether too much hope has been placed in the miraculous type of healing.

'The patients of even the most gifted healers have relapses. I've known people who go to—I won't give his name—who have had immediate benefit, but it wears out in a few days. I think they should return to that healer and have a *course* of healing!

'And yet, I have seen hunchbacks straightened in public healing demonstrations that remained straight. I have seen a boy carried on to the platform because he couldn't walk, a boy of ten or eleven, who walked off the platform. I was acting as chairman and Harry Edwards was the healer. I said to the mother, "How long is it since he walked?" and she said, "He has never walked." I regard Harry Edwards an extremely gifted healer. I wish we could get more healing like this.'

'Have you found that the attitude of the patient is important?'

'The main thing is that he does not set up any kind of opposition. It is best if he can maintain a strictly hopeful attitude, without any sense of "I wonder if it will fail?" That is a negative thought, you see. But an attitude of faith on the part of the patient is *not* necessary.'

'Animals,' he went on, 'are easier to heal than persons because they don't know they are being healed. I would also say that absent healing, as applied to people who don't know they are being healed, is often extremely effective.

'I had a case of a woman who was dying. She had suffered a uterine haemorrhage for twenty-five days and somebody phoned to ask if I would do what I could. I gave her treatment and the haemorrhage stopped in twenty-four hours. She recovered completely. She did not know she was being treated!'

I asked Brigadier Firebrace to please explain the radionics method which he said he had used in this case. As I understood it, from the explanation given by the US physicist William Tiller, to an Academy of Parapsychology and Medicine symposium in California, radionics involves use of a rather mysterious instrument, best-known of which is the 'De la Warr Box' made in England. According to Tiller's theory, the instrument can be tuned into the 'wavefield' of the patient through a 'witness', usually a spot of his blood, and can detect any abnormalities and then send out healthy waveforms, expressed in numbers, to correct the condition. Firebrace gave a slightly different interpretation :

'There are a number of opinions, but I have decided myself that it is a form of mental telepathy—the conveyance of symbols which you, the operator, consider are healing numbers, for a particular disease. You implant your belief in those numbers which you set on the boxes and that is transmitted telepathically to the patient. I don't think there is any more in it than that. Now the late George De la Warr would not have agreed with me, but that is my belief.'

'Then it is a psychic process involving the mind rather than the box?' I said.

'It is a psychic process. I do not think that everybody could operate that box. And I think you can operate without a box. I know so-called radionic practitioners who only write the numbers down on a bit of paper. They don't use the box at all. So I think it is mental telepathy, but with a good intent, a healing intent behind it. The great thing is the belief and the intent of the operator. You've got to believe that what you are doing will help, do you see?' He said the box is an aid in keeping straight which numbers are associated with different parts of the body and which are helpful in various diseases.

I asked him about his personal religious beliefs.

'I am unorthodox,' he said. 'I believe that the true basis of all religions is one. I think truth is expressed in different forms, and I have respect for all religions. I would not put a label on myself. I am interested in the spiritualist philosophy—I do not consider Spiritualism a religion. I think we survive death. I personally have had enough evidence to convince me to a very high degree that it is possible to communicate to a limited extent with those who have died. I've done it myself. But I don't accept it as a religious belief. I think they overemphasise it actually.'

Brigadier Firebrace noted that the College of Psychic Studies, which has undertaken serious research on the matter of survival, does not consider 'the fact that if you communicate with Tom, Dick or Harry it constitutes a religious act', and he is of the same opinion.

'I'm primarily a researcher,' he said. 'My interest is the study of the super-physical, that which is beyond the physical. I have studied every form of psychic phenomenon.'

'When you are healing,' I asked, 'can you describe to me your state of mind? Do you meditate?'

'It is a calmness of mind. Yes, you can call it meditation. But I don't go into that deep Eastern meditation in which I think there can be a lot of self-deception. Personally, I don't care what anybody else does. It's in the calmness of mind that Spirit can approach you, and to get calm in this present world of ours is not too easy.'

'Do you try to attune yourself to a Higher Power?'

'Yes, and simply through calmness, and the belief. Not through any invocation necessarily.'

'Do you try to sense a one-ness with the Universal consciousness?'

'I try and hold to that, as truth, but at that moment I don't make a direct effort. If I need it, it will come, do you see?'

'And what is your attitude toward the patient?' I asked.

'It must be a desire to help and the belief that you *can* help. If you are doubtful, then you won't succeed. And if you are not feeling well it is almost bound to induce some kind of subconscious doubt in your mind.'

Now what about karmic suffering? I asked him. Did he believe it could be the cause of illnesses that weren't helped by healing?

'I believe there is such a thing as karma, that is to say, that we come into this world with certain advantages and very likely with some disabilities. Now our task in this life, and it is all very difficult, is to make the most of the good which has been given to us, not concentrate it entirely on the self, and to *transmute* the difficult aspects of our life onto a higher plane. This is how I try to look at the problem of karma.

'I've seen examples where severely afflicted people have tried to do this under very difficult circumstances and have won happiness. Their physical disability does not always disappear, but they rise above it,' Brigadier Firebrace said.

16. Spiritual Healing at the SAGB

THE SPIRITUALIST ASSOCIATION of Great Britain is housed in a cream-coloured mansion in Belgrave Square, and there I discovered a hive of psychic activities that go on 'round the clock'. Not only do they have training classes and psychic development circles where people can develop and increase their healing abilities, but there are healing clinics where anyone can walk in and be treated free of charge.

The head instructor in healing is Ursula Roberts, well-known as an excellent healer and clairvoyant. She gives three classes a year, each lasting six weeks, with twenty in a class; the cost—£1.05.

On my first visit, I investigated the Spiritual Healing Clinic on the third floor (conveniently, I had a sinus condition that really needed treating).

After a short wait with some friendly older people, I was directed toward the treatment rooms past a sign that read, 'Silence is Requested. God is Giving Proof of His Existence by Spiritual Healing. Meditation on this is Desired'.

A beautiful young Indian woman in a crisp white coat stepped forward and led me to her cubicle, behind a curtain. Her name was Doreen Gatland and she had a soothing, gentle manner. She asked me to sit on a low, square stool and after I told her about my sinus, I asked how she had happened to become a healer and what sort of training she had taken.

As a child growing up in Bangalore, she said, she had wanted to be a doctor, and a few years ago, feeling on the verge of a nervous breakdown, had come to this clinic on the advice of a friend. The treatment was wonderfully relaxing and she decided this was the kind of healing she wanted to do. Her healer encouraged her by saying she already had the ability, and when an ailing neighbour asked for healing, she agreed to try.

The experience was very draining, however, and her husband, an Englishman, urged her to find out the proper way to do it. So she enrolled in a psychic development class at the SAGB. After six months the teacher told her she had learned enough to give healing, she said.

Before treating my sinus, Mrs Gatland meditated briefly. Then she placed her hands on my head. Slowly she moved them up and down my spine and then put her fingertips over the sinus cavities. I felt a deep penetrating heat. She said she saw a lovely purple light which she sees 'only occasionally'. (With eyes shut I saw blue!)

'We always ask people with serious illnesses to see a medical doctor first,' Mrs Gatland continued, 'and we will give healing in co-operation with medical treatment. And if it is obvious that minor medication or certain foods will be helpful, we suggest them.' She thought AH Antihistamine would be good for me. I thanked her. My sinuses seemed a little clearer. I dropped a donation into the offering plate as I left the clinic.

A few minutes later I was sitting in the lounge with Thomas Johanson, Secretary of the SAGB, a warm outgoing man, perhaps in his early fifties, with wavy, collar-length hair, who had been a portrait painter with work hung in the Royal Academy, and later a technical writer and illustrator in electronics.

I asked him if he would kindly list all the healing services offered by the SAGB, and he said there were twelve healing clinics, each with a leader, all open seven days a week. About one hundred healers worked for the Association and they treated five to six hundred people weekly.

Then, he continued, there was a band of healers who conducted absent healing nightly at ten o'clock for those sending in their names to him with a description of their illnesses. This also applies to sick animals. Then, on Tuesday evenings, psychological healing was available, and it was extended to people suffering from obsessions. There were also Ursula Roberts' training classes for healers, and psychic development classes.

I asked him to describe a psychic development class.

'Well,' he said, 'you must first be interviewed by the leader to find out if you are suitable material. Then you sit around in a circle, limited to twelve in a very quiet room, with a leader at the head. The leader shows you how to concentrate and go quietly within yourself. Some in the group may be natural trance mediums so the leader must sense what kind of influences are impinging on his students since there are psychic pitfalls. You have to keep out the wrong kind of influence. After a little time you'll see or hear impressions or symbols. It's the leader's job to tell you what the symbols mean. Many ministers come to sit in these classes. They'll say they want to be able to see and hear things psychically. Often the leader will inform them that they are natural healers. Basically, the participants learn to attune mentally to the psychic healing force through prayer and meditation.'

'How can a person tell if he's a natural healer?' I asked.

'If he has a natural compassion for his fellow man, is sad whenever they suffer and has the inborn desire to help them, and I don't think this type needs any training whatsoever.'

'Not even a simple course in anatomy?'

'Anatomy doesn't need to come into it at all. Just ask yourself who or what is doing the healing? I say—and most would say—the healer himself cannot heal. He is acting for a Higher Intelligence. Do you suppose for a moment the Higher Intelligence needs the personal awareness of that person on earth?'

'Doesn't the healer have to know something about the human body to make an accurate diagnosis?' I asked.

'It's not ever necessary for the healer to know what the person is suffering from. It's only necessary to know he needs help. Diagnosis is not healing. Suppose the person's got a pain and you know it's in the heart. Do you switch on a special technique? If they've got a pain you put your hand on it and ask for help, that's all.'

I asked him if he had any special advice for would-be healers?

'Yes, there's one practice that is happily dying out—combing the aura, or cleansing it. I was instructed by a very old and established healer and he told me it was essential. Start at the head and go down to the feet and throw the stuff all over the place! This I decry for the simple reason that the first day I went into clinic work I realised I was treating people who were apprehensive, despondent —doctors had given up hope for them. I realised a healer's first job was to make a patient perfectly at ease and calm and that these motions would frighten the life out of them! So I didn't bother and they were healed anyway! I still find old healers doing it, but I don't allow it in my clinic.'

'Do doctors ever come to the SAGB?'

'Yes, and I have found that many osteopaths and chiropractors are natural healers. Medical students often come here wanting to know if they are naturally gifted. I find that many doctors use their psychic healing gift subconsciously.'

Would he, I asked, compare the faith healing practised by Christian Scientists with the Spiritualists' approach to healing?

'In Christian Science, man is created perfect and disharmony is created by man himself. And, as man is capable of creating disharmony and disease, he has the ability to eliminate it, and does so by complete faith in God. Of course, very few of us can do this . . . The Spiritualist invokes help not only from Divine Spirit but also from helpers in the spirit world who come forward not only to inspire the healer regarding diagnosis, but also to add their prayers that the healing power can flow through the patient. That is basically the difference.'

'Can you estimate how many Spiritualist healers there are in your member churches? Or in the Spiritualist sect?'

'Well, the SAGB, which is one hundred years old this year, is a commonwealth of twenty-seven Spiritualist churches, all with high standards, stable finances and a good, respectable platform, and all have their own healing bands. There must be a few thousand Spiritualist churches, though it's difficult to count them because any person can set up a Spiritualist church—you can convert an old stable and nothing can stop you! Then the Spiritualist National Union, with about five thousand members—the SAGB has 8,000— has a Healing Guild, not as large as the National Federation of Spiritual Healers, and the Greater World also has healer members. Greater World emphasises Christ's teachings. They and the SNU share the same Spiritualist philosophy but differ in administration.'

That afternoon Mr Johanson arranged an interview for me with Eileen Roberts, president of the Union of Spiritualist Mediums, and it was most enlightening.

Mrs Roberts, blonde, with a predilection for pink—her chiffon scarf, dress and even her glasses' rims were all pink—was serenity itself. 'Everyone can, to some extent, do healing through the mind,' she said confidently. 'And the desire to help another is really enough to commence it.'

She added that everyone has magnetic healing powers, if they're healthy, but through meditation they come to a higher awareness and a recognition that there's something more than themselves operating in the healing.

Identifying the three layers of consciousness as (1) your normal (2) your subconscious—'everything that's gone into your make-up, your experience'—and (3) your superconsciousness or higher consciousness, she gave this formula for activating the healing energy:

'Through meditation close your mind to the normal consciousness of things around you and listen to your subconscious. Listen to all the thoughts that are stored away, extraneous thoughts, until you reach a certain stage of stillness. Then focus your mind with a desire to help someone. That desire is itself a spiritual quality, therefore it stirs Higher Self and begins to activate the healing energies of life. You find new thoughts, new ideas, a greater desire to help and be of service.

'It is really the Higher Self becoming conscious of an at-one-ment with the universal forces of energy. The healer must have a sense of affinity for all living things and therefore with his patient. One could say there's no separateness between living things.

'The healer, with development, becomes conscious eventually of being in a stream of energy, or that it's flowing through him. He may not, of course. He may merely have a great desire to help and a serenity he transmits to his patient.

'I think it also has to be recognised that healing can take place when the recipient is unaware of any healing being sent to him, either while he's asleep or deeply involved in material work, because it's the patient's Higher Self which accepts the attunement to the energy being received. The patient can be attuned by choice, but need not necessarily be. Animals and babies are healed in this way. Even those who don't believe it possible are healed. If it's done by absent healing it can manifest and assert in people who are unbelievers or even against it.'

'Would you say that spiritual healing is on a higher level than the other psychic abilities?' I asked.

'I'd say yes. It's not just a psychic power, it's a spiritual power. You can have a lot of excellent psychics who work on a very material level and use their power of perception in relationship with the sitter, whereas a healing medium attunes himself always to a higher level of sensitivity and spiritual awareness.'

'Do you work as a healer as well as a medium?'

'When called upon, yes. My work is not especially to develop healing power but I've endeavoured to use my mediumistic powers wherever needed, and in my early years I found I could be used for healing,' she said.

'Do you still work at perfecting your psychic abilities?'

'Certainly. I would insist there is no such thing as a fully trained instrument. We should all be open to receive further instruction and training.'

I asked: 'What is your conception of spirit helpers or spirit doctors?'

'I believe they exist, most definitely. Those dedicated to the business of healing in this phase of life will still have the same interest and desire to heal in the next. It's a spiritual quest on their part to help others to heal.'

'Is it true that you pace up and down like a caged lion before giving a demonstration of clairvoyance?' I asked, referring to an interview with her I'd read in *Psychic News.* 'Isn't that just the opposite of what a healer does to prepare himself?'

'It depends on what you're working for,' she said, smiling. 'In healing, I'd say, yes, you need quiet and meditation in order to reach the superconsciousness through the universal relationship. But in mediumship, clairvoyance, clairaudience, you need your psychic energies activated. My own auric field has to be stimulated!'

My final question, 'Do you see any connection between spiritual healing and world peace?' brought a warm, spontaneous reply.

'Yes. In my opinion, if man could release his potential to assist his brother through the mediumship of spiritual healing, he could revolutionise the world, because he would help man to recognise his inner spiritual self!'

Since one of my chief objectives in coming to England had been to find out what kind of training courses were available for would-be healers and which were considered the best, my next quest led me to Ursula Roberts, whose classes at the SAGB had been highly recommended to me by several knowledgeable people.

Fortunately, she had written down her healing philosophy in a slim booklet entitled *Hints for Healers,* and when I talked to her she assured me that it was just as complete and accurate a picture of her modus operandi as she could give me verbally. This made it easier for me to make a few comparisons between the instruction available at the SAGB—and the NFSH, whose study course for trainees was based on *A Guide to Spirit Healing,* by Harry Edwards.

For example the preliminary steps suggested are very much the same : the student should set aside fifteen to thirty minutes each day, or three times a week, to develop his 'spiritual faculties'. He should find a quiet place where he will be undisturbed and sit upright in a chair, perhaps with arm rests in order to be perfectly comfortable. The light should be dimmed so that the optic nerve is not stimulated. He should relax completely and breathe deeply for a few seconds, then say a simple, spontaneous prayer to God.

At this point, however, the two teachers would lead their students to higher consciousness by varying spiritual routes :

Ursula Roberts instructs, 'Dwell in thought upon an aspect of goodness, such as mercy, compassion, love, purity, peace, endurance, strength, self-sacrifice, forgiveness, self-control. Think about this aspect of goodness, how it should be expressed. How you have seen it in the life of another person. The manner in which it should influence your actions. How it was expressed by Jesus Christ . . . If you find it lacking in yourself, pray for guidance that you may achieve it . . .

Harry Edwards says : 'Let the mind be gently contemplative, thinking of contact with the spirit people and of the purpose for which the attunement is intended—to heal the sick, take away pain and to remove causes of disease . . . Let your mind dwell on beautiful things, take a mental holiday in a garden of beauty. Float in your imagination down a peaceful river. Contemplate the idealism portrayed in the Scriptures.'

Ursula Roberts calls this process 'concentration' while Harry Edwards calls it 'mental abandonment', explaining that since one can't make his mind a blank by mental effort or concentration he should 'dwell lightly' on these uplifting ideas.

After much practice, they both say, the student will sense an attunement. In Ursula Roberts' words : 'It is as if Silence comes to us, rather than we going to it. When it comes, after due preparation, it is as if a powerful stillness holds the mind and every particle of our being in such deep tranquillity that it saturates every aspect of our person and leaves us forever longing for an opportunity to experience such bliss again . . . You should now feel utterly at peace and in tune with Infinite Goodness. You may feel as if the room is full of light, or you may feel the presence of your guardian spirit friends . . .'

And in the words of Harry Edwards: 'Attunement is a subtle condition, very difficult to describe in words. It is a semi-in-between state between consciousness and spirit awareness. There is a modern teenage word that is somewhat near an explanation . . . known as being "sent". It is the essential factor a healer needs to establish en rapport with the source of the healing and the recipient. Healers possess the high motives of love and compassion for the sick. Healing from spirit also has these two great qualities. Thus it is, that through love and compassion from spirit, blending in with the same qualities in the healer that the attunement is brought into being . . . It requires no technique, it is a blending of high motives.' At another point he puts it this way: 'When there is any transmission . . . there must be attunement between transmitter and receiver. If we are to act as transmitters for the spirit forces, we must possess some spirit quality to enable us to do so.'

Both teachers then suggest ways to deepen the attunement by spiritual development, praying for others, living according to a code of high values, fasting to eliminate accumulated impurities stored in the cells and so forth. They then each prescribe ways to attune with the patient when doing contact healing.

Ursula Roberts: 'One way is to hold the hands of the patient for a few minutes; another way is to place your hands on the head of the patient or on his shoulders. We call this establishing contact, and while you are doing this the spirit helpers should be able to examine the patient through the psychometric link created by the contact of your hands.'

Harry Edwards: 'The healer feels a sympathy for him or her and then seeks to "blend in" with the patient. After inducing in them a relaxed state, it is well for the healer to spend just a moment to deepen his attunement with both spirit and patient. By this, we have the perfect state of healer attuned to spirit and to the patient, bringing about a state of "oneness" with all three.'

Both healers also advise students against giving diagnoses:

Ursula Roberts says, 'Leave the guides to deal with the illness their own way. You will find they will convey to you a strong impression as to the *cause* of the trouble and this you will explain to the patient. The cause may be different and far removed from the symptoms diagnosed by the doctors . . . Do not have any thought as to what is wrong with the patient . . . You are simply a channel for the Love Power.'

Harry Edwards says, 'As a general rule it is not advisable for the healer to offer diagnosis. Firstly, he may be wrong—and remember in passing that medical diagnoses are also often wrong—secondly, the patient may be overimpressed by the healer's comments, and so they induce a state of mental anxiety . . . they can so easily be misunderstood.'

What do the two teachers say about the 'healing guides' and the 'healing energies' and their relation to healing? Here are a few samples:

Ursula Roberts: 'What do the healing guides do? These unselfish souls come to blend their healing magnetism with ours. In this way they reinforce our healing magnetism and make it very much stronger. Without their aid, we find that a medium soon tires, because the patient can absorb magnetism directly from the medium. With their help, we find that the medium can give help to numberless patients and feel thoroughly revitalised when he has finished, because the guides are able to draw power from a more spiritually advanced realm than can be touched by the medium . . . Our guides can pour into the etheric mould created by our thought some of the spiritual magnetism they possess. Thus, if a patient has a crooked bone in his arm and the healer, while he has his hand on the arm, holds in his mind the vision of the bone as it should be, an etheric mould is created, into which the guide may, if he wishes, pour a healing magnetism. This mould can then be applied to the arm somewhat after the nature of a plaster cast and in time the arm should straighten.'

Harry Edwards: 'It seems a logical assumption that through the healer's faculty of attunement with Spirit he is used as a transformer for the change, becoming like a laboratory where the spirit forces are converted into physical ones through him and are directed by the guides to the site of the healing need.

'Hard and fast ideas should be avoided. It need not be the healer's hand that is the terminal for the flow of healing energies to the patient. They may flow to the patient direct. The fact is that a chemical change is induced within the patient . . . In absent healing . . . a similar process of transformation takes place through the spirit self of the patient.'

The four study courses of the NFSH are, of course, more comprehensive than Mrs Roberts' booklet. Of special interest is the history of spiritual healing, beginning with primitive man 100,000 years ago, based on anthropological writings and running right up to the present. It suggests that Jesus of Nazareth was 'trained by the Essenes, a strict Jewish sect that widely practised spiritual healing' and it notes the role of Spiritualism in the mid-19th century in 'recapturing the gifts of the early Christian Church'.

Of even more importance is the section on ethics in Study Course No. 1. Some sample regulations for healers :

> 'Do not practise dentistry.
>
> Do not treat venereal disease.
>
> Do not attend women in actual childbirth or within ten days thereafter unless emergency.
>
> Do not sell herbal medicine unless sold in a 'shop'.
>
> Do not sell even in a shop medicines other than those produced by drying, crushing or comminuting a plant or plants.
>
> Do not treat animals by physical as opposed to spiritual remedies.
>
> Do not publish any advertisement offering to treat cancer, tuberculosis, Bright's disease, cataract, diabetes, epilepsy, glaucoma, locomotorataxy or paralysis.'

If a healer is asked to treat the child of parents who have not sought medical attention for their child first, he should obtain a signed statement from the parents to the effect that they were warned by the healer to call a doctor in to see their child.

17. Distant Healing at the College of Psychic Studies

THE COLLEGE OF PSYCHIC STUDIES, I was told, has a very efficient Distant Healing operation. They keep complete and accurate records on every recipient, the idea being to measure the results of their healing bands' efforts.

Founded in 1884, the College is non-religious, non-profit, and 'fosters a spirit of free inquiry into the psychical field'. A prestigious institution because of its integrity, it has a library of 10,000 books on psychical research and related fields, the most comprehensive of its kind in Great Britain, and it offers conferences and lectures open to the public.

The idea of pinning down the results of group healing statistically interested me greatly because I had always wanted our ARE healing group in New York to do some kind of follow-up. We were always sending healing to long lists of people requesting it, most of whom never notified us of their progress or lack of it!

Arriving at the College's building at 16 Queensberry Place, South Kensington, an old-fashioned town house of fading elegance, I inquired at the desk how I could send Distant Healing to my cousin in Virginia Beach who was going through a painful recovery after the removal of his right lung. I was given a form to fill out as follows:

Please return to :

The Healing Secretary
College of Psychic Studies Ltd.
16 Queensberry Place,
London, S.W.7

APPLICATION FOR DISTANT HEALING

This healing does not replace medical treatment but is intended to supplement it.

The patient (or sponsor) will be asked to report briefly once a month on progress made.

First name and surname of patient

Mr
Mrs
Miss ....

Address of patient, ONLY if patient will report

....
....

(IF patient CANNOT report Name and Address of sponsor who will then be responsible for report)

....
....
....

Does the patient know that healing is being requested? ....

If not, please give reason ....

Age category of patient:
Infant   Child   Teenager   Adult   Elderly
(please tick)

Complaint ....

When did it start? ....

Give brief details ....

State preferred time for healing, during which the patients are asked to rest quietly if possible.

Mondays from	11.00 to 11.30 a.m.	
Wednesdays	9.30 to 10.00 p.m.	
Tuesdays and		
Fridays	3.00 to 3.30 p.m.	

Notes on healing and instructions for subsequent reports will be sent to the patient or sponsor on receipt of this application.

I filled in the information and was assured that the Healing Secretary, Rosemary Beard, wife of the College's president, Paul Beard, would be in touch with my cousin.

There are several healing bands of six to twelve members sending Distant Healing at the four half-hour time periods, and all are volunteers, the desk attendant informed me. Mrs Beard's job is to write each patient and ask for a report, and in three weeks to follow-up with a second letter, and so on until the patient no longer needs help.

(Many weeks later my cousin wrote to me in consternation because he had neglected while on summer vacation to make his report within the month and had received word that the healing would stop since he apparently no longer needed it. He quickly shot off an air mail letter of apology and had the healing reinstated. He got steadily better and wrote me recently to say, 'I'm feeling much better than three months ago and I wrote Mrs Beard of the CPS to that effect, thanking her for their help and implying they could "turn off" the healing now. By the way, is there any way I can make a contribution or donation to them? And is it proper to do so?' I suggested he ask Mrs Beard about the proprieties.)

As I understand it, this is a research programme of the college and presumably the results will be announced when enough data has been collected.

18. The Quakers and Healing

I HAD SEEN no trace of spiritual healing activity during my twelve years of active membership in the Society of Friends, although I had been told by a knowledgeable fellow-member of the Fifteenth Street Meeting in New York that George Fox (1624-1690), the founder of Quakerism, had mentioned spiritual healing in his letters and that a hard-to-find Quaker pamphlet by Henry J. Cadbury told of his 'miracle' healings.

Then, just before leaving for England, I read in Leslie D. Weatherhead's encyclopaedic book, *Psychology, Religion and Healing*, that there was a London-based Friends Spiritual Healing Fellowship. He also mentioned a Quaker pamphlet entitled, *The Place of Spiritual Healing in the Society of Friends*, in which Dr Howard E. Collier, a medical man, and Sydney A. Hurren, a member of the Institute of Hygiene, sought to stimulate interest among their fellow Quakers in spiritual healing work.

According to Weatherhead, Collier and Hurren hoped to convince Friends that spiritual healing was 'something they can and ought to be doing', that they should prepare themselves for it and develop Quaker Healing Groups, while studying the techniques, methods and effects of spiritual and group healing. They also proposed that Friends 'proclaim a "Gospel-Message" concerning Health, Disease-Prevention and Healing'. For more information, readers were referred to Friends' House, Euston Road, London.

In London, I inquired at Friends' House, as suggested, and found that the aforementioned Fellowship, now re-named the Friends'

Fellowship of Healing, was founded back in 1936 and that the very timely-sounding pamphlet by the two Quakers was written in 1938! The Fellowship's secretary, Joan Hackwell, was away at a conference, however, and I had to wait a few weeks before being supplied with the information I needed by mail.

'The Fellowship consists of forty Prayer Groups whose members regularly uphold those for whom prayer is asked,' Miss Hackwell wrote in a cordial letter, 'with a Postal Group of isolated members and about four hundred other individual members who share our views.

'Although we have grown steadily over the years, we have not so far been successful in getting Friends generally to accept spiritual healing as part of the Quaker ministry,' she continued, 'and we are not yet officially recognised by the Society, even though there is much more interest and understanding of our work than was formerly the case.'

Despite the lack of official recognition, the Fellowship carries on a lively programme, it appears. Their quarterly journal *Towards Wholeness* has subscribers in Canada and the United States, they offer Conferences and Retreats and arrange for speakers to address the various Prayer Groups for Healing. They help form new groups, run a library and offer a score of pamphlets with titles such as *George Fox: Healing and Spiritual Regeneration* and *Health, Healing and the Quaker Faith,* all published by the Fellowship. Twelve tape recordings on healing may be borrowed without charge if the borrower pays the postage.

Of special interest to me were the two Guest Houses run by the Fellowship. Claridge House, in Lingfield, Surrey, was opened eighteen years ago. A new expansion of it, 'Lattendales', opened this year. 'In this setting of lovely garden and pleasant countryside, and supported by loving care, many are finding renewed courage and a deep sense of the healing presence of God,' says the leaflet, giving the atmosphere of Claridge House.

The Chairman's Appeal for 1972 gives a vivid picture of their healing activity:

'We rejoice to see Bob back at work, his ulcer cured, cheerful confidence replacing his former anxious mien; B., of no religious conviction or affiliation, thanks us warmly for our love and prayers that she is convinced we were instrumental in bringing serenity to her husband in the last months of his long illness, prepared him for the journey ahead and contributed to a peaceful passing; X came to us emaciated, without courage or hope, and returned to greet life with joy and gratitude, a light step and a longing to help; Y's back is straight and free from pain after twenty years of suffering.'

Adding an ecumenical note, chairman Bernice Joachim gave members the feeling that spiritual healing is on the upsurge everywhere : 'It is wonderful to read about, and increasingly to meet, others in all denominations and countries discovering this power of Healing, a making-Whole of body, mind and spirit. The Holy Spirit is increasingly finding channels, "ordinary" men and women, through which to work and answer the challenge and need of our time . . .'

Along with this current information, Joan Hackwell sent me an amazing little orange booklet, *The Gift of Healing in the Life of George Fox*, by Edmund Goerke, a minister and overseer in the Society of Friends and an American. In it, some dramatic healings are described by George Fox in his own quaint language :

In 1672, when visiting Friends in Shrewsbury, New Jersey, Fox saw a man in his party thrown from his horse. The man landed on his head and his neck appeared to be broken.

'. . . I came to him and felt on him and saw that he was dead, and as I was pitying his family and him . . . I took him by the hair of the head, and his head turned like a cloth it was so loose, and I threw away my stick and gloves and took his head in both hands, and set my knees against the tree and raised his head, and I did perceive it was not broken out that ways, and I put my hand under his chin, and behind his head and raised his head two or three times with all my strength and brought it in. And I did perceive his neck began to be stiff and then he began to rattle, and after to breathe. And the people were amazed, and I bid them have a good heart and carry him into the house. And then they set him by the fire, and I bid them get him some warm things and get him to bed. And after he had been in the house awhile he began to speak . . . The next day we passed and he with us pretty well, about sixteen miles to a Meeting in Middletown.'

Another was the case of James Claypoole in 1683, who was 'mighty sick of the stone that he could neither lie nor stand'.

'He was in such extremity that he cried out like a woman in travail,' wrote George Fox. 'I went to him and spoke to him and was moved to lay my hand on him and desired the Lord to rebuke his infirmity. And as I laid my hands upon him the Lord's power went through him. And his wife had faith and was sensible of the thing. And he presently went off asleep and presently his stone came forth . . .'

Referring to Cadbury's pamphlet, *George Fox's 'Book of Miracles'* Goerke writes that Fox performed in all about one hundred seventy 'divine healings and revelations', of which he kept a catalogue.

Another precious item Miss Hackwell sent was a copy of the Collier-Hurren pamphlet, which is now out of print. I feel sure it will be back in print before long however, because few medical doctors have shown such a beautiful grasp of the need for spiritual healing as a complement to physical healing as the late Dr Collier.

Taking George Fox as his model, Dr Collier realised that he had to be healed spiritually himself, by looking into his own nature and motives ('an insight undimmed by false pretence, a knowledge which tears away the mask of our own self-delusion') before he could sense 'by sympathy the inward state of sufferers'. He writes :

Little by little I began to see myself as I was, self-centred, anxious about many things, a tangle of conflicting and incompatible purposes.

On a sunny November morning I was descending a hillside when I became aware—with deep emotion—that a clean cut must be made with the past. I must cease striving for my own ends and purposes, must cheerfully embrace whatever plans or purposes God might have for me : must be prepared to be well or ill : must subject my hitherto dominant self to the one purpose of the Lord of Life for me. As I did so, a deep peace followed and spread out to joy. For inward strife and chaos were given peace and joy ! At such times we experience a lightness of heart, an adventurous abandon which he who calculates chances in the lottery of life can never know or comprehend. From this time on my physical health steadily improved. Here we find, I am persuaded, the essential living core of Spiritual Healing. It arises from a glad submission of the self as a whole, as a personality, to the will of God for us. To heal is to make whole : to be healed is to be made whole. It was in this manner that the Healer came to me . . .

'This mingling of the vital forces of the Self with the Life of

Reality as a Whole constitutes a spiritual experience. Every spiritual experience is a healing.

I believe that most diseases start within the personality rather than in the parts, and that permanent and progressive healing starts there also. I am sure that health is largely determined by the attitude of the personality to its life problems.

'When the first move towards harmony of the self with reality is made upon the spiritual level of experience, a change of the relationship between self and God takes place. This change spreads by degrees throughout all of the lower level. Thus the soul's change modifies both mind and body, both the internal environment and its instrument. A new factor has entered into the total situation, and if that factor be both powerful and persistent it can alter, and I believe it does in fact alter, both mental habits and physical states.

During real spiritual experiences a new factor, which is a healing power, is set free within us by reason of the entry into our personality of unselfish, God-derived motive-power or energy. This new power comes from the Reality to which we have related ourselves in spiritual exercises. That power is the Creative Logos, the Holy Spirit of God. It is God as Creative Love, the Life-Builder, the Christ . . .

And what have been the results that I have seen? I have seen the chronic bed-ridden walk, "evil spirits cast out", unexpected recoveries occur from physical illness, operations, poisonings, heart diseases, blood pressure and even growths. These are as nothing, however, to the still clearer evidence of disease prevented and health established.

'If we are wise we shall make no extravagant claims for Spiritual Healing, shall hold out no promises of Healing, but shall try to help people to seek the "First Thing" first, in the hope and confident expectation that a large measure of the other needful things like Health will be "added unto them".

In another section, Dr Collier outlines an imaginary Friends' Meeting for Worship 'where a concerned group are met with the intent that they and others shall be healed'. He compares the plan for worship with a symphony of four movements. Interestingly enough, the stages he prescribes are very much like those used by Ursula Roberts, Harry Edwards and, indeed, spiritual healers everywhere, in reaching attunement. Collier takes us one step further, however, to what he calls 'personality healing'.

1 On entry Friends gather quietly and seek to become poised and balanced. Rigidity and slouching have equally to be avoided. Every muscle should be fully relaxed as circumstances permit, and be careful to relax the jaws and eyebrows.

2 Having prepared the body, prepare the mind. Gently and gradually disjoin the mind and move the centre of attention from the outward to the inward quiet centre. If the thoughts stray (and stray they will) very gently shepherd them back towards their fold. It may help to hold in the mind some thought of wisdom of beauty, of truth or of goodness—an act of love or the remembered scent of hay in summer, or the sound of wind in the grasses on a sun-bathed hill.

3 The quiet centre slowly moves from the creature to the Creator : from Nature or from Man to God : from Self to Christ. In the deepening silence, a sense of corporate unity in worship begins to be felt. At such times feelings and thoughts are transferred, the alert and open mind feels the needs of others. This is because in Him we have Unity and are together with Him in worship. He is the link between us and between ourselves and God. The human group catches a glimpse of Jesus the Christ, the object of their worship, and quietly, dispassionately and humbly each one compares himself as he is with Him whom he has seen. This comparison brings a measure of true self-awareness. Patient, quiet, entirely unhurried self-analysis is inevitably accomplished. Such self-criticism should never be used as a stick to beat ourselves withall, but rather it is an objective, unimpassioned looking at ourselves as we stand revealed in the light that streams from Him whom we worship.

4 There arise living streams of felt life-emotion, pulses of love and of emotion towards God and toward our fellows, for at last we are free of the thralldom of self-passion. Then it is that the Word of Power springs to life, in the Meeting. "I will not leave you comfortless." "Take up thy bed and walk." "Thy sins are forgiven thee." Within the Meeting the Healing Power is moving; the creative stage of worship has been reached. Not only more and deeper self-knowledge, but power also comes

to enable us to change and to be changed. And in this experience there is a joyful resurrection to a brighter life and to a fuller health.

Finally, my informant at the Friends' Fellowship in London, although she knew no similar organisation to theirs in the United States, gave me the name of a Friend in Southbury, Connecticut, just a few miles away from where I was living, and said she was the organiser of a prayer group for spiritual healing.

19. The Questionnaire for Healers

In june, 1972, a forty-part Questionnaire (see appendix) was sent to one quarter of the 4,000 healer-members of the National Federation of Spiritual Healers. About fifteen per cent filled it out and mailed it to me in order to give more complete answers. All will be turned over to leading researchers and should add to our understanding of the psychic healing phenomenon. The information they contain will certainly shed light on spiritual healing practice in the only country where it has attained the momentum of a 'movement'.

A rough preliminary survey of the replies brought out such facts as these :

Spiritual healers in England are mostly males, by nearly two to one. A few husbands and wives work together. The great majority heal in sanctuaries in their own homes. They also heal in churches, hospitals and in the patient's home. One healer wrote, 'In my home, in the street, any place !' Most of those replying indicated that they carry on everyday jobs and do their healing in the evenings and at weekends.

The average age at which they began to heal is thirty-seven. The greatest number were in their thirties and forties, but they may have discovered their gift at any age between five and the ripe age of seventy-one.

In answer to Question 21 ('What is your religious background, if any?'), a varied picture emerged. The greatest number wrote 'Church of England', and the next largest grouping was 'Church of England, now Spiritualist' or 'now free-thinker'. Next in order came 'Methodist' and 'Spiritualist'. There were also a small number of Presbyterians, Baptists and Quakers. Two wrote 'Jewish' and one of them enclosed a letterhead imprinted with a Star of David and the heading 'Jewish Federation of Spiritual Healers'. The other enclosed a card identifying himself as having been formerly a Savile Row tailor. One healer said he had been a Sunday School teacher in the Church of England, then turned Catholic, but after becoming a healer left the Catholic Church because it did not believe in spiritual healing and became a Christian Spiritualist. Several listed themselves as 'Non-Conformist', or wrote 'not fond of labels'.

One healer wrote, 'I was brought up in the Church of England. I found it to be full of cant. My most satisfying period of conventional religon was Wesleyan Chapel when I was in my teens. I have since searched via Buddhism, philosophy, etc., but I am back to the basic formula—treat them as you would be treated; and also, Thy will be done.'

A lone Scottish member wrote from Argyll, 'Presbyterian since early Scottish youth. Still a member of Church of Scotland but, oh dear, I sit in church and feel I could tell the minister a thing or two about the world of Spirit.'

The great majority wrote 'yes' to Question 19 ('Do you think that every human has the inborn psychic ability to heal and that it can be developed, at least to some degree?'), the number dissenting being fewer than half a dozen. Many added amplifications, such as, 'If they have love and compassion and are humble in all that they do' or 'a confident outlook and positive thinking by the healer should lead to improved power, and success brings further success'.

When asked if they charged a fee, accepted donations or mailing expenses for healing, none said they charged a fee. (The NFSH discourages the practise.) Many, however, said they accepted donations and that patients insisted on giving free-will offerings. But the majority made very definite statements that they had never taken any fee or donation of any kind.

Of special interest to American healers and their supporters are the replies to Question 9 ('Have you ever been harassed, criticised or inconvenienced by the medical profession or law enforcement officials or others because of your healing activities?'). In the entire sample of 150 all but half a dozen said 'No'. The forms of harassment were, in any case, mild. One said, 'I have been criticised by the nursing profession and also by one doctor.' Another said, 'Very occasionally staff in hospital not very co-operative.' A third said, 'At times, but we all have to be tolerant of each other.' A fourth said, 'by doctors, not the law.' Only one, a woman in North Wales, seemed to have a problem. 'Yes, many times,' she wrote.

Not a single healer mentioned harassment, criticism or inconvenience at the hands of the law. One healer wrote, 'No, I am a law officer and my customers are also many policemen.' He signed his Questionnaire 'Police Constable ————' and gave a London address. A woman in Swansea, South Wales said, 'No. The police actually call to make appointments.' Some other replies : 'No. I've always received great encouragement.' 'I am allowed to visit the local hospital here at any time at the request of the patient and am always welcomed by the nurses.' 'Not at all. In fact my own doctor is aware of my work and applauds me.' 'I have been encouraged by doctors. Was once inconvenienced by a Catholic priest.' 'In one of the hospitals where I was healing the nurse put a screen around the patient's bed just as she would for a doctor.' 'Each time I've visited patients in a hospital to administer contact healing nurses and other members of the medical staff have treated me politely and helpfully. I'm keeping my fingers crossed that it continues this way.'

To Questions 24 and 26 ('Are any of your patients referred to you by doctors?' 'Do you have any doctors as patients or have had at any time?') one third of the sample said 'yes' to either one or both questions. Here are some answers :

'I often have GPs on my Absent Healing list' (Walter Roger Smith, High Wycombe, Bucks).

'Occasionally doctors send me patients and I have had many doctors for patients, also surgeons, sisters and radiologists' (George Sparks, Northolt, Middlesex).

'I cured one doctor of cancer and another of arthritis. Both were German' (H. H. Potter, Southampton).

'A lot of doctors believe in spiritual healing and send their patients to me' (Donald Maycock, London).

'An eye specialist told a patient of mine to keep coming to me as I was doing more good than he could' (W. G. Laflin, Ipswich, Suffolk).

'One doctor asked for help for his own child' (Mrs G. V. Hawke, Plymouth).

Several said 'not yet' or 'not knowingly' or 'we always hope'. Margaret Rushford of Kingsley, Surrey, wrote, 'Not to my knowledge. People don't have to declare themselves to me. Healers don't pry into other people's lives.' One healer said that doctors came to see him 'but either under cloak of secrecy or anonymously'.

An entire book could be written reporting the responses to Question 1 ('At what age and in what manner did you discover that you had the ability to heal?'). Many told astonishing stories and described the most eerie experiences. Here are a few :

> Many years ago I fractured my right patella and subsequently osteo-arthritis set in. Two London hospitals told me there was no cure. Pain and swelling was intense. I was still in the Army and on one occasion during leave the pain was almost unbearable. For many years my wife and I had been interested in psychical research and—to take my mind off the pain—she suggested we have a "sitting". Only the two of us were present and almost immediately I became completely stiff (not in trance) and heard clairaudiently, "You have the gift of healing which you must use. But healing, like charity, begins at home". I then felt as though warm water were being poured over my bad leg. After the "sitting" all swelling and pain had disappeared. Next day, against my wife's strong advice, I climbed down a cliff path near our house without return of pain. The next day I walked eight miles. Since that time, 1947, I have never had a return of serious pain in the leg. In view of this a healing circle was formed . . . Harry Edwards visited Bude. I was his Chairman and he taught me and others on the platform his method of healing which I have adopted ever since.— Major F. McDermott, Bude, Cornwall.

> 'I was a nurse in a mental hospital (had formerly been an opera singer and won several competitions). I turned to Spiritualism and found I had been a healer all my life. A dumb woman suddenly spoke when I was doing mental nursing and she completely recovered. Another woman who was unable to use her arm, suddenly lifted her arm and touched my hair. The doctors were baffled and so was I. While doing private nursing I had an urge to massage the very thin legs of a woman bedridden for twelve years. This I did every day for three months. The woman suddenly got out of bed and walked . . . My husband and I were having a glass of wine in an hotel. A man entered and suddenly couldn't move. He had a stroke. I went over to him and gave him healing. I slowly uncurled

the man's fingers, straightened his crooked face and made him walk again . . .'—Mrs Doris Liffen, Lowestoft, Suffolk.

On an occasion I took my wife to Mr Harry Edwards. My wife's turn came and she sat before him. He ran his fingers down her spine. He knew neither my wife nor me. He turned to me sitting some fifteen feet away, beckoned to me and told me she had a curvature of the spine. I knew this. Medicos had told her so. He spoke and said, "Would you care to heal this?" And when I declared it was impossible, he took my hands, looked at them and said, "You have healers hands. Place them over that part of the spine". I did as requested and he put his hands over mine, told my wife to bend to the right and to my surprise, the spine moved back into place. His advice to me was to go and join a healing group. I did.—A. E. Phillips, The Healing Brotherhood, Hemel Hempstead, Herts.

I had a double strangulated hernia that necessitated immediate surgery. But I was a "bleeder" (haemophilia) and if operated on would bleed to death. My blood fluctuated every few hours, that is, it was sometimes normal. It was decided to operate and the surgery was a success, blood OK at the vital moment as it were. Then on the fifth day the stitches gave way. My family gathered at my bed for my passing . . . I was aware that my senses were unnaturally acute. As my family left my bedside I had an overpowering sense of guilt . . . I then prayed perhaps the first real prayer of my life. I asked if there was a superior power, help me! Then I was aware that I was looking down on my bed and seeing myself, a shrivelled old man, a pitiful, lifeless thing. My next awareness was of my lying on the bed and an entity clothed in a beautifully coloured hood and cloak, very bright in shade. They were colours beyond description. This something or entity was at my side and laid two hands on my body and moved slowly around the bed, the hands travelling down to my feet and up the other side, and remained at the left side of my head for a while. Suddenly the entity was gone. In a few days I demanded to be sent home and after making myself a general nuisance, an ambulance took me home to the comfort and care of my family. I made a speedy recovery, and then many unusual healings began to occur . . . —James Ernest Hulett, Birmingham.

Healer Phyllis Palmer said she discovered she could heal when her daughter collapsed with a spinal sinus and she heard a voice say, "Heal thy child". She placed her hands on her daughter and she recovered.

Charles Henry Philpot said he had 'a funny feeling' in his hands and was told it was the 'means of healing'. He learned how to do it properly and has been healing ever since.

J. Parker of Warwickshire wrote that a friend with spinal trouble was told in a dream 'that I could heal him'. The friend asked for Parker's help and within a day he was healed.

'At thirty-eight I saw a vision of my dead grandmother,' wrote Dennis Mitchell of Plymouth. 'She told me I had the gift of healing.'

'Joined Manchester Society of Psychic Research. Was told I would make a good healer. Attended a healing circle. "Gave power", and before long was accepted as one of the assistant healers,' said Charles MacIntyre of Argyll, Scotland.

'At fifty years, an impulse to relieve migraine from which a friend had suffered for many years. Hands were laid on head. No return attacks after that,' wrote Peggy Esther Lupton of Brighton.

Conclusion

It is obvious that a spiritual healing explosion is taking place in England and that the healing power is being channelled generously through the hands of thousands of English men and women in all parts of the country.

Many have taken the initiative in developing their gift, others have been 'recruited' in strange ways, apparently from Spirit. Many were told by mediums and healers that they were naturally gifted. Others say they were told while sitting in a psychic development circle that certain healing spirits wanted to work through them.

In taking these people at their word, we are fortified by the knowledge that they could not have become full healer-members of the National Federation of Spiritual Healers without proving that they have been able to heal people.

Indeed, membership in the NFSH has clearly given status to England's healers. Led by an awesomely gifted president, Harry

Edwards, members quite obviously take pride in their organisation's ideals and its insistence on high standards of ethics. And, judging from their replies to the Questionnaire, they appear to be generally serious and of high calibre.

NFSH healers make a strong impact on the public with their annual 'Healers' Day' demonstration and mass healing, usually held in Royal Festival Hall, London. On these occasions, over one hundred white-coated members share the platform with Edwards and, at the end, give healing to any of the thousands attending who ask for treatment.

As a corporate member of the United Nations Association and by sponsoring the International Fellowship of Healing, England's healers' federation projects its message outwards, that spiritual healing is God's gift to all humanity and that people of every country, creed or colour can benefit from it equally since all are of the same Spirit. Wisely, it is not saying that spiritual healing is a panacea. It is proposing that people all over the world join in a 'great experiment' that gives hope of relieving world tensions as well as much individual pain and suffering beyond the help of medical science.

Not only do the more articulate leaders of the NFSH express these world views. They seem to be shared by rank-and-file members, and I'm sure by many unaffiliated healers. For example, in mailing out the Questionnaire at Federation headquarters, Joan Robertson, the RAF Wing Commander's widow who helped me tirelessly, said almost casually, 'It doesn't matter how each member of a circle develops his healing gift if their collective power can help mankind.' (At the Spiritualist Association of Great Britain I also met healers who fervently believe that spiritual healing will bring the world closer together in brotherhood and peace.)

The National Federation of Spiritual Healers also keeps tabs on healing research going forward all over the globe, and representatives of Life Energies Research Inc. of New York serve on its research committee. Through its chairman, Marcus McCausland, I first learned of Dr Barbara Brown's controlled studies of healers and patients at Sepulveda Veterans Hospital in California and of Russian discoveries by two doctors that white blood cells—a main defense against disease—increase in number when patients feel positive emotions and decrease when their emotions are negative—certainly a finding significant to spiritual and self-healing.

What are the implications for America of the 'healing happening' in England? While in both countries official medicine is chilly towards them, England's healers have shown that by maintaining a cooperative attitude and by being discreet it is possible to interest individual doctors in spiritual healing, not only for their patients but for themselves. The English experience also shows, I believe, that this long-term wooing is greatly aided by the healers' having their own prestigious professional organisation.

Predictably, America's healers soon will be seeing the need to organise, whether for better healer-doctor relations or to explain their work to the churches and to the public. When this happens, what better model can they follow than England's National Federation of Spiritual Healers with its study courses, membership hurdles and insistence on the Hippocratic Oath for healers? Some Americans may find the English belief in spirit doctors hard to accept, but many leading psychic researchers are convinced that they exist. (The widely studied English medium, Douglas Johnson, told me, 'Yes, I believe the healer is helped by spirit entities, or else I'm dotty, and I don't think I'm dotty! I've seen them'.)

As a surrogate for Harry Edwards, America's healers may look to such organisations as Life Energies Research, the Academy of Parapsychology and Medicine, the Foundation for Parasensory Investigation, the SFF and the ARE for guidance. Already a growing number of New Age doctors are not at all cool to spiritual healing, undoubtedly because of the recent vigorous activity in the field of these organisations.

A hopeful sign to America's healers is the defiant note sounded by Dr Robert G. Brewer at the ARE conference reported elsewhere in this book. 'The way I see it, healers have a special thing to offer,' said Dr Brewer, 'and I don't see why we should subjugate any one kind of healer to another. We should all be working together! As time goes on we will be criticised and may be ostracised. But who cares? It's you people who give us the power to go forward.'

Meanwhile, America's healers can speed up their organisation if they act on their own initiative and join the NFSH-sponsored International Fellowship of Healing, whose motto is 'The Hands of Healing Encompass The World'. (Address: 'Shortacres', Church Hill, Loughton, Essex, England.) And, rather than wait for good healing trainee schools and classes to grow up in America, they might enrol in the NFSH's correspondence courses by writing to the same address.

The next step—when enough people have developed their gift of healing to make a worldwide movement—will be to present a programme for healer-training to the United Nations, to be administered by the UN's World Health Organisation.

PART THREE

Probing the Healing Mystery

20. Investigating Psychic Healing and Self-Healing

IN THESE unpredictable times, when an antique Chinese concept of healing has become the newest thing, there is growing hope among those exploring new ways of relieving human suffering that the next 'innovation' in Western medicine will be psychic healing.

Its acceptance as a viable therapy by the medical profession should be hastened by the breakthrough obtained in recent years by a handful of intrepid research scientists.

Risking the disdain of their more conservative colleagues, these researchers have invited into their labs people claiming to have 'healing hands', and they have tested this legendary gift in scientifically impeccable experiments.

Two of these pioneers, a biologist and a biochemist, have measured the effect of 'the laying-on of hands' on plants, animals and body enzymes. And a third, a psychologist, by analysing the mental states while healing of a score of respected healers in England and the United States, and combining this knowledge with mystical teaching of other cultures, has devised a system of teaching healing that has effected cures in a number of volunteers having medically verified ailments.

In a category by itself is a radiation field photography technique, developed by the Russians and now being used in other countries for healing research, that shows streams of light flowing from a healer's hands when beginning a healing treatment.

Other significant research is under way in the area of self-healing and its relation to psychosomatic medicine. By means of biofeedback techniques, subjects have learned to bring under conscious control certain bodily functions such as rate of heart beat and hand temperature which are normally automatic.

Much is also being learned by observing practising healers and verifying the results of their healing treatments in a wide range of illnesses. And helping to round out the still-fragmented picture are the efforts of a young physicist who has constructed a theoretical base for the psychic healing process, his idea being to encourage other scientists to consider the possibility that there might be seven levels of substance or energy in the body, each obeying a unique set of natural laws.

All this information was brought to the public in three historic conferences on paranormal and unorthodox healing in California during 1972. The number of people absorbing it was limited, however, to the seating capacity of three large auditoriums and by the high price of tickets, tapes and transcripts.

One conference, in May, was on 'Psychic Healing and Self-Healing, the Transcendent Human Potential', sponsored by the Association for Humanistic Psychology in San Francisco, and another, in October, was the symposium on 'The Dimensions of Healing' sponsored by the Academy of Parapsychology and Medicine and put on twice—at Stanford University in Los Altos and a few days later at the University of California in Los Angeles, the two universities cooperating through interested departments (Industrial Engineering and Materials Science at Stanford and Continuing Education and Health Sciences at UCLA).

While the AHP's conference lasted only one day, the Academy's two symposiums extended over eight days, altogether. Formed in 1970 by a remarkable group of scientists and physicians, its aim is to 'provide a catalyst for the study of all forms of paranormal and unorthodox healing'. More expressive of its state of awareness is its credo, that 'spirit and matter are somehow one' and that 'it is the essential purpose of man to seek the meaning behind all human experience if the true nature of healing is to be found'. President of the Academy is Dr Robert Bradley, the Denver obstretrician and natural childbirth pioneer, who has also led the way in using hypnosis and ESP in treating psychosomatic disorders.

Thelma Moss, PhD, assistant professor of medical psychology at UCLA's Neuropsychiatric Institute, acted as moderator and set the tone for the gathering in a provocative programme editorial, which read in part :

'Psychic healing poses an intriguing paradox for our scientific times. It is indeed interesting that with our exploding technology, certain scientific laboratories are beginning to find some evidence —if not verification—to support ancient occult concepts . . .

'Actually, in the recorded histories of civilisations around the world, there is repeated reference to an invisible energy which is, naturally, called by various names, in various cultures. The ancient Egyptians called it "ka"; the Chinese, "ch'i"; the Yogis, "prana"; the Hawaiians, "mana", etc. Whatever the name, this invisible energy has traditionally been linked with a healing power which can be channelled through the healer to the patient. Typically this healing power was bonded to religion and ritual, and became the special mystery of the medicine man, the shaman, the witch doctor—the holy man. Over the course of time, as the ritual became more elaborate, the healing became less effective. And the religious ritual came to be regarded by many, in "the age of enlightenment", as superstitious nonsense.

'But not always. In China, the concept of the invisible energy, ch'i, was encoded into a medical model—acupuncture—still in use today. This ch'i is presumed to course through meridians in the body with special points on the surface of the skin through which the energy can be manipulated. Recent Chinese research has discovered that certain acupuncture points produce anaesthesia deep enough to remove a lung or brain tumour while the patient sips tea or eats fruit.

'Miraculous? No more than the hundreds of operations reported by the surgeon Esdaile in the 19th century, who anaesthetised his patients through "magnetic passes" made by the hands over the body, after which entire limbs were amputated, the patient feeling nothing. For this technique, Esdaile was indebted to Mesmer who had postulated an invisible "magnetic fluid" by means of which he could cure patients, either with iron rods, or simply his hands.

'Perhaps this practise of "magnetic passes" is related to the Biblical practise of the "laying-on of hands" by holy men, which apparently resulted in miraculous cures. Even today similar healing power is claimed by many churches, chief among them the Christian Science church. This church was founded by Mary Baker Eddy, after she had been healed of chronic invalidism by an uneducated clockmaker Quimby, who had only accidentally, in his mature years, discovered his healing power after learning the techniques of hypnosis.

'Can it be that all of this lore, ancient and modern, is only super-stition? Or are our present-day scientists learning in the laboratory basic facts about an invisible energy which might be harnessed for its curative power?'

Early in the programme, Dr Moss introduced Dr Bernard Grad, the McGill University professor from Montreal—probably the first research biologist to ask a healer to administer the laying-on of hands to a lab mouse.

'The question is whether there is a life force,' Grad began. 'Most biologists will say that you just can't study it because it's too vague an idea, so no experiments are done in this field.' He then outlined a series of his own experiments that drove home in dramatic fashion the reality of an unseen force that heals and stimulates growth.

He had learned that a Montreal man, Oskar Estebany, claimed to have had particular success healing thyroid diseases among hospital patients in Hungary with the laying-on of hands. And since Grad himself had worked in that same area when obtaining his degree, he hit upon the idea of inducing enlarged thyroid glands (goiters) in mice by removing the iodine from their diets while Estebany would try to slow down the gland's growth in half the animals.

On a screen, the biologist flashed a graph indicating the growth rate of the thyroid glands of the two groups of mice. The two up-turned lines soon parted company, a red line on the bottom rising only slightly. 'There was really an inhibition of the growth of the thyroid glands in the healed animals, which was very surprising and gratifying to me,' he said.

Next, he again gave the mice a low iodine diet, but this time rather than have Estebany apply his hands directly, Grad had him 'treat' some material that was put in the cages of half the mice. The results were the same! 'The healing energy is apparently transferable through an intermediate object,' the biologist said. (I couldn't help being less scornful of the so-called miraculous powers that have been attributed to sacred relics and the bones of the saints!)

Another test, Grad continued, was the reverse of the first. If he put the mice with goitres back on their normal diet of Purina Fox Chow with a full quotient of iodine, will their goitres shrink faster with healing help from Estebany? The answer again was 'Yes'.

Grad then reviewed his wound-healing experiment on mice that has had such wide circulation in scientific papers and journals. Projecting on to the screen pictures of the wound patches in their various shapes and sizes sustained by the mice in the interests of science, it was possible to compare those taken at three intervals over a space of two weeks. It was startling to see how the wounds of the healed mice, pictured in the centre strip, shrank to pin-point size or vanished by the fourteenth day while most of the others had healed only partially.

Grad next experimented with barley seed which he planted in pots filled with peat moss. 'I first watered them with a one per cent salt solution to make them sick so they would have a condition to overcome in addition to growing,' he said. And, rather than carry the plants to the healer, he found it necessary only that the healer treat the solution that was to be poured on the plants.

He also discovered that the healer needed only to treat the first watering with the saline solution, its effects lasting apparently through all the successive waterings.

In preliminary runs, the solution was treated by the healer in open beakers, then the controls were tightened up and it was placed in sealed bottles 'just to make things difficult for the healer'. When the seedlings began to sprout seven to eight days later their height was carefully measured and the average growth per day added up for each group, marked X and Y.

'We didn't know which group had been treated by the healer,' Grad said, 'but on the fourteenth day the sprouts in group X were much higher than those in group Y. This sort of thing does not. happen by chance.' He showed us a picture of the two groups so we could compare them. Group X was obviously longer and more luxuriant than group Y.

In a repeat of the experiment, the only difference being that neither group received 'healed' water, there was no difference at all in the growth rate of the two groups!

'Believe me,' he commented, 'it still is surprising and a source of continual amazement that we can be blind to this life force just because we can't see it.'

Grad concluded by describing an experiment that showed the effects of emotion on plants, a man with a psychotic depression having clearly inhibited plant growth—compared to the control— after holding the saline solution and sprinkling it on the plant. The biologist felt this was dramatic evidence to back up the traditional belief that a doctor's bedside manner is a critical element in healing.

'There are forces at work here so powerful that they can lead to unusual changes in a patient,' Grad said. 'So, you see, we must be careful of bio-energetic pollution.'

Sister Justa Smith, PhD, a biochemist and chairman of the Natural Sciences concentration at Rosary Hill College, Buffalo, took her cue from Dr Grad and invited the obliging Mr Estebany into her laboratory to see if he had a way with enzymes.

Her increasingly admired experiment with the kindly Hungarian-born healer has resulted in a flurry of invitations to speak at an international Parapsychological Association conference at the University of Freiburg in Germany, and at all three of the aforementioned California symposiums on healing.

She started her working thesis: 'Many biochemists agree we're going to be able to show that all illness is due to some malfunction of an enzyme, since the enzymes catalyse the metabolic reactions of each cell. And so, if enzyme failure is a cause of disease, a healer would have to be able, in some way, to affect an enzyme.'

Happening to meet Dr Grad personally when he lectured at her college's Human Dimensions Institute, Sister Justa told him, 'If this Mr Estebany really is a healer, he certainly ought to be able to affect an enzyme system.' And she asked Grad's help in obtaining the healer's cooperation for further experiments.

Fortunately, Mr Estebany, a retired colonel in the Hungarian army, shared the biochemist's desire to shed more light on the phenomenon Grad had uncovered and was equally curious about his apparent successes over the years healing his countrymen.

A foundation grant from the fund set up by the late Chester Carlson, the inventor of Xerox, made the experiment possible and Estebany agreed to spend a month on the Rosary Hill campus.

Sister Justa was guided by original research she had done for her doctoral thesis, in which she discovered that a magnetic field increased activity of the enzyme trypsin while ultra-violet radiation damaged and slowed it down.

So she would test the effect of Estebany's 'healing hands' on the enzyme trypsin, she said, and compare the result with the effect of a magnetic field on the activity of that enzyme.

And, acting on Dr Grad's point that she was having a healer heal a perfect enzyme, she would damage one sample of trypsin with ultra violet light and have Estebany try to overcome that condition.

When Sister Justa gave a detailed account of this experiment in San Francisco, she paused a minute 'to make one thing straight'.

Crisp, cool, attractive, with a pleasant manner, she told her confrères, 'I've had a few Catholics ask me which order I belonged to. I still belong to the Franciscan order and I hold a position in it. So I'm really a bona fide nun even though I've kicked the habit.' After the appreciative laughter quieted (she wore a becoming slim-waisted dress with knee-length skirt) the biochemist returned to her experiment.

'Now the enzymes I used were purchased and were highly purified in crystalline form,' she explained. 'I experimented *in vitro,* meaning in glass, not *in vivo,* in living things.'

Elaborating, she said, 'One of the reasons I used this technique was because so often when people are healed by a paranormal healer or, if you like, a psychic healer, the cure is immediately attributed to their own imagination. They simply *thought* they had an illness or psychological problem, or whatever. I didn't think anybody would say this of enzymes, of these crystals!'

And so the design of the experiment was set forth : Every day new solutions of the enzyme trypsin would be prepared in hydrochloric acid and divided into four capped bottles. One would be retained in the native state as a control; the second would be held in Estebany's hands for up to seventy-five minutes; the third would be damaged by ultra-violet radiation to reduce its activity to 68-80 per cent and then treated by the healer the same as batch two; the fourth would be placed in a high magnetic field of 8,000-13,000 gauss.

Sister Justa recalled that when she first handed Colonel Estebany the little flask of enzyme solution that looked so much like water, he searched her face questioningly and said, 'What do you want me to do?'

'I said, "Well, Mr Estebany, I don't know. What do you do when you treat people?" and he said, "I put my hands on them." I said, "Then put your hands on them. That's what I want you to do."

'So, each morning this man would sit there in the lab as long as I wanted him to, with his huge hands around this little vessel. Much of the time his eyes were closed. I was very curious. What was the man thinking? What does he really do? Once I said to him, "Do you pray?" and he looked up very pleasantly and said, "I pray, don't you pray?" I never really found out whether the man meditates. Frankly, part of the time I think he slept. But I don't think that matters because of the results we got from the experiments.'

While Estebany sat in a room by himself, he was visited every

fifteen minutes by a technician whose job it was to pipette out a constant amount of the enzyme solution from the healer's flask and put
it into another vessel which was immediately covered with foil so
that nobody could see the coding on the bottom of it.

'The experiments were run as a double blind,' Dr Smith emphasised. 'I never did the work myself. I wasn't going to be accused of
having the power to change anybody's solution! So I hired these
technicians who really didn't know what was going on. But they
were very well trained at assaying this enzyme. More than that they
were only curious, and they didn't know which sample vials they
were running until the run was over and then somebody else would
come in and take the code from the bottom and put it on the chart.'

The final measurement of enzyme activity was done automatically, she said, so there was 'no possibility of fudging numbers or
human errors'. She explained briefly how this was done :

'In order to measure the activity of an enzyme, it has to react on
something and that something is called a substrate. The particular
substrate I used was chromogenic, meaning it gave off a colour.

'When the enzyme breaks a bond in the substrate (benzoyl-Dt-
arginine-p-nitroanilide hydrochloride), it breaks into two compounds
and one is yellow. The spectrophotometer measures the activity of
the variously treated enzyme samples by measuring the amount of
yellow added per minute.

'The more yellow added, the more active the enzyme,' she continued. 'It's all automatic, you see. And the rate of increased enzyme
activity is traced automatically on a strip chart recorder.'

When the experiment got under way and the results began appearing in the form of sloped lines on a graph, Sister Justa could hardly
believe her eyes.

'Estebany's hands had increased the activity of the enzyme to a
degree comparable to that obtained in a magnetic field of 13,000
gauss!' she said.

(Comparing that to the earth's magnetic field, the latter is a mere
.5 gauss.)

When the enzyme was exposed in the magnet for longer than an
hour the activity went much higher, so it was only in the first hour
that the effects were comparable, she explained.

Strangely enough, the other sample Estebany had treated, the one
damaged by ultra-violet light showed just about the same slope on
the graph.

'What this said to me is that these enzymes I was buying as highly purified were not all that perfect to start with,' she said, 'otherwise how could Estebany affect these two batches, both the damaged and the undamaged, in about the same way? Upon investigating, I found that the enzymes are purified by a process called salting-out, and that it would be utterly impossible to get all the salt out of the product.'

She next attempted to measure any possible flow of magnetic force from Estebany's hand with a gaussmeter, placing it between hand and enzyme during repeats of the experiment. It registered nothing.

Sister Justa speculates that the energy exchange in healing might be activated by a surrounding psychic energy field and that there might be a whole new spectrum of energy we know nothing about yet 'except for the evidences that are produced, for instance, by a healer'.

As for any healing effect of magnetism, which the experiment suggests, she said others were following up that line of research. However, she thinks the results of treatment by a healer and by a magnet must be 'of a different nature'.

Chiefly, her experiment has measured the effects of psychic healing on an organic substance critical to the healing process in the human body. 'We were not able to measure the amount of energy coming out of the man's hands. What we were able to measure,' she emphasised, 'is the effect of the healing energy on something else.'

Sister Justa then proceeded to outline an important follow-up experiment that was able dramatically to measure those indirect effects *in vivo*, rather than *in vitro*.

Working out a plan with a young Buffalo physician to test the effectiveness of psychic healing on his patients, they arranged for Estebany to have an office in the same medical complex as the young physician and his colleagues. The healer was assigned a nurse and given twenty-four patients who agreed to cooperate in the experiment.

'One of the doctors screened the patients to make sure they wouldn't be harmed by postponing their own treatment. They were given an examination and diagnosis and ushered into Mr Estebany's office,' said Sister Justa.

'Estebany immediately sent two of the twenty-four to a psychiatrist—I've always felt this helped them too. Perhaps they never would have gotten to a psychiatrist otherwise. The remaining twenty-two patients were asked to return as often as he felt necessary and until he felt their treatment was completed.

'At the end of the experiment, twenty-one people said they felt much better. Only one man said he felt no different,' said the researcher. 'I don't believe too many physicians have that kind of batting average!'

Reportedly, the response of the doctors to their patients' statements of well-being was less than enthusiastic. She felt this was certainly understandable.

'We're asking something tremendous of these men. Remember, they've given a great deal of themselves and made a lot of sacrifice and studied very hard to come to this knowledge they have. And here's a man who hasn't studied at all, with really no medical education, and he's able to do the same thing! I think we'll agree this would be a hard thing to accept,' and she added, 'It's so easy to say, "It must have been psychological". But the fact remains that enzymes are not psychological and Estebany did affect that enzyme system . . .'

When I interviewed Sister Justa in her lab at the college, I asked if the results of this experiment would soon be published. She said, 'Every time I approach this young doctor he says he's going to.' She suspected, however, that he was reluctant to issue the report for fear of upsetting his colleagues.

She conceded that there were obvious weaknesses in the study, too many kinds of complaints having made comparisons difficult. 'Unfortunately, we couldn't order the illnesses. We had to take what came. I hope some time we can get into a clinic where only one kind of illness is being treated, like glaucoma,' she said, adding that Estebany has had particular success with that condition.

There was a sequel to these experiments with Estebany that tended to corroborate Grad's observation that a negative mood or emotional state while trying to heal can cancel out the healing power. Sister Justa told all three conferences exactly what happened.

When Estebany returned to campus in the Autumn to resume tests a new set of circumstances had sprung up, and the results he got in this new atmosphere were quite different.

'During the summer Estebany had lived in the dorm,' she said. 'The campus had been beautiful and peaceful, with an older type of student enrolled in the summer sessions. He took long walks in the evenings, everyone adored him and fought to sit next to him at mealtimes, and I had much more time to be attentive to his needs.

'Then, in the autumn, college was in full swing and he had to live off campus and be dependent on his hosts for transport. I was very busy running my department and had little time for him when we weren't doing the experiments. The weather was bad and a personal problem, which I'm not free to divulge, had him very upset.

'Under these circumstances, Estebany did not affect the enzyme, nor did he heal anybody,' Sister Justa declared. 'All of this convinced me that the healing ability can be blocked.'

She recalled that all healers she has known who were effective, and certainly Estebany, shared two outstanding characteristics— utter tranquillity and absolute confidence. 'They're not cocky, not braggart, but very sure of what they're doing.' Nevertheless, when Estebany was so disturbed by external factors, she said, he was not able to function as a healer.

Other follow-up tests that autumn turned up more surprises.

First, Sister Justa had people who made no claim to healing powers hold the enzyme in the manner of Estebany, and they had no effect upon it whatever outside the standard deviation from the control.

Second, she took a group of local people who said they had some healing power and their results were very erratic. 'I think everyone has *some* healing power,' she noted, 'but these people, perhaps, doubted themselves.'

Then, the next summer, Sister Justa used three people with considerable reputations as healers, although short of Estebany's forty years of experience. With this group she used different enzymes, one of them nicotinamide atazine diphosphate, the function of which is the release of ATP, the energy-giving compound of the body.

She paused to explain that she was well aware that not all enzymes should be speeded up for good health. It depends upon the enzyme and what its function is in the body.

In this case, all three psychic healers *reduced* the enzyme's activity, she said.

Because the function of that particular enzyme was to release an energy-giving wallop, Sister Justa thought there must be some error in their work, so she had it run repeatedly over and over again. But she got the same results each time.

'Then I really examined what this enzyme does, and I found that although it releases ATP, releasing it *faster*—by increasing the enzyme's activity—would have released the ATP so fast that it would have been wasted.'

So in this case it was more therapeutic that the ATP be conserved by a reduction of the enzyme's activity—and that's precisely what the psychics did.

The biochemist also used an enzyme from human blood rather than the crystalline form, with the idea in mind that if she used an enzyme more living she might get a different result. It was, indeed, different. Neither of the healers lowered or elevated its activity one whit. She thinks the non-activity might be attributed to impurities that were present.

Finally, she had them also try to affect the trypsin, the original enzyme that had responded so exuberantly to Estebany's touch. 'All three of them affected trypsin in the same fashion as Estebany,' said Justa, 'but not in the same amount nor as consistently as Estebany.'

The final trio of tests suggested to Sister Justa that this technique might some day be used 'to test the healing ability of a person, and to sort out the charlatans in the business'—in other words, to separate the sheep from the wolves under a nationwide programme for licensing healers.

To her audience of over a thousand in Ackerman Auditorium at UCLA, Sister Justa gently deplored the fact that she is sometimes criticised for her research with healers by her fellow Catholics.

'I received a telephone call the other day, and a voice asked, "Does the Church know what you're doing?" I could only answer, "Not everything, really," "But do they know you have a healer out there?" I paused a few minutes before answering. Then I asked, "Can you recall who it was who first healed by the laying-on of hands?" There was silence. I guess that settled the matter.' Sister Justa then asked a rhetorical question, 'If we Christians can't accept this kind of healing, who should?'

The discussion—with slides—of Kirlian photography, and seeming evidence that this technique has at last made the invisible healing energy visible, were fascinating highlights of the Stanford and UCLA symposiums.

Most of the audience were aware—since undoubtedly they had read that fresh breeze of a book, *Psychic Discoveries Behind the*

Iron Curtain—that this is a major contribution of the Russians and that some of their best scientists have been using it to study healers and the acupuncture process.

Before reporting the efforts of US researchers to replicate the Russian findings, it is important to flash back for a minute to the pioneering work of Semyon and the late Valentina Kirlian and Dr Vladimir Inyushin and his colleagues, which is told dramatically in the book by Sheila Ostrander and Lynn Schroeder.

(It was appropriate that these two attractive young psychic sleuths from New Jersey turned up at the Los Angeles sessions where they took a bow and stirred up an appreciative commotion.)

The book reports that some time after Semyon Kirlian, an ace electrician, and his wife, a teacher and journalist, had discovered the luminous 'energy body' surrounding and interpenetrating the physical body, using a high-frequency electrical field photographic technique they had developed, they found it was possible to detect disease in both plants and humans *before* it strikes by the appearance of blurred or shadowy areas in the energy body.

In later studies, the Kirlians found that when they were nervous or harried the high-frequency photos reflected it. Suddenly the coloured flares of light in the energy body of a hand would go into a tailspin, then unwind and fade out of focus. After a while they were able to decipher these seemingly chaotic shifts.

A shot of vodka was found to stimulate a discharge of light around a fingertip. Disease, emotional states, even thoughts and fatigue made separate and distinct impressions on the volatile energy body which came to be known in certain Soviet scientific circles as the 'bioplasma body'.

By the 1960's, the Kirlians were given official recognition in the form of a specially equipped lab, better living quarters and a go-ahead to the scientific community to look into their invention.

Interest in the Kirlian process has centred about Kirov State University of Kazakhstan in Alma-Ata, where a group of biologists and others led by Dr Inyushin have carried out exciting experiments with the Kirlians' power generator hooked up to a huge electron microscope.

The co-authors report that these scientists have been able to watch the bioplasma body replenish itself with oxygen. 'Breathing, it seems, charges the entire bioplasmic body and renews our reserves of vital energy and helps to equalise disturbed energy patterns,' they wrote, adding that this tied in with the Yoga teachings that prescribe deep-breathing exercises for good health.

Issuing a lengthy paper in 1968, entitled 'On The Biological Essence of the Kirlian Effect', Professor Inyushin and his colleagues made a statement that was of far-reaching significance to medical research :

'With this concept of the biological plasma body, we can open new paths to understanding the growth of cancer, tumours and other diseases.'

A top medical professor was similarly quoted by the American writers. Dr S. M. Pavlenko, Chairman of the Pathology-Physiology Department of the First Moscow Medical Institute, put it this way : 'Kirlian photography can be used for early diagnosis of disease, especially cancer.'

Most dramatic, perhaps, was the account of experiments carried out by certain unnamed Soviet scientists with the healer Alexei Krivorotov of Tbilisi, Republic of Georgia. A retired colonel, he practises in the same office as his son, a medical doctor, and the son refers patients to his father.

The elder Krivorotov reportedly moves his hands up and down the patient's body without touching it and generates intense heat, which his patients describe as 'burning through' them, although tests show no change in the temperature of the skin of either patient or healer.

Quoting a 'reliable source', the two psychic reporters listed a few more reactions of patients. 'If an inner organ is diseased, patients often report feeling tremendous heat pouring from the spot, almost, they say, as if the organ is being choked.' The healer himself can feel this warmth radiating from the patient and can diagnose exactly where the illness is, they said.

The co-authors then reported the provocative tit-bit that quickened healing research in the West : extensive experiments had been made of Krivorotov using Kirlian apparatus to photograph his thumb while healing, and it showed a very different pattern of energy coming from his skin than was noted when at rest.

Was the elusive healing energy at last caught on photo paper?

'At the moment when he seemed to be causing a sensation of intense heat in a patient,' wrote Ostrander and Schroeder, 'the general overall brightness in Krivorotov's hands decreased and in one small area of his hands a narrow, focused channel of intense brilliance developed. It was almost as if the energy pouring from his hands could focus like a laser beam.'

And they summed up with another provocative conclusion, that the Russians' preliminary work with the Kirlian process so far seemed to indicate that 'psychic healing involves a transfer of energy from the bioplasmic body of the healer to the bioplasmic body of his patient' and that changes on this bioplasmic level were eventually reflected in the physical body and healed it.

Not many months after the book appeared, two Kirlian photographs of Krivorotov's thumb were reproduced in the US magazine *Psychic* (see May/June, 1971). The first, taken at rest, showed dots of light with a few short flares around the tip. The second, reportedly taken when he was 'asked to heal', showed flowing streamers of light bursting outward. The pictures accompanied a story by Dr Thelma Moss telling of her trip to see for herself these intriguing developments. Entitled 'Searching for Psi from Prague to Lower Siberia', it reported in lively style, among other adventures, her meeting with Professor Inyushin in Alma-Ata.

Unfortunately she was unable to put a foot inside any laboratories working with the Kirlian process, since official permission was not forthcoming, although she was given several published scientific articles by Inyushin and others describing their work in detail. In interviews, however, she was able to get at least verbal verification of many of the wonders reported in *Psychic Discoveries* . . . as well as new information.

The characteristic colours of various parts of the body that are revealed in Kirlian photos impressed Inyushin as significant to our understanding of disease as well as health and organ function, wrote Dr Moss, recalling their interview.

She seemed most intrigued, however, by the ability of Russian researchers to see acupuncture points on the body with the aid of Kirlian photography, since locating these points is one of the worst hurdles for practitioners.

By using the 'tobiscope', which lights up on acupuncture points, it is possible to double check their position by comparing them with the vivid light flares seen at these points in Kirlian pictures.

According to Inyushin's colleague, Dr Nikolai Shuisky, laser beams are being applied to acupuncture points and some cures have taken place. Dr Moss was told that a laser beam directed to an acupuncture point above the upper lip, for example, will stop an epileptic seizure within seconds. (It does not cure epilepsy, however.)

A number of severe arthritic cases have also responded to the laser beam treatment, they told her, and she was assured that if properly directed to the acupuncture point there is no tissue damage and no pain is felt. (Some Russian researchers with Kirlian photography appear to link the bioplasma luminescence with the 'Vital Energy' that is involved in healing by acupuncture.)

Returning home to her lab in California, Thelma Moss and her associate, Kendall Johnson, were the first parapsychologists to set up a workable Kirlian-type apparatus and to put it to work immediately on healing research.

It was not easy. The sheaf of schematic diagrams given her by Russian scientists were difficult for American electronic experts to decipher, some calling them 'infeasible' and 'absurd'. But Ken Johnson took over the project and put together a simpler version, using a lower-frequency range of 100 to 4,000 cycles per second. (The Kirlian set-up has been described as 'a specially constructed high-frequency spark generator or oscillator that generates 75,000 to 200,000 electrical oscillations per second'.)

In the Russian original, the power source is attached to two insulated plates, between which the object being studied is inserted with photo paper. When the power is switched on, the high frequency field created causes the object to radiate its bioplasma or energy body on to the photo paper. No camera is necessary.

Ken Johnson's American-made apparatus works with one plate and an insulated grounding wire. According to the Californians, many of their pictures resemble those made by the Russians' high-powered method.

In July, 1972, Moss and Johnson unveiled their first 'radiation field photography' pictures in *Psychic* magazine and seventeen of them were ranged across two pages.

Concentrating her radiation field photographic apparatus on the study of different states of consciousness, Dr Moss has found that the steady intake of alcohol over a long evening increased the size of a fingertip 'corona discharge' while its colour changed from lavender to a 'rosy glow'.

A study of cannabis intoxication done in association with the National Institute of Mental Health showed a general increase in size and luminosity of the corona; a gifted psychic in deep trance produced a corona that was brilliant blue-white.

Her studies of three self-styled healers, strangely enough, produced photographic effects opposite to those reported by the Russians : at rest, their fingertip coronas were bright and expansive, and during an attempted healing the coronas shrank. (The Moss pictures, although not highly magnified like those of Krivorotov's thumb, have these rather neat coronas rather than flares and streamers of light as seen in the Russian pictures.)

The people 'healed' appeared to draw the power out of the healer in this Moss-Johnson experiment, their finger coronas expanding and the healer's shrinking during treatment. (Magnetic healers who use their own energy in healing might well make this sort of picture. In other types of psychic or spiritual healing, the healing energy seems to come from the outside and to flow through the healer. Indeed, later Kirlian experiments with the Rev. Gordon Melton and Dr Olga Worrall showed expanding coronas while healing, in line with the effect produced by Krivorotov, suggesting they were doing the latter type, in which the healer's powers are reinforced from outside himself.)

In any case, Moss and Johnson did not mention finding the 'narrow focused channel of brilliance' said to appear in Krivorotov's hands when causing a sensation of deep heat in a patient.

At the twin symposiums on 'The Dimensions of Healing', Dr Moss—a dynamic one-time actress and a founder of the Actor's Studio—described her most recent studies of psychic healing, using her adaptation of the Kirlian photographic process.

In a series of slides, she showed that a psychic healer was able successfully to treat plant leaves that had been wounded by gashing.

On the screen she projected the radiation photo of a leaf on which red splotches had appeared in the damaged area as though it were bleeding. Then, after a healer had placed his hands over it, the leaf appeared to have regenerated.

Another leaf, gashed in the centre, was treated by a San Francisco healer who made magnetic passes over it, she said. A layer of whitish stuff appeared over the gash, and after a few more 'magnetic passes', the hole in the leaf closed up. Dr Moss commented that the healing seemed to come from the outside rather than from within the leaf.

Finally, she showed a radiation photo of a leaf with a 'giant' hole in it, and she followed that with a slide taken a few minutes after the leaf had been given healing at a distance. The hole had clearly shrunk in size and looked as though it might heal. A later slide showed the hole closing up further, but eventually the damage proved too extensive and the leaf apparently gave up the struggle.

Pointing to a mass of bubbles that appeared in the wounded area of a test leaf, Dr Moss observed that 'the occult literature might call these "vitality globules in the prana" '.

A man who boasted of having a brown thumb was asked to 'zap' a freshly plucked leaf at a distance. On the screen, she showed that one side of the leaf turned almost all black and, compared to the control leaf, the difference was striking.

'This energy is a force, and perhaps it can be directed two ways,' Dr Moss cautioned, 'and if so, we have to be very careful how we use it.'

Douglas Dean's plunge into Kirlian-type high-voltage photography was not far behind that of Moss and Johnson. He was able to obtain the apparatus from a Czech source in the spring of 1972.

It was ordered originally by Sheila Ostrander and Lynn Schroeder, who live not too far from where Dean teaches at the Newark College of Engineering. And so, when the precious apparatus came to them straight through the mail they loaned it to Dean, who had photography facilities and dark rooms at the college.

At the California symposiums on healing, Dean announced with some elation that he had obtained high-frequency radiation photographs of a healer's fingers that 'seem to agree' with the two Russian photographs of Alexei Krivorotov's.

(Dean, a past president of the Parapsychological Association, is known for having engineered the PA's successful bid to membership in the prestigious American Association for the Advancement of Science in 1969. A tall, burly Briton, he has studied Physical Chemistry and Electro-Chemistry at Cambridge and holds a Masters in Science.)

Before the Czech apparatus arrived, Dean worked with Paul Sauvin, a research technologist from West Paterson, New Jersey, and they turned out some very good Kirlian-like pictures with a $39.95 machine that hairdressers use to make hair stand on end for brush-cuts, that generates 25,000 volts.

Then, upon receiving the Czech outfit in April, they began working with the New Jersey healer Ethel DeLoach, seeking evidence of 'what healers do'. But first Dean put his own finger on the strange 10 × 15 inch copper plate table insulated by plastic and varnish on to which would be developed 40,000-volt pulsed square waves of about 50 cycles per second and upwards of 50,000 Herz frequency.

'I knew Kirlian had worked at it for thirty years, and I asked someone if he still had his fingers,' said Dean humorously. 'I was assured that he did. So I took it into my dark room and placed my finger on the plate. I switched it on for three seconds and 40,000 volts went through the film, through my finger and down through my feet.'

All Dean felt was a tingling! And the very first picture that came out, he said, was 'gorgeous'.

(The photo papers he uses in his experiments are Kodak black and white, 4 × 5 inch, long exposure, or Kodachrome X20 film, emulsion upwards, or Polaroid colour pack of eight, the pack wired directly to the output of the secondary coil.)

In May, Dean wrote a paper concluding that the DeLoach pictures confirmed the Russian findings that 'healing generates increased energy emanations'. He read the paper and showed the DeLoach photographs to the public in New York on May 25 at the First Western Hemisphere Conference on Acupuncture Kirlian Photography and the Human Aura, sponsored by the Foundation for Parasensory Investigation, and a week or so later at the second annual seminar of the Jersey Society of Parapsychology.

At the latter event, Mrs DeLoach was shown giving a healing demonstration live on television, and TV projectors showed it on a large movie screen to a capacity audience.

At the California symposiums on healing, Dean began his slide show by presenting on the screen the two Krivorotov pictures Thelma Moss had brought back from Russia. He pointed to the small flares coming out of the skin when the healer was at rest and then to the 'spurts of light' when asked if he would do some healing.

Dean then flashed a high-frequency picture of the tip of Mrs DeLoach's third finger, left hand—a Roman candle effect with diaphanous emissions of light from the rim of her long nail as well as from the finger itself! 'She had been asked to think of healing,' Dean explained. 'The emanations are much bigger than when she was at rest.'

A picture of the same finger in colour showed Ethel when she was busy healing—with the other hand. Blue flares extended about two inches outward and, down toward the middle of the finger was a bright splash of light shaped somewhat like a ballet skirt, the flares pointing away from the fingertip as though in the direction of her other hand. The audience gasped. 'With the other hand she was healing a man with a wen, and it disappeared the next day,' Dean noted, 'so I think we can assume healing was really taking place.'

Dean confided that his paper concerning the high-voltage photographs of Mrs DeLoach healing has met with a mixed response. It was well-received when he read it at the May and June events in New York and New Jersey, and also at the second international parapsychology conference in Moscow in July, but when he proposed to read it at the Edinburgh international meeting of the Parapsychological Association, it was rejected by the conservative contingent. 'They just did not believe it possible,' he said.

Writing in the newsletter of the Jersey Society of Parapsychology, of which he's president, Dean told members he had the impression that many brilliant young minds were 'itching to break out' from the influence of this conservative element which he feels has held back progress for some time.

At the Moscow gathering, for example, which Dean wrote up for the *National Enquirer*, he found Russian parapsychologists 'going all-out to harness psychic force', and among their feats in the area of healing he witnessed was a further development of the Kirlian process that makes it possible to take colour motion pictures of the aura or 'field' that appears to surround the human body, now being studied by Russian doctors as a means of diagnosing illness.

'There was the human aura, as the psychics have described it, before my eyes—flowing from the body of the subject in wave after wave of vivid colours,' wrote Dean. I gazed fascinatedly as colour succeeded colour, each with its own significance as to the state of mind and body of the subject.'

21. Lawrence LeShan

DR LAWRENCE LESHAN probed the healing mystery by studying a select group of healers for clues, and when these led in every direction he dug deeper and found that they shared a common core of experience of which they were unaware.

'I had to tease and analyse it out, and I found they all go into an altered state of consciousness. I then analysed that state of consciousness,' says LeShan, who is a University of Chicago-trained clinical and research psychologist.

After much study and practise going into that altered state, LeShan is now hailed as 'the man who scientifically trained himself to become a healer'. He teaches his method in workshops, and the number of his pupils is fast growing.

Listing a few of the healer-subjects he interviewed or worked with or whose writings he studied, LeShan names Harry Edwards, Ronald Beesley and George Chapman among the Britons and the Worralls, Agnes Sanford, Edgar Jackson, Katherine Kuhlmann and Carmen Barazza among the Americans.

How did a psychologist become interested in the paranormal? A big, dynamic man with a salty sense of humour, LeShan traces his interest in 'ESP and all that jazz' to nine years ago when he read about Dr Grad's work with the healer Estebany, and certain scientific studies in the Journal of the American Society for Psychical Research.

'I looked into it and I tried to understand it,' he recalls, 'and I soon decided the paranormal was an important area to study. Unfortunately most people prefer simply to look away from it.'

In his lively lectures before the ASPR in March, the Association for Humanistic Psychology in May and the American Academy of Psychotherapists in October, LeShan told how he had chosen healing from the entire range of psychic activity, by a process of elimination.

'The telephone,' he said, 'will always be better than telepathy. Clairvoyance? It's a whole lot easier to reach for the letter-opener . . . I decided psychic healing was the most potentially useful.'

A man with a cool, no-nonsense approach, LeShan says he estimated that ninety per cent of all claimed healings could be 'thrown out' as mere instances of hysterical or misreported symptoms. But the ten per cent remaining were a solid residue and he found it 'absolutely unquestionable that the phenomenon exists'.

And so, since psychic healing is obviously impossible in the minds of most people, and yet occurs, he would have to produce a theory that would account for the paradox, construct a framework that would make psychic healing acceptable to the culture. And if it was ever to be a useful cultural tool, it would have to be made 'teachable'.

Reviewing the stages of confusing information he was given at the start by his healer-subjects, LeShan recalled that 'some said God did it, some said spirits did it, and some said the healing was done by some unknown and undetectable kind of energy'.

He had no quarrel with those who attributed the healing to God, but the Spiritualists' belief was hard for him to accept. 'If a spirit told me he had been dead five years I'd find it very hard to take anything else he said seriously,' LeShan quipped. 'However,' he added, 'I may have a block there.' As for the energy explanation, that seemed, perhaps, more reasonable.

He next studied his healer-subjects' behaviour during the healing session. What did they say they did, and how was it related to biological changes in the patient? He found some faced North, some South, some took anything metal off their bodies, some prayed to God and some thought of Brahma. He then rooted out the 'commonality factor' which all seemed to share, at least in Type I, which he called 'the prayer method', and he was later to make it the basis of the coherent theory he was seeking:

'In the prayer method the activity is within the healer's own head, mind, person. He doesn't try to heal but tries to merge with the patient for one moment to know completely another way of being in the world—a oneness, a feeling of caritas, love, absolute concern. At that moment the healer is perceiving in the deepest sense that the universe is constituted on other lines, that we're all one. The patient is very much the centre of it and is merged with the healer as part of it . . . All is one. Nothing is alone.' He found that healers associated these moments with biological changes in the patient.

In his subsequent studies, LeShan began to realise that this metaphysical way of perceiving reality sounded very much like the more thoughtful statements of Einsteinian physicists. Indeed, he discovered that sensitives, mystics, and physicists, three groups of individuals with different goals and methods, were all in complete agreement on the concept that there were two ways of being in the universe, that there was the world of the many or the everyday commonsense world, and the world of the one, or the field theory of the universe.

In his lectures, LeShan has a little fun with his listeners by reading off several quotations he's collected expressing this idea of oneness. Asking for a show of hands, he'll ask, 'Was this said by a physicist or a mystic?' On most occasions the majority guesses wrong. For example, the phrase, 'The stuff of the universe is mind stuff' is usually pegged as the utterance of a mystic. 'Wrong,' says LeShan, 'a physicist said it.'

But how does the healer's attainment of this state of oneness affect the health of a patient? LeShan says he was influenced here by the writings of George Bernard Shaw and Alexis Carrel on Lourdes. Shaw had called the shrine 'a blasphemous place' because the absence of wooden legs and toupés implied a limitation on the power of God, and LeShan glimpsed the truth that so often underlies Shaw's most flippant statements. And in Carrel's account of watching a miracle healing at Lourdes he thought he found more of the answer. 'Carrel was watching an open cancer through a lens when the healing occurred. He knew that every now and then when a cancer dries up it follows a course, and this cancer was following that same course but about five thousand times faster than he'd ever seen it happen.' Was it possible that in psychic healing the body is helped to heal itself at a stepped-up pace?

Putting it all together, what seemed to be happening was this: the healer, with his caritas and the concept of physics on which he is operating, welcomes the patient home to the universe. The patient recognises this at a deep personal or subconscious level and at that moment his body's self-repair mechanism is stimulated to function closer to its potential. LeShan feels this is the major type of healing and is the kind done by many individual healers, Christian Scientists and prayer circles.

Type 2, on the other hand, represents an effort on the part of the healer to heal, and he does not go into an altered state of consciousness, according to LeShan. 'He perceives a current of energy flowing through his hands and being passed through the area of the wound. The juice is turned on, so to speak, and sometimes healing results.'

He doesn't know how this unnamed energy works, but he knows that the sensations of heat or cold people report when under treatment are not picked up by a thermometer.

Comparing the two, LeShan suggests that Type 1 is reasonably permanent and that with healing of Type 2 the symptoms often come back.

LeShan's next step was to try to emulate the healers of Type 1 in the hope that if he could attain the same altered state of consciousness he, too, could heal.

For the next year and a half he steeped himself in the writings of mystics, from Evelyn Underhill, St Teresa of Avila and St John of the Cross to Patanjali, Sankara and Jacob Boehme, he says. He then studied the leading teachers of Zen, Yoga, Sufi, Hasidism, and the Christian tradition, took what mystical training and exercises he needed out of books and put it all into sequence of exercises designed to alter consciousness in the direction indicated to him by the healers. 'I then tried it on a patient and I got results.'

The patient was a young woman with a badly scalded hand, he said. It was swollen, the skin was shiny, and she couldn't remove her rings. This first time he used both types of healing for good measure, and in fifteen minutes all her symptoms disappeared.

Another early case was a woman with arthritis in both hands. She didn't believe in psychic healing and read a newspaper while LeShan went into the altered state of consciousness. Both crippled hands were suddenly free and she could flex them!

A sty in a woman's eye disappeared just as suddenly. But then, a good friend who really wanted to be healed of painful muscle spasms in her lower back showed absolutely no improvement after two deep sessions, he said. He emphasised that it is impossible to predict when healings will happen and when they will not.

Feeling he was now ready to teach what he had learned to do, LeShan organised a seminar. He deliberately chose people who had not had psychic experience so that they could approach it with fresh eyes. Many were psychologists. All were people who could endure discipline and hard work, he says. They met two nights a week from 7 to 12 p.m. over a six-week period. 'I've never seen a group so exhausted.'

The workshop course as it now stands consists of three kinds of exercises :

(1) Mental discipline—exercises to train the mind.

(2) Exercises to loosen the usual concepts of time and space.

(3) Exercises to lead step-by-step to the special altered state of consciousness associated with psychic healing.

An important part of the training is the tuning of the personality so that it is emotionally at home in the world of the one. In one exercise the student tries to feel that he and his patient are together inside a bubble. In another he concentrates on a match for long periods in order to still the mind and allow the consciousness to expand. 'Training the mind is a lot harder than training the body,' LeShan told one of his audiences, 'but I've found no one who could not learn this method.'

His students work only with patients who are under a doctor's care for the ailments being treated, unless it is a minor complaint. Results are recorded and kept for scientific purposes.

'Patients who face the group report a feeling of being tremendously loved and cared for and in forty to fifty per cent of cases we do get results.'

In an interview, LeShan summarised the transmission he believes takes place between healer and subject during the 'uniting' and I was struck by the emphasis he placed on the need for the healer to experience this sense of caring.

'The altered state is very close to the consciousness in which telepathy takes place,' he said. 'In this telepathic transmission the two become one in a metaphysical sense so that a communication is established between them and the dualism is temporarily cancelled. But in order to have this unity in multiplicity established you have to really care about the person, and unless there's that primary concern it's just an empty and meaningless exercise.'

(LeShan's belief that the healing takes place on the telepathic level ties in with the findings of Russian researchers that the energy or bioplasma body can be affected telepathically, as reported in *Psychic Discoveries Behind the Iron Curtain.* Kirlian photography also reportedly indicates that healing takes place on this bioplasmic level which is tied in with the psychic consciousness.)

LeShan can't help wondering what would happen if a culture 'that's going to hell in a handbasket', could accept the fact that we are all one and can heal each other. 'Maybe it could save us. At least it could help,' he says.

Judging from the impact of LeShan's speeches wherever he appears, the indications are that he is reaching a good-sized section of the culture that is uninterested in the simpler, less intellectually rigorous approaches to healing.

Following are some of the questions LeShan was asked by audiences in New York, and his replies:

Q. How can you say your theory applies to a Spiritualist healer like Harry Edwards?

LeShan: 'He does the same merging of self with patient. It's the same procedure with a different explanation system.'

Q. What do you think of people who criticise you for taking a non-spiritual approach?

LeShan: 'They bring all the saccharine and sugar and diabetes into it that the movement needs.'

Q. Why do you meditate lying down?

LeShan: 'Because there are fewer body signals to interfere with your meditation.'

Q. Just what kind of meditation do you teach?

LeShan: 'It's very, very highly disciplined. Its a form of meditation that's much more disciplined than Yoga.'

Q. What kind of research are you doing now?

LeShan: 'How to get deeper into the altered state. What activity of the subject will make him most responsive. What is the best way for healers to work—in groups? In the next room? In a circle? We're trying to understand it better, do it better.'

Q. Are you doing any research on failures?

LeShan: 'We're studying them equally.'

Q. Do you think egoism stops healing?

LeShan: 'I deeply believe so.'

Q. How do you know healings aren't merely due to suggestion?

LeShan: 'Well, it has worked with colicky babies, people in

comas and at a distance. That should make it perfectly plain that it's not all due to suggestion.'

Q. But aren't there lots of illnesses that are just too far gone to be helped?

LeShan: 'An Englishwoman who had a 28-pound tumour was healed in this manner. A psychic healer named Mrs Sammons worked with her late into the night. Both dozed off, and in the morning the woman's abdomen was flat, the liquid was gone and the bed was dry. There are a few cases of this kind.'

Q. You seem to prefer Type 1. What's wrong with Type 2?

LeShan: 'It implies we're separate. I'm not trying to meet and unite with you, I'm going to heal you. Look at this, Zap! It attracts people who like power-trips. It not only prevents individual spiritual growth but blocks the personal growth that would make healing possible, in my opinion.'

Q. When you meditate on the oneness is there any other input of a spiritual nature?

LeShan: 'You can say "faith, hope, and caritas, these three, and the greatest of these is caritas".'

Q. Then you are perfectly willing to quote St Paul?

LeShan: 'Certainly.'

An independent researcher who has done most of his work on a foundation grant, Dr LeShan works in cooperation with Life Energies, Inc., 563 Park Avenue, New York, a group of scientists and other professionals whose purpose is to seek scientific confirmation of psychic healing and other unexplored aspects of man's potential. He has written a monograph, *Toward a General Theory of the Paranormal* and has a new book out, entitled, *The Medium, the Mystic and the Physicist*.

In winding up our interview, LeShan recalled with some satisfaction that when he presented his theory on healing at a Wainwright House seminar in Rye, New York, there were a number of healers in the audience, among them the Worralls. 'At the end they came down to me and one said, "We'd like to talk to you. We want to congratulate you as a body. You're the first person who has managed to articulate what we're trying to do".' It was a moment Lawrence LeShan is not likely to forget.

22. The Academy of Parapsychology and Medicine

THE ACADEMY OF PARAPSYCHOLOGY and Medicine symposiums on 'The Dimensions of Healing', in covering a wide range of paranormal healing practises, devoted a full day to the study of acupuncture and another to the latest developments on the biofeedback frontier.

These sessions were designed for physicians and other interested professionals rather than the general public, and in a smaller auditorium I watched Sister Justa Smith, in the interests of science, lift herself nimbly on to an operating table where she remained motionless for over an hour while Dr Harold O. Saita showed how the acupuncturist makes his diagnosis, using a kind of meter that measures the energy flow at various points on the body. After assessing Sister Justa's physical state, and stopping short of sticking her with needles, Dr Saita, a kindly, soft-voiced Oriental who is now in private practice in West Vancouver, Canada, was peppered with questions from local doctors. (The symposium planners were pleased to have been able to produce three adepts at acupuncture who spoke good English and were also familiar with Western medicine.)

In the bio-feedback lectures, Elmers Green, PhD, and his wife, Alyce Green, PhD, two Menninger Foundation researchers, explored the possibilities for self-healing and building 'psychosomatic health' in hitching oneself up to electronic instruments that let you see how your body is functioning.

The theory is that if a person can 'see' their tension or heartbeat rate, and can watch its fluctuations on a meter, he can practise 'making the meter go down' and in so doing learn to manipulate the underlying psychophysiological problems that caused the tension or fast heartbeat. By observing one's temperature readings or brain-waves on a dial, a person may learn to control normally automatic functions for better health, creativity and self-realisation. The Greens described their exciting research with the distinguished Indian Yogi, Swami Rama, who came all the way from Rishikesh in the Himalayas to Topeka, Kansas, and co-operated good-naturedly in showing how he could stop his heart from pumping blood for 17 seconds, and other amazing feats of self-control.

The Academy's president, Dr Robert Bradley, spoke up for the therapeutic use of spirit communication, combined with hypnosis. With his wife, Ruth Bomar Bradley, the author of the book *Psychic Phenomena: Revelations and Experiences,* Dr Bradley says he developed this method of treatment after moving into an old house in Denver inhabited by poltergeists. Such spine-tingling experiences as having his cigarette lighter float through the air and out of range when he reached for it, led him to the studies he later put to use in his medical practice.

'Assuming the patient's religious beliefs encompass these concepts,' Dr Bradley explained, 'the concept of karma, or purposeful reincarnation, can be explored by age-regression to former life experiences, especially if this life inventory produces no logical etiology of behaviour problems.

'The former life or lives may give a clue. The reassurance of the continuity of life, the chance through free will to balance the scale tipped by ego errors, the "never alone" feeling imported by subtle spirit communication can all be sources of useful trance suggestions to those patients oriented to these beliefs . . . I have found it even more effective in achieving self-confidence and serenity than psychotherapy.'

Dr Bradley said he was apprehensive about going into hypnotherapy, although he had his certificate in trance induction training. But he had cases he hadn't helped 'one iota' and felt he needed an effective new tool.

And so, being a firm believer in spirit guidance as a result of numerous experiences, he went to see Arthur Ford, taking with him a list of 20 questions on an index card in his shirt pocket. He happened to be attending a hypnotists' convention in Philadelphia and knew that Ford lived in the neighbourhood.

'The voice of Ford's spirit guide, Fletcher, came through and said, "Doctor, you need not be afraid. We are with you always. We will guide you and help you and work through your subconscious mind." He then answered all my questions, *in sequence* accurately,' Bradley said, adding that he had time and again used the hypnotic regression technique, with spirit help, to good effect.

Giving an example, he said a waitress with a sixth grade education and a defeated attitude in this life was regressed to a life in the last century in which she was well-educated and a creative writer. Bradley gave her the suggestion under hypnosis that she make it her main hobby, and now writes poetry and is studying to be a reporter.

The doctor said he thinks spirit communication is going on constantly and that he got his ideas on natural childbirth and for his lectures either in sleep or from spirit sources. He once wrote, 'I think the greatest crime of the century is that our children grow up to become adults still retaining with them the silly fantasy of Hallowe'en. The only thing they know about spirit communication is from that silly childhood fantasy of evil.'

In his experience using regression to past lives in baffling cases, Bradley has come to believe that 25 per cent of homosexualism is a 'karmic assignment' and that's why it's so hard to treat. A homosexual may have had five previous lives as a woman and now he's trapped in a male body while in the soul crossover the female is deeply embedded. And if this person once ridiculed homosexuals, he now has the 'privilege' of experiencing that ridicule in this life.

Dr Bradley has also made a forceful observation on the need for doctors to practise 'the laying-on of hands' to supplement other healing therapies. 'As doctors,' he said, 'when we're making rounds to sick people or post-operative patients, we should be encouraged to put our hands on the patient. I think we are transmitting the force that you have heard about . . . going from a stronger person to perhaps a weaker person under stress.' And, referring to the Kirlian photographs showing energy coming from healers' hands, he added, 'If I had my way, extrapolating into the future, I think Kirlian photography should be used to evaluate every medical student before he's allowed into medical school to calibrate his healing capacity.'

Full of exciting ideas for putting information from past lives to work therapeutically, he'd like to see studies done of mentally retarded children and senile people in old folks homes in search of soul memories and foreign languages. And he feels mediumship and spirit communication can be valuable in a religious type of treatment that would help people overcome a fear of death.

Bradley said he's appalled that so many middle-aged women come to him suffering from depression and spastic colons who follow the same pattern : when he starts age-regressing them, he finds they are good church-goers, well-versed in all the creeds and dogmas, but when he gets them in an altered state of consciousness their only problem is 'they're scared to death of death'. He has concluded that there's something wrong with the religions that make people so morbidly fearful of dying.

When I asked Dr Bradley if he believed in the existence of spirit doctors, he shot back, 'Don't worry they're there. Perhaps not many, but their numbers are increasing !'

Dr William McGarey leads the effort of the Academy of Parapsychology and Medicine to stimulate professional inquiry and research in acupuncture.

The new-old Chinese method of healing, he points out, is not only serving as 'a bridge between East and West' but also between parapsychology and medicine, since the subtle, unidentified body energies involved in acupuncture are equally challenging to psychic investigators and doctors.

Dr McGarey, with Dr James Rhee, conducted the Academy's truly historic Acupuncture Symposium in June, 1972, at Stanford University attended by over 1300 doctors—the largest such event ever held in the Western World—and it was shared with thousands more doctors when a videotape of the panel was presented to the American Medical Association convention meeting in San Francisco.

In his talks before the twin symposiums on healing in October, Dr McGarey conjectured that the arrival of acupuncture in the West after 5,000 years is 'part of a movement of consciousness we're all involved in, a great change in the way we look at our bodies'. We are at a take-off point in understanding our bodies and body energies, he added, and perhaps acupuncture is bringing about the awakening.

He then enthusiastically described a case in which acupuncture, medicine and parapsychology 'converged' in a single patient, opening up far-reaching possibilities of treating pain quickly and simply. The therapy was described to him by experts at the Osaka Pain Clinic in Japan, he said.

The patient suffered painful third degree burns of the left axilla (armpit). The Japanese doctors reasoned that if the energies of that area could be drained off to another part of the body it would heal faster. So they put aluminium foil over the burn and ran a wire from the foil to a meridian point in the patient's right leg (diagonally opposite quadrant, assuming the figure-of-eight flow of body energy or life force described by psychics). Within ten minutes the pain had disappeared. McGarey wrote it up for his state's medical journal, 'Arizona Medicine' and it was published.

McGarey had an unexpected need to apply the technique when his twelve-year-old son, David, was badly burned in the palm of his hand in a boyish experiment with 'mud, fire and water' in the backyard. A pipe his son was holding in his hand exploded and when the pain hadn't subsided in an hour, he wrapped the hand in aluminium foil and ran a wire to the meridian point in the opposite leg. In 25 minutes all the pain was gone. His son's hand was a bit numb and had a blister, but no more pain. McGarey said he repeated the technique successfully on a very painful case of sunburn. 'We don't know why it works but, anyway, it does.'

Giving us a few ABC's of the Yin-Yang philosophy that underlies acupuncture, McGarey informed us of a number of its uses other than for anaesthesia, which has received the most publicity. Projecting on to the screen slides of two cardiagrams, one very irregular-looking and the other obviously normal, he said they had been taken before and after acupuncture and within fifteen minutes of each other. 'It is very satisfactory in heart conditions,' he said.

The doctor commented that in the West we know that each cell of the living organism is essentially a galvanic battery and has the capacity to transform energy. 'The regulation of the electrical voltage level in the cells may constitute the mechanism through which acupuncture works,' he said.

Dr McGarey's interest in acupuncture appears to stem logically from his fifteen years working with the Edgar Cayce concepts of healing which also recognize a mysterious flow of energy through the body. As medical director of the Edgar Cayce Foundation's clinic in Phoenix, Arizona, he cooperates with over 200 doctors as they utilise Cayce therapies in their practice. He also runs annual medical symposiums which are well-attended by MDs from a broad area. (The sixth met in Phoenix, Arizona, in January, 1973.)

Relating acupuncture to the work of Western researchers, many of whom present findings at his symposiums, McGarey noted that several are using electrical currents in healing. He told of a stubborn case of an ulcer that had been cured by inducing into it a low current of electricity. Another researcher, Robert Becker, had regenerated the leg of a rat, 'tissue, bone and cartilege', using electric current of a very low voltage, McGarey said, and he is convinced that some day this sort of thing will be possible for human beings.

'Instead of removing a mangled limb, in the future we'll regenerate it,' said the doctor; 'in fact there may come a day when a breast that has been removed surgically can be regenerated.'

Offering a Cayce concept, McGarey said, 'God's energy manifest in man is electrical in nature, a vibration. The same force you call God in action. Seeing this, feeling this, the body becomes revivified and, as related to spirit, mind and body, all three are renewed.'

In closing, he brought up two intriguing electrical appliances that Edgar Cayce so often recommended in the readings. Known as the Wet Cell Appliance and the Radio-Active Appliance (re-named the Impedance Device), they are described in detail with diagrams in an ARE pamphlet written by Cayce's son, Edgar Evans Cayce.

Illustrating the modus operandi of the latter, he said two wires from the device were fastened to metal plates that were attached to the patient's right wrist and left ankle or left wrist and right ankle, much as in the Osaka Pain Clinic therapy. 'The device would not do anything of itself, but body-produced energy would flow through it, be clarified and be put back into the body and put where there was too much or too little.' Its effect was to equalise the body's 'electronic force', according to the pamphlet, and it was prescribed mostly for insomnia, poor circulation and nervous tension and less often for deafness, obesity, arthritis, neurasthenia, debilitation and abnormal children. Research on both devices goes ahead, although slowly, and early results have been promising. Apparently, when Cayce prescribed them, his patients were often lax in their use or other treatments were given in combination, making a scientific evaluation difficult.

These devices also assumed the figure-of-eight of energy in the body, said McGarey, noting that the centre of the '8' two or three fingers to the right of the umbilicus is the point where the life force enters the foetus embryo, according to the readings.

'But healing of the body by electrical energy was not all Cayce talked about,' McGarey continued, 'he suggested other physical therapies which are just as important for total well-being as spiri-tual and mental healing.

'Take the Castor Oil Pack. You place a flannel cloth saturated with the oil over the abdomen, cover it with plastic and then apply a heating pad. It's a treatment that's at least 50 years old, but I use it successfully with appendicitis.'

(In the monthly 'medical research bulletins' he writes for the ARE Journal, McGarey is always reporting new therapeutic uses for the Castor Oil Pack. For example, in the July, 1972, issue of the Journal, a Shillington, Pennsylvania surgeon is said to have found it wonder-fully helpful in relieving 'malaise, fever, low abdominal tenderness and pain' following a hysterectomy that developed complications. In that same issue, another doctor reported that good old Atomidine and Glycothymoline, two more Cayce standbys, were excellent for healing canker sores of the mouth when applied locally, one at a time.)

At the ARE clinic where his wife Gladys, also an MD, works with him, McGarey has been dealing with the problem of epilepsy for the past four years and has started more than twenty-five patients on the Cayce therapy, among them their own son. Following are some excerpts from an article reporting progress:

'Seventy-five per cent of all epilepsy cases are termed either idiopathic of cryptogenic, implying thereby that we actually don't know the causes. Thus we are dealing with the unknown. In Edgar Cayce material, there are suggestions as to what may really be the etiology of these seventy-five per cent "idiopathic" cases. The spinal cord and several lymphatic patches are involved in this explana-tion . . .

'He said that the karmic influence in epilepsy was usually the basic problem . . . The karmic result is usually either a spinal lesion or a lacteal lesion, or both. In thirty-seven of the seventy-nine cases on which Cayce gave readings, both types were present. The spinal lesions were not in the spine itself, but in the spinal cord or portions thereof—perhaps the posterior ganglion or the autonomic sympathetic . . .

'The philosophy of the Cayce material suggests that the first goal of therapy is the improvement of the co-ordination of the nervous system within the body. The second is to re-establish normal nervous system function by restoring or regenerating tangled nerve ends. The third is to bring about the healing of the body . . .'

Amazingly, Cayce 'saw' functions of the body as easily as he saw organs inside the same body, McGarey once said, giving tribute to the great medical clairvoyant. 'It was the fact that he did these things so many times and was so consistently correct whenever he could be checked that made this capacity so unusual and attractive to study. For, in this consistency lies the most powerful argument for the accuracy of concepts that grow out of Cayce's statements to a multitude of people.'

Tracing back to its roots in the dictionary, the word 'meditation' means 'to heal'. It is generally agreed among parapsychologists that it is the one universal and safest method of self-healing as well as an essential to the sending of healing to others. And now, the healing effect on the body of meditation appears to have been given a solid scientific base, judging from experiments reported in the *Scientific American*. (See February, 1972.)*

In this context, the presentation of Haridas Chaudhuri, PhD, at the Academy of Parapsychology and Medicine symposiums couldn't have been more timely. Adding information from his own resources on how 'meditation therapy' can produce healing, he filled in areas beyond the purely physical measurements that provided the scientific data.

A specialist in East-West cultural understanding who radiates

The Physiology of Meditation, by Robert Keith Wallace and Herbert Benson. The findings are based on a study conducted both at the University of California at Irvine and the Harvard Medical Unit in Boston City Hospital of 36 volunteer adults, ages 17-41, 28 males, 8 females, who had been meditating 2-3 years using the easy-to-learn transcendental meditation technique. A complex of measurements were taken at regular intervals, the results showing a sharp decrease of oxygen, slight increase in acidity of arterial blood, marked decrease in blood lactate level, slowing of heartbeat and considerable increase in skin resistance. Electroencephalograph (EEG) showed intensification of slow alpha brain waves and some theta wave activity all indicating what the writers termed a 'wakeful hypometabolic state.'

'In these circumstances,' they concluded, 'the hypometabolic state, representing quiescence rather than hyperaction of the sympathetic nervous system, may indicate a guidepost to better health.'

kindliness and warmth, Dr Chaudhuri spoke in practical terms without sacrificing beauty of expression. He is president of the California Institute of Asian Studies and the Cultural Integration Fellowship, a participant in various international UN conferences and author of, among other books, a *Philosophy of Meditation*. His topic was 'The Healing Potential of Psychosomatic Integration.'

'There is a built-in healing power in the human system,' Dr Chaudhuri began. 'The more we maintain harmony, the more we enjoy health and creativity. The more disharmony and discord between elements of the human personality, the more we suffer disease and ailments.'

Through 'meditation therapy', he said, healing can be produced psychosomatically, because the mind can be trained to affect the body in such a way that we can tap the sources of well-being and long life. For, in meditation this mentally directed or psychosomatic health is fed by spiritual energy, he said.

Listing the essential elements of meditation therapy he began with the art of breathing.

'Breathing is a very significant kind of continuous communication with the universal life energy, and there is a constant interaction as you harness vital energies.'

Next in importance is getting into a very relaxed state.

'There is a reduction of blood pressure which is good for the heart, a reduction of heart beat, a reduction of ionised lactic acid salt particles in the body due to anxiety, the root of many psychosomatic ills.'

Then, as you practise the silence, anxiety is released before you can settle down.

'You need the help and guidance of a guru. But the divine guru, God himself, appears in response to your prayer. He takes the poison and swallows it. Where else would he put it? He takes it upon himself . . .'

'Next, you dive into the depths of your mind and you find the treasure in your unconscious psychic, and in doing this you catch a glimpse of your true self.

'Most of our ills are estrangement from our true self. Ignorance of the true nature of self is responsible for most of our suffering . . . So many feel they are failures in life. They attract failure because they have lost touch with the inmost centre of their being. Some suffer from an inflated self-image. This is how we develop delusions of grandeur, lack of perspective in regard to oneself.

'Soon there is an increase of the energy level and of the consciousness—without intoxicants.

'The serpent is the symbol of energy and when in the course of meditation you get high and increase your energy, you are intoxicated with celestial snakebite! There is an awakening of spiritual energy which is dormant in humans at the base of the spinal cord.'

Finally, he said, there is the unexpected surge of energy, with a sudden, spontaneous rhythm.

'You have the feeling it's the divine power. Man's experience of the divine in this life, divine communion. Those who have felt this supernatural power of the Holy Spirit, also described by the Hassidic mystics, know that it is a reality. It is the profoundest potential of man, every man.'

(Referring to Dr William Tiller's theory of the seven energy levels present in man, Dr Chaudhuri said, 'We are doing similar research and we are discovering many things about the human potential'.)

'And so, in the course of our meditation if we pursue it along proper lines without going astray to the goal—blissful communion with the Supreme Being—the higher centres of consciousness are activated—a wonderful experience in terms of humanity as a whole.'

Dr Chaudhuri added that when we unfold to these higher fields of energy the heart centre is opened and we are able to experience ego-less love, perhaps for the first time. 'And there is a social dimension also, since you throw out vibrations of joy and love to the community when you are illuminated on this level.'

It was these vibrations of love that people responded to in Christ, he said, and that was the secret of his healing power. 'They felt the joy of love, the joy of faith.'

And when the chakra between the eyes is opened, he said, the meditator experiences at last cosmic consciousness. 'Your horizon is expanded, and you realise your function and value in the universe. At this moment of total truth the highest healing power is realised, and by transmitting the cosmic power thousands could be healed!'

After that there is no limit to the changes that might be brought about in the world, according to Dr Chaudhuri, and he smiled benevolently. 'In this self-healing power and in healing others we will become a global unity, functioning as an expression of the divine healing power.'

When Dr Chaudhuri appeared as a panellist, he was asked to outline the best method for meditation to be used every day by the beginner. He listed these four steps:

1 Relax, let go in mind and body.

2 Look within self. Focus on the true nature of self. Who am I? What is the essence of my being? Think of self as a unique creative centre of the cosmic whole.

3 Relate self to fellow beings. Send out vibrations of love to all fellow beings, and we can bring about a profound change of heart. As we get trained we can spontaneously radiate love and peace.

4 Total self-giving to the Supreme Being. Ultimate Reality or Cosmic Reality. No thought, reduce the mind to nothingness, to total self-givingness, to light and power and love.

23. Five American Healers—Jackson, Rolling Thunder, Schwartz, LeShan, Worrall

PRACTITIONERS as well as investigators of psychic healing were well-represented at all three California events. The Humanistic Psychologists invited, aside from Dr LeShan, no fewer than three healers, all with very different approaches. Edgar Jackson, Rolling Thunder and Jack Schwarz appeared as their own witnesses, but their impeccable reputations helped to make their accounts of incredible healings more credible.

Soft-voiced, understated, wearing a grey business suit, Edgar Jackson, D.D., is one of the nation's leading spiritual healers. His background is formidably respectable—Yale Divinity School graduate, an ordained Methodist minister, studied at Yale Institute of Human Relations and New York's Post Graduate Centre of Psychotherapy.

A specialist in crisis psychology and crisis management, nine of his books have been professional book club selections (*Understanding Prayer* is recommended by Dr LeShan as a 'must' for would-be healers). Now teaching at Royalton College in Vermont, the Rev. Jackson works with a healing group he has trained that reputedly does high-powered healing. He has estimated that in the past two decades he has administered the laying-on of hands, along with prayer and meditation in the Quaker tradition, over ten thousand times.

In his talk, Dr Jackson described four particularly poignant cases where full healings occurred. One involved a concert pianist with heavy financial obligations who had been told by his doctor he had a bad heart and must give up concert work immediately. After spiritual healing, his cardiagram returned to normal and he was able to continue his career full tilt. Another was the case of a woman with an acute psoriasis covering most of her body, making the slightest contact painful. 'I told the woman that I did not believe it was in the divine plan that she should suffer to this degree, and I asked her to pray with me.' The condition, which had been of long standing, cleared up within a few treatments.

'I don't fully understand, I am just describing,' Dr Jackson told his listeners. 'But I think you can help another person by stimulating a process.'

Rolling Thunder wore a flat-crowned hat with three feathers. Born a Cherokee, he serves as a medicine man for the Western Shoshone Indian nation, his wife's tribe having adopted him. Chosen for this work in his early youth, he was apprenticed to a teacher who supervised his rigorous training and discipline. He is now not only a spiritual leader for his people but also a legal adviser and powerful spokesman. An authority on man-nature relationships, he is concerned with the well-being of all people and the environmental conditions that are threatening the health, particularly, of Indians.

The healing power comes from the Great Spirit, says Rolling Thunder, and he himself is only the instrument, having no special power of his own. He believes the Great Spirit works through people who have prepared and purified themselves.

When I asked Rolling Thunder to expand a little on his philosophy of healing, he said, 'There should be more respect for the Great Spirit's life plan and respect for animals and all nature and for each other,' and he added, 'People ought to learn this before they ask for healing and other benefits.'

'So many people want these things,' he continued, 'before they've earned the right to have them. They may be healed, but you're dealing with an awful lot of power. A person being a healer should approach the Great Spirit humbly.'

He said it was very difficult to heal people in a modern society properly because they're so impatient. 'They want everything here and now.'

Rolling Thunder told very little about cases of healing, and more about the failure of certain white men to treat the Indian with respect and especially to understand his healing traditions. 'When the medicine man is called to heal someone, they prepare for him to stay, and give him a meal. If he wants to meditate they don't harass him, they make him comfortable, and they always bring him a little gift of tobacco,' he said.

I asked if he does absent healing, and Rolling Thunder said yes, but he didn't prefer to. 'I like being in a person's actual presence, to do it directly when possible. I feel better that way.'

Jack Schwarz is a tall, gaunt-looking Dutchman who found at the age of nine that he had healing ability. At fifteen he was able to demonstrate self-healing and also how to control pain and bleeding. Coming to the US in 1957, he became director of the Conscious Research Foundations and lent his gifts to a number of research projects in such areas as the investigation of cerebral memory patterns and psychometric diagnosis, and lately to studies of the voluntary control of internal states at the Menninger Foundation.

Before Schwarz appeared on stage to speak on 'The Integral Way of Self-Healing and Prevention', he was shown on the screen by Dr Elmer Green, with whom he worked in the Menninger project. The audience gasped when Schwarz thrust a long needle straight through his biceps without a drop of blood appearing. (When Green asked if he'd do it again and bleed a little, he did that too, but only after asking the permission of his unconscious.)

After that, one expected Schwarz to be a tight-lipped Stoic, but instead he was gentle and at times fervently spiritual as he outlined the method he teaches at his Aletheia Psycho-Physical Foundation in Selma, Oregon, for attaining higher states of consciousness and learning to extend conscious control over previously unconscious sections of the brain. Dr Green said of Schwarz ecstatically, 'He learned to turn on all the different brainwaves at will!'

Olga Ripich Worrall was the only healer sharing the platform with the parapsychologists, doctors, and physicists at Stanford and UCLA. Although petite in stature, her manner was spirited and confident.

Fixing her reading glasses, she read her speech with liveliness and precision. She began with a review of psychic healing through the ages (beginning in 3000 BC) and deplored the fact that no one has been able to reduce it to a law or embody it in a form acceptable to science.

'If a disease is cured by unconventional means, the diagnosis was wrong, or it's obviously a case of spontaneous remission, or "It cured itself",' she said. 'When science can study spontaneous remission we will take a giant step toward understanding unconventional healing.'

What is responsible for healing? she asked, 'The healer? The patient? The environment? Medicine? The wisdom of the body? The intelligence of the cell? God? The operation of a law? Perhaps all. What matters is that it works,' she said. 'All any healer can do is provide the conditions.'

As for the actual source of the healing power, 'There's a certain something out of which comes everything,' she said, 'Supreme Intelligence, Omnipotent Will, Immutable Law, timeless, spaceless, the majority of people call this source God and so do I.'

In the years since 1915 when she and her husband were actively engaged in healing they never took money, not even love offerings or gifts, she said. And she has not only healed adults and children, but cats, birds and horses as well. 'Even plants respond to this mysterious energy.'

Listing a few of its applications, she mentioned scar tissues, diseases of the kidney or spleen, strep throat, alcoholism, emotional disturbances, cancer. 'A woman asked for my prayers for a tumour and under my touch it reduced to half its size. The pain stopped. She came to me again and I touched it. The tumour was softer and smaller and the inverted nipple had popped out. But all arrangements had been made for surgery and the doctor insisted on performing the operation as scheduled. What would have happened if he'd waited? Today that woman is minus a breast.' A shock went through the audience.

She then told a happier story. This time it was an abdominal tumour and very large, the size of a head. The woman was sent by a medical doctor to her weekly healing service at the New Life Clinic of the Mount Washington Methodist Church in Baltimore. She placed her hands gently over the tumour, and the woman later reported a sensation like 'a corkscrew turning in my stomach'. Six months later she was back at her job as a nurse and the tumour was completely gone. 'If we're to demand the respect of the public,' said the doctor, after examining his patient, 'It's our obligation to understand this phenomenon.'

The nurse was free of pain after that first touch and she never took any more pain medication, she said. 'This happened in 1956.

I saw her two years ago and she's fine. Maybe we might say it's a cure . . .'

She then told of a child that had suffered fifteen traumatic operations on her brain, and meningitis. Her head was heavily bandaged and she wasn't expected to live. After Mrs Worrall placed her hands on the child's head she never had another operation and has done well, able to attend a school for retarded children.

It happened that a witness to one of her healings was in the audience, she said 'A woman came to the altar of the clinic with a lump the size of a goose egg on her face. She explained that doctors would not remove it, for fear facial paralysis would result. I placed my hand on it, but it didn't respond. So I blessed her and dismissed her. Then, as she was walking past two women on the way to her seat, they saw the lump melt before their eyes.' It was one of those two women who was there in the audience, and she could testify that she saw it, Mrs Worrall said.

She referred her audience to the book, *Your Power To Heal,* by Harold Sherman, for further accounts of her healings.

'The experiences I have given you should help to establish the reality,' Olga Worrall said as she gathered up her papers. But before leaving the platform she put in a pitch for chiropractors, telling one more story about a young man's dramatic recovery by that method.

'I'm the aunt of three doctors, one of them a psychiatrist and I'm always telling them they're missing the boat,' she said. 'I'd like to suggest that everyone get acquainted with the importance of the spine. It has a great deal to do with health and they don't learn about it in medical schools!'

As a parting shot, she recalled that a child of twelve, judged to be mentally retarded, was treated by a chiropractor at her suggestion. The child was recently re-evaluated and found to have an IQ of 130.

'I suggest everyone work together for the purpose of healing the whole man,' Mrs Worrall said and, with a little flourish of her hand she added, 'God bless you and love you!'

During every intermission she was pressed by crowds of people wanting healing, and she gave one young student who was about to have abdominal surgery the laying-on of hands while everyone watched. An assistant collected a stack of written requests and Mrs Worrall promised to send healing to all of them in her nightly nine o'clock prayers.

(Those requesting healing are asked to join her in five minutes of spiritual communion with the Divine Presence, and she suggests that they anticipate, by sensing or intuition, an actual demonstration of the Divine Power.)

When we thought we had heard everything, the wind-up speaker for the Humanistic Psychologists' conference offered some surprising information suggesting that there may be hundreds if not thousands of great healers practising in the United States of whom most Anglo-Saxon Americans are completely unaware.

A Pennsylvania State and University of Florida-trained clinical psychologist who teaches at West Georgia College, Horace Stewart, PhD, told us he became interested in psychic healing after working in a Georgia state hospital with black patients. They kept telling him they were there because they'd had a hex put on them and they wanted to be treated by their own healers, he said.

'Like most people coming out of a traditional background I found it a whole weird sub-culture, terrifying, exciting, wonderful, and unknown to white people. I had some students do a survey and they found 40 natural healers practising in just one county of Georgia. And they had been doing it for years!'

Stewart obtained a grant from the National Institute of Mental Health to study the Afro-American healer, and among the most interesting people he studied was Ma Sue. 'She is close to 100 years old. It's fantastic to listen to all the things she's done,' Stewart said. 'You can get the flavour of the Afro-American healer from her.'

(Ma Sue appeared briefly in a television documentary on parapsychological research entitled 'Psychics, Saints, and Scientists' put together by Hartley Productions and shown on a number of educational stations in 1972. Ma Sue is shown sitting serenely in her porch rocking chair, and she answers questions in a gentle, soft voice, quoting passages from the Bible. One of her patients, sitting beside her, told how she had healed him after he had been run over by a truck.)

In Dr Stewart's opinion, 'psychic healing is all bound up in the human potential'.

I knew a little about the Mexican-American practitioners of curandero, and an interview with one of them in the *Enquirer* convinced me that they too were doing psychic healing. A burly, grandfatherly-looking man named Apolonia Leon who works with

the mentally ill in Metropolitan State Hospital in Norwalk, California, had this to say about curandero:
'The power is not mine to transmit, but God's . . . By touching the patient I transmit to him the healing force. It takes great concentration.' And explaining his approach, he said his patients are given three ten-minute treatments a week. Three for strictly psychological reasons. 'In this manner, the patient imagines himself to be better after the first treatment, his condition is greatly improved after the second and cured after the third. There is something about quantities of three to the human mind that makes things seem valid.' Several people were quoted as being cured of depression by Leon, who was brought in by a Mexican-American social worker, Ignacio Aguilar who, reportedly, holds degrees from the University of Mexico and the University of Southern California.

By chance I learned more about these unsung American healers at the dinner served to the participants at the Humanistic Psychologists conference downstairs in the huge ultra-modern Masonic Auditorium in San Francisco.

Sitting across from me was David G. Edwards of Pacific Grove, California, a social worker with the San Benita state-county health services who said he ran the out-patient clinic. He was well aware of the good work of the curandero practitioners, he said.

But he was sorry to say that there was little co-operation between them and the regular doctors, and he gave me a sad picture of their relationship. 'We would like to co-operate with them, but they are not very eager to co-operate with us.' He rounded out the picture:

'I represent the mental health services and we don't have any professional inhibitions about working with them, asking for their help or telling them what we think should help the patients. But it's pretty hard to get them to come down and talk to us. They're pretty scared of the officials. They just stay away from the establishment because they don't think white Anglo-American doctors are going to help them—because a lot of them haven't.'

At the American Academy of Psychotherapists conference in New York in October, my horizons were unexpectedly expanded in another direction—Africa. Richard Katz, PhD, who lectures on social relations and teaches trance and meditation at Harvard, gave a fascinating account of his findings, subsidised by another NIMH grant, that the Kalahari Bushmen apparently raise the same healing power in their bodies through trance-dancing! And what Dick Katz had to say fitted right into the theory that we are all healers. 'There's no limit to the number who can become doctors,' he said. 'There's no shamanistic idea that he's got it all and we're waiting till he can release it. It's much more widespread. It's an expandable, uncontainable substance. All you have to do is go to a dance and you'll get some!

'The healing power is literally floating around, it isn't totally within people. It's the life force, and they call it "medicine". You can go as deep as you want in it, but you have to bring it up so you can do curing, pass it through you to the person who needs it.'

24. Controversial Issues

ONLY ONCE during the three California conferences on healing did sparks fly, but matters were quickly smoothed over in gentlemanly fashion. The issue was whether or not the mind control courses that are sweeping the country are beneficial or dangerous.

Elmer Green, in his bio-feedback talk, made a blanket indictment of them as dangerous and also irresponsible while acknowledging they are based on a good principle; the use of self-suggestion while in a meditative state to overcome bad habits, become more productive and healthier.

On the other hand, Dr Carl Simonton, a young radiologist who practises in an Arizona veterans hospital, said that in a mind control course he'd learned exciting ideas for self-healing that he'd put to use with great success in his practice. He had taught his patients how they could speed up the healing effects of the radiation treatment by going into the relaxed meditative state taught by most mind control courses and visualising on their mental screen how the immune mechanism—which he describes to them in detail—is working to overcome their illness.

As evidence, Simonton showed a series of coloured slides in which angry cancers dwindled rapidly down to nothing.

When the two men met on the same panel later that afternoon, Green said he didn't disagree with Simonton, but he was worried about the wrong people running the mind control courses. 'A lot of people are being catapulted into the altered state of consciousness unprepared,' he said, adding that he had seen a programme of a mind control school, submitted to him by the State of Kansas, that had to do with 'going into another person's body, using visualisation techniques, and manipulating.' What if they're on a power trip? he asked. Didn't the student have to be taught ideals and moral responsibility in using these methods?

Simonton replied that the course he took was strongly oriented to ideals and moral responsibility. Conceding that they have 'a lot of room to grow and improve their techniques', he urged that whatever regulation occurs be done 'not for limitation, but for protection'. He had found the criticism of psychiatrists flawed by the fact that none of these critics, to his knowledge, would take the course.

Replying to Green's charge of danger to the psyche, he said, 'Among all the people I know, many of them my friends, none have suffered psychiatric disturbance—change, yes, but disturbing change, no.' (Having taken the Silva Mind Control course, which I found to be a beautifully stimulating experience, I liked Simonton's constructive attitude.)

Two scientists on the Academy of Parapsychology and Medicine panels tossed into the arena some daring theories on the universal laws that govern psychic healing.

Not too hard to grasp were the ideas of Henry K. Puharich, MD, a former research scientist at New York University Medical Centre and a pioneering investigator of psychic healers.

Dr Puharich began by suggestiong that healing can be viewed from two levels, the biological and the cosmic, and that the most intriguing aspects of it—the appearance and disappearance of tissue—are on the cosmic level.

He then hypothesised the manner in which healing of the cosmic variety reaches the human body on the earth plane. Perhaps, he said, a 'galactic brain' on the cosmic level interacts with and over-powers a 'local brain' on the biological level, while healers, acting as transducers, manipulate the flow of healing energy between them.

'When tumours disappear,' Puharich noted, 'I'm sure Olga Worrall will tell you she's only an intermediary.'

Concentrating on what seemed to him the fundamental pheno-menon in the big gap between medicine and healing—the mind powers of the 'transducers' that have to do with making matter appear or disappear, Puharich said he spent a year studying an unusual young man in Israel who had these powers in abundance—Uri Geller, now 26, a former Israeli Army paratrooper, who apparently takes his fantastic gift lightly. He uses it to entertain his friends, said the doctor, and he has no philosophy.

'I've had him independently checked by five scientists, repeatedly. He can make such things as gold, steel and organic materials appear and disappear, and he can do it under laboratory conditions. When a physicist sees this his whole world of matter collapses!' The researcher added that these feats of Geller's are repeatable, the kind orthodox scientists are always challenging parapsychologists to come up with.

Puharich then proposed a drastic step—that all the laws of physics be 'put to the test'.

'For example, if such a person as Uri Geller makes something disappear and doesn't bring it back, a fundamental law of physics has been violated, the classic law of the conservation of energy which says we can account for every bit of energy even if it changes form.'

He is confident that such tests will demonstrate that these psychic phenomena don't fit into the framework in which we live, and the result, he is sure, will be an extension of the boundaries of physics, bringing medicine and healing together.

'I firmly believe that we're dealing with pure law. We're just on the first step of an infinite ladder which we've been calling the universe,' he theorised further. 'I think it's a matter of probing into different spaces . . . of extending our powers to reach into those spaces.'

Some years ago, Puharich made an intensive firsthand study of the late great Brazilian healer, Arigo, watching and verifying many astounding cures. He feels that Arigo's claim—that everything he did was programmed by a spirit entity (Dr Fritz)—is one of the most challenging problems facing parapsychologists. Speaking before the Academy in 1971, Dr Puharich said he couldn't discount the spirit doctor thesis because he couldn't disprove it. Indeed, the weight of evidence made it apparent to him that Arigo, who had no medical education whatever, was working with an intelligence far beyond that of the greatest and best-trained medical diagnosticians within Puharich's acquaintance.

In trying to explain how a radionic device is used to make health diagnoses at a distance through a sensitivity to radiations from the patient, Dr William A. Tiller, a buoyant, bearded physicist, was led to postulate the nature of those radiations and the role they play in healing.

As chairman of the Department of Materials Science at Stanford and a world authority on the science of crystallisation, Tiller tends to boggle the mind when hypothesising the seven levels of substance of man, each obeying its own natural laws ('following the Yoga philosophies') and each in an ascending scale of fineness and energy with different types of radiations.

For clarity, he projected on the screen a series of finger-like curves representing the basic components of the human aura as well as the relative characteristics of each level of substance.

Beginning at the left with the lowest level, the physical, he pointed to a puny, crooked finger. Next came a taller but still irregular curve for the etheric substance (or, as the Russians would say, bioplasmic), then a smooth, symmetrical but skinny finger for the astral substance, reality', he indicated the curves for the four higher levels of substance together between an entity's reincarnations.' Then, crossing a line representing a step from 'temporal reality' to 'indestructible reality,' he indicated the curves for the four higher levels of substance, which he termed the intuitive mind, the intellectual mind, the spiritual mind and the spirit substance, the shapes of the three mind substances building up and rounding out and the spirit curve appearing smooth-shaped and perfect.

These seven substances, Tiller said, may be imagined to exist everywhere in nature and to interpenetrate the human body, being within the physical atom and organised in various patterns in the body. He suggested we think of them in terms of 'seven transparent sheets containing seven different circuit patterns, each in a different colour', all put together.

In healing, he theorised that there's a 'ratchet effect' as energy transfers take place between these levels of substance. For example, a mind image concerning a physical change in the body creates 'a coherent potential distribution' on the etheric level which in turn causes changes in the energy patterns of the etheric body. This in turn effects the physical level of substance and finally manifests as changes in the energy patterns and atomic reorganisation of the physical substance !

'All illness has its origin in a disharmony between the mind and spirit levels of the entity and that of the universal pattern for the entity,' suggests Tiller. 'This disharmony works its way to the physical level via the ratchet effect. Permanent healing and wholeness require that harmony with the universal pattern exist at the mind and spirit levels. Thus, healing at the physical, or even the etheric level is only temporary if the basic pattern at the mind and spirit level remains unchanged.' The concept, it seemed to me, brilliantly explains at least some of the failures of psychic healing.

In another dazzling set of postulates, Tiller links the chakras—the seven psychic centres of Hindu philosophy—on the etheric level of substance in our bodies with the seven major endocrine glands on the physical level, and suggests that the two systems can be tuned and balanced so as to tap 'primary energy streams from the cosmos'. The endocrine/chakra systems, having attracted maximum power to the body, says Tiller, they can then send it out to others in the form of healing, love, and other spiritual qualities.

I was suddenly aware of a crackling bundle of energy in the seat beside me—a small, black-haired woman who appeared to be Japanese. She was from Hawaii, and had flown in from Honolulu just for the symposium, she later told me. Her name was Hawayo Hiromi Takata, and she wore fire-engine red slacks, a tunic splashed with tropical flowers and her hair very short and straight.

Mrs Worrall had just finished speaking and Mrs Takata could hardly contain her admiration. 'She really knows what she is talking about,' she said to me, eyes sparkling. The rest of the speakers made her very impatient. Then she mentioned that she, too, was a healer and practised in Waikiki. I quickly made a date with her for lunch.

When we had filled our trays and found a table, her story began tumbling out. 'I studied in Japan under a great master,' she said. 'I am a teacher of healing. What's the sense of having a good mind if the body is riddled with illness? I believe in the very simple method. It takes me only four days to teach it, and two hours a day. Why struggle for years when you can have it so quickly? I teach it to housewives who can use it practically every day.'

Then you believe we are all healers? I asked.

'Yes, *true*. We are all born with it,' she said. 'But I am the engineer, the technician. You buy a new TV, you have to plug in the socket and get the energy. I give my pupils the contact with the great universal life force that does the healing—I have the secret of how to tune into it!

'From the first day they can use their hands to heal. The fifth day I teach ideals and principles.'

How did you learn how to do it? I asked, and she told me her teacher had been Chujiro Hayashi of Tokyo who had been the chosen disciple of Mikao Usui, founder of the Usui System. 'He had a PhD from Chicago, an old Japan scholar,' she said. Initiated in her thirties she was made a master in 1938, after going up by degrees. There were seven chosen to be teachers but all the others have passed on and today she's the only living teacher of the system. 'It is a method Usui revived from the Buddhist scriptures, a way of tuning into the *reiki*—that's the Japanese word for "universal force".'

I was amazed when she said she was now 72 and had been practising and teaching healing for 37 years. There was not a line in her face and her body was slim and sprightly. 'I am an old woman,' she said, smiling, without a hint of self-pity.

'I was very much impressed by Mrs Worrall,' Takata continued. 'She is getting results! That's more important than a lot of words. Of course, it's a good thing these fine young scientists are doing all this research, otherwise the healers would not be recognised. But when are they going to crack through and get going? How long will it be? Another twenty years?

'In Honolulu we had a forum with the AMA. The president of the AMA tested me. He wanted to know what I did, and the meeting lasted from eight in the evening until one in the morning. At the end he asked me, "All right, Takata, I think I understand you and what are you doing. Do you recommend that all doctors learn this?"

'I said, "Not only doctors but ministers, too." And I explained that in a church you have a large congregation and if the minister can help them by fixing their aches and pains they will listen to his sermons! The doctors know the techniques of medicine and psychiatry, and if they learn my treatment, I told him, the art of healing will then be a complete whole.'

I asked if she did the laying-on of hands and absent healing. She replied, 'Yes, but it's a higher degree. I learned it direct from the master.

'He would tell me, "There is no such thing as I *think* so." He was *positive*. If you were not positive he just bawled you out. He'd say, "That's the wrong attitude. *It shall be done.* It's not you, it's the cosmic energy doing it. How dare you doubt the energy?" '

Takata said that since reaching 61 she has not worked fulltime. But she gets up at 5 o'clock and at 6.30 plays a few holes of golf. On Thursdays she plays 18 holes and on Saturdays does her washing, ironing and cooking, and puts her food in the freezer. The last two years she's been travelling all over the world. 'But when I'm home, I *work.*'

'I like teaching in groups of 10 to 12 because there's more competition,' she said briskly, 'and they can compare notes.' Her pupils come to her by word of mouth, and she teaches many doctors and their wives, and even a few celebrities. She named a famous American heiress but made me promise to keep it confidential.

I asked if she would give a few details of her lightning four-day course, and she was willing—up to a point.

'The first lesson, I explain the universal life force, what it is, and I explain the workings of cosmic energy and how to make the contact. I manoeuvre it so that they have it. So far I have never made a mistake. They come to the lecture and they get it from me.

'The second lesson is how to use it. This is a demonstration of applying the healing from the neck up, eye, ear, nose, mouth, glands of the neck. I teach them how.

'The third day I teach them how to treat the organs in the front of the body. The fourth day I teach them how to apply it to the back. I take the body in sections so they don't forget or they'd get mixed up.

'The fifth day is the mental and spiritual lecture—mental attitudes, meditation. When they acquire this reiki it is a complete treatment for the physical body, the mental and the spiritual being.'

She said it also applies to plant life and animals and even to goldfish. 'Anything that has life accepts it,' she said, 'and with babies it's much, much more simple because the cause of the sickness is new. When it comes to chronic illness, it takes time. I work on the cause and the effect. Remove the cause and there shall be no effect! Isn't that sensible?'

She added that she gives her pupils the energy over five days, little by little because it's so powerful. 'I have to test them and see if they're doing it right.'

But *how* do you plug into the universal life force? I asked, trying not to sound impatient. 'It's a secret,' Takata said firmly, 'but before I die I want to teach as many people as I can, spread it to as many people as possible and create many teachers.' When I asked if there was any danger of the secret dying with her, she said, 'I will reveal it in 1973.'

A Buddhist, she said, 'We healers recognise God because the healing power is the God power.' She accepts contributions to her church.

For healing lessons she charges a fee. 'Not too much, not too little, for some it's free. In a group it's cheaper.' Most of her pupils are just plain ordinary people with common sense, she declared.

In brief, Takata says her method is a way of making contact with the healing power quicker, and it comes straight out of old Buddhist scriptures.

I asked if her pupils learn to heal themselves and her eyes flashed. 'That's Number One. If they can't do that what is the good?

'I have been asked to write about it but I have no time,' she said as we walked back to the auditorium, and when we were settled in our seats and the next speaker was announced, she muttered 'Scientists and all their theories are okay, but when? *When?*'

Since my chance encounter with this dynamic little Hawaiian healer I've wished many times that I had a 'quicker' way of making contact with the healing power, that I knew the old Buddhist secret for speeding up my development as a healer . . .

An esteemed member of the parapsychology fraternity ever since he conducted ESP tests en route to and from the moon, retired astronaut Edgar D. Mitchell (the sixth man to walk on the moon) was the banquet speaker for the Academy of Parapsychology and Medicine symposiums. Taking a prophetic look at the future of psychic healing in the United States, he listed four crucial steps that needed to be taken, leading to its full acceptance.

The greatest need of the moment, he said, is 'to bring orthodox medicine together with the psychic scientist so as to make the psychic healing event credible to them at the highest level'.

Mitchell—warm, direct manner, rusty beard—compared this uncertain stage of healing to that of acupuncture when the first two Americans went to North Vietnam and China and brought back glowing reports only to be rebuffed—until Dr Paul Dudley White went over and came back with the same story. Unable to ignore a president's physician, the medical community was obliged to take a look. The result was the AMA began studying acupuncture.

'I feel recognition of psychic healing and psychic surgery will come about in the same way,' Mitchell said. 'It will be just as cogent an event in the Western World.

'So far, the medical profession sees it as evil, or denies that it exists,' he continued, 'but those of us in the field know better than that. We're in the same position in the Academy as the first two who went to North Vietnam and China.'

Mitchell next emphasised the need for deeper research, and he revealed his own studies of a virtuoso healer he's found named Norbu Chen, an American who, having had training in a Tibetan technique of healing, has adopted a Tibetan identity.

In three months of observing Norbu Chen, he has seen cases of hepatitis remissed in four days as opposed to six months, gall stones removed without surgery and arthritic conditions in which the calcified deposits started to disappear in a few days, he said. 'In one severe case, where the limbs and face bore the signs of deformity, it was possible to watch them slowly return to normal. It was quite unbelievable. . . .'

(Questioned later on Norbu Chen's healing technique, Mitchell said he uses chants to raise his vibration level, and then goes into a meditative state, and when he has reached a certain level of consciousness he says he 'shoots' his consciousness and gets a return of energy which he channels to the patient.)

Mitchell invited Norbu Chen to Houston so that his healings could be documented by Mitchell's research organization*. 'Some real, viable evidence has been recorded on X-rays and by other measures appropriate to the disease and we're amassing a file,' he said. 'These preliminary cases have been verified by doctors and some have been sympathetic. But it's premature to publish a report. More time must elapse before it can be seen if the cures are lasting, especially the cancer cases which must be watched for several years.'

Mitchell added that he'd like to see healing research done by a team from many disciplines. 'But they should become "generalists" who are able to step out from their own point of view.'

The third need, as Mitchell sees it, is a certification process for healers similar to the licensing process required of doctors. He warned, however, that healers' licenses could be denied for all sorts of unfair reasons since the ego of the medical practitioner is very much tied up with 'those pieces of paper'. Indeed, 'if the Great Healer himself were around today he'd probably be brought to court for practising without a license!' said Mitchell.

* Now called the Institute of Noetic Sciences.

The astronaut conceded that it's not unreasonable for healers to be looked upon as frauds and charlatans because 'there have been many' but he would 'raise Cain' not against the ignorant, but against those in the medical profession who are unable to admit ignorance and go on to a higher level of understanding.

Mitchell predicted that as psychic healing advances, more and more people will seek to bar the incompetents, and he agrees that any who are proven unethical should of course be barred from practise. 'But we must find out *how* they should be examined and *by whom* I urge you not to make the requirements so rigid that you bar those whom they are designed to protect.'

If such unreasonable restrictions are avoided, he envisions healers becoming valuable adjuncts to hospital staffs and clinics, and setting up their own professional organisations such as the NFSH in England. The title he suggested was a large mouthful : 'The National Federation of Spiritual Healers, Etheric Surgeons, Shamans and Medicine Men.'

(Mitchell did not make any specific suggestions on how a healer could be 'certified' and I wished he had mentioned Sister Justa Smith's 'enzyme test'—the kind of objective measurement of a healer's abilities that could not be used arbitrarily.)

Fourth in Mitchell's list of needs is the training and education of psychic healers.

'After the first general gains in respectability, they will want to gain full standing in the profession,' he said, while conceding that some old-timers might think going to school was ridiculous. He was sure, however, that many others would be glad to take advantage of further training.

'Some have come by their healing ability hit or miss, or they've stumbled on it or been pushed into it. But even a great healer like Kathryn Kuhlman says she hasn't the slightest idea what happens when she is healing! Maybe with training and understanding she might improve her performance.'

He predicted that doctors might want to train their own psychic healing ability, and he's convinced that many of them use their gift already 'whether they say so or not'.

Dwelling a moment on the mind control courses which teach psychic diagnosis, Mitchell admired their attempts to do the same kind of thing Edgar Cayce did. 'Of course they are nowhere near the proficiency of Cayce, but the interesting thing is that there is some diagnostic ability apparent and I'd like to put the improvement of psychic ability on a statistical basis. 'Whatever you may think of them, there's something going on in these courses that's worth looking into.'

Mitchell suggested that the Academy itself would be performing a great service if it set up advanced training courses for accomplished healers.

In concluding, Mitchell compressed the four needs in the burgeoning field of psychic healing into four words—recognition, research, certification and training. And to these he added 'a standard of ethics'.

'We must keep in mind that the aim is to put it to the service of humanity,' he said, 'and to keep our ego out of the way of service.'

Index